Language and Literacy Learning in the Early Years:

An Integrated Approach

LANGUAGE AND LITERACY LEARNING
IN THE
EARLY YEARS
An Integrated Approach

Susan B. Neuman

Temple University

Kathleen A. Roskos

John Carroll University

HARCOURT BRACE JOVANOVICH COLLEGE PUBLISHERS

Fort Worth   Philadelphia   San Diego   New York   Orlando   Austin   San Antonio
Toronto   Montreal   London   Sydney   Tokyo

Publisher	Ted Buchholz
Acquisitions Editor	Jo-Anne Weaver
Developmental Editor	Tracy Napper
Senior Project Editor	Katherine Vardy Lincoln
Production Manager	Mandy VanDusen
Designer:	Carol Kincaid
Compositor	Octavo Design & Production

Library of Congress Cataloging-in-Publication Number: 92-073422

ISBN: 0–03–076846–2

Printed in the United States of America

3 4 5 6 7 8 9 0 1 2   039   9 8 7 6 5 4 3 2 1

To our children, David, Sara, and Tyler

It's snack time in Ms. Moore's class. The children, seated at tables around the room, have just been served their milk and snacks. A conversation begins:

Jeremy: Hey, Where's my chocolate milk?

John: A little boy in China drinked it.

Jeremy: China?

John: Cause I readed that Chinese book and it did this: "abra-cadabra—poof!" And then your chocolate milk just disappeared.

Jeremy: It disappeared?

John: Yup, everything just disappeared. Everything 'cept this book. This little book is magic...

PREFACE

*L*anguage and Literacy Learning in the Early Years: An Integrated Approach is intended to be used by preservice and inservice teachers enrolled in prekindergarten education courses and to provide a guide for administrators currently working in childcare programs. The book is also designed to be used by childcare providers and in courses for parents and parent groups.

The aim of this book is to provide a framework for understanding the beginnings of language and literacy: how young children come to know and to use spoken and written language in ways that connect them to life around them. It is designed to help teachers build on what children bring to oral language, reading, and writing, and to enhance developmentally appropriate language and literacy activities. It advocates an **integrated** approach in which young children are actively engaged in meaningful and functional language and literacy events, thereby learning "a language for life."

But children do not engage in these activities alone. Adults, as well, must participate and support their efforts. Therefore, many early education programs have raised the important issue: How can adults appropriately assist young children's spoken and written language development in prekindergarten programs? How can we effectively teach "a language for life?"

This book addresses these questions. The first three chapters provide the important foundation for examining language and literacy experiences and developing appropriate practices. Chapters 1 and 2 focus on children's development of language, in oral and written form, and on the importance of an integrative view of language. Chapter 3 then describes how early childhood programs may ease the transition between home and school, providing more opportunities for children to engage in functional language activities as they bridge these two learning environments.

From this framework, the book moves on to practical classroom applications, answering the critical question: What would the program look like? Chapter 4 describes design principles for preparing physical settings where language and literacy may flourish and provides applications to a variety of early childhood classrooms. Chapters 5 and 6 take on the complex question of how to plan for integrated language and literacy learning experiences in classrooms. Here, the focus is on how these processes may be taught through children's explorations of themselves, their community, and their world. We take the stance that planning for language and literacy learning *must* be embedded in broader curricular goals that seek to develop children's knowledge, language processes, and dispositions. It is through these explorations that children develop and grow as speakers, listeners, writers, and readers. Chapter 7 describes **"instructional mainstays"**—activities that many teachers will want to use in creating integrated language and literacy experiences in their classrooms. Finally, Chapter 8 describes the critical issue of assessing children's language development and growth. We offer teachers concrete strategies, such as creating portfolios, observations, and checklists to examine children's behaviors in the context of their use.

This book, therefore, enables teachers to enhance language and literacy holistically and in a developmentally appropriate manner for young children. It responds to the increasingly widespread demands for curricula well suited to the needs and interests of children, serving in stark contrast to the rigid, formal pre-reading programs that focus on isolated bits of language or a curriculum trickled down from the elementary schools.

Each chapter in *Language and Literacy Learning* begins with an overview ("At a glance . . .") that allows instructors to preview the contents of each chapter with their students. Following each chapter are review ("Let's review . . .") and applications sections ("Let's explore . . .") designed to encourage students to consolidate information and to seek out new experiences that will enhance and extend their understanding of young children. Finally, the book contains several appendices featuring additional children's literature selections, technology, and teacher resources, all to invite further explorations.

This book grew out of the research and classroom experiences of the authors, both of whom have been engaged in early childhood education for more than 15 years.

ACKNOWLEDGMENTS

We owe a great deal to the many children whose experiences with oral and written language became the basis of this book, and to the Directors of childcare programs, their teachers, aides and parents who so graciously welcomed us into their settings. In particular, we'd like to thank Susan Turben, Early Childhood Specialist in Cleveland Ohio; Colleen Olson at Cuyahoga Community College, Cleveland; and Willa Web, Little Neighborhood Center Head Start Director, Philadelphia. We would also like to thank the reviewers of the manuscript—James Christie, Arizona State University; Linda Gambrell, University of Maryland; Carol Vukelich, University of Delaware; and Mona Lane, Oklahoma State University—who offered invaluable and thoughtful suggestions, and Jo-Anne Weaver, Tracy Napper, and Katherine Lincoln for their assistance and careful editing. Finally, a special thanks to David B. Neuman, photographer extraordinaire.

CONTENTS

Language and Literacy

Causes Of

- needs

- demands

- intentions

Properties Of

- stability

- versatility

- predictability

Acquisition and Learning

"a whole series of little inventions and discoveries"

Teaching Principles

- knowledge

- environmental design

- function

- connectedness

- appropriateness

- insightfulness

CHAPTER 1

Learning Language and Literacy as an Integrated Process

Adam (age 4): We have a baby in mom's tummy—a real one.

Teacher: No kidding! That's exciting news. When is the baby going to get here?

Adam: It's a lotta miles. Four miles away in August.

Teacher: What are you going to do when the baby comes?

Adam: I'm gonna play with 'em and talk to 'em and read to 'em. I'm gonna stay with my baby and never leave 'em alone.

The Beginnings of Language and Literacy Learning: Human Demands, Needs and Intentions

*L*anguage! What would we do without it?

Continue to communicate, certainly. We would use our bodies to gesture and dance. We would use our faces to smile and frown. We would use our voices to shout and sigh. But our desire to understand and to be understood would undoubtedly go unmet. We would be, as Robert Frost writes, "desolate and lone."

We want language. Pushed and pulled by the communication *demands* of the human community into which we are born as well as our intense *personal need* to connect with others like us, we pursue spoken and written language. Fortunately, the unique biological structure of humans accommodates this pursuit. In addition to physical adaptations of their vocal tract, humans seem "wired" with a swift ability to acquire the oral

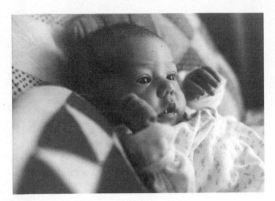

Babies smile.

Moms and Dads smile back. And make noises, exaggerating the movement of their lips and tongue.

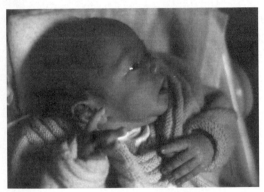

Babies try to imitate these facial movements and sounds. They coo and wriggle in response. Suddenly they move their hands.

Moms and Dads watch. They gesture back, touching their infants, uttering corresponding sounds and coos.

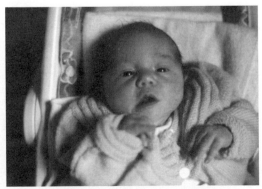

Babies watch and respond . . . more wiggling and gurgling . . .

language of the cultures into which they are born. The first evidence of this ability is the infant's gaze-following and switching reflex—which seems terribly modest when considering their profound implications. The baby's ability to look in the same direction as its mother, to fix attention and then burst into activity, is actually a form of turn-taking. And turn-taking paves the way to speech and literacy. What begins with looking and wiggling soon gives way to speaking and listening, writing and reading.

We are witnesses to the wondrous beginnings of these linguistic processes whenever we watch parents and babies together. Their looking and smiling games are examples of turn-taking in action.

In this quite natural way, adults and babies take turns at communicating. The interplay of their gestures, sounds, and expressions is a form of prelinguistic "chat." Although not yet spoken and written language in the ways we know them, these "chats" form the foundations of speaking and listening, writing and reading (Menyuk, 1991).

Because babies seem so adept at engaging another human in this way, some have suggested that such behavior is *intentional*—a primitive attempt to make social contact (Bruner, 1978; Trevarthen & Hubley, 1978). Being specially equipped with the capability to interact, it appears babies waste no time in sharing themselves with others. As early as six weeks of age, they are busy doing so. Even though their early contributions to the human conversation surrounding them may be only gestures, cries and coos, these are nevertheless their first "bids" to get involved with the vast, culturally diverse world within which they find themselves.

Properties of Spoken and Written Language: Stability, Versatility, Predictability

Babies, then, are born ready to communicate, needing language to get on with living. Their intent is to survive and, in the process, develop a loving relationship with another human being (Donaldson, 1984). Lacking speech, they use a form of **proto-language** to do so: gestures, expressions, and voice tones. But even in their earliest cries and babblings, they are beginning to use a language for real reasons: to interact with others, to inform others, and to indicate their wants. Ever so quickly, babyese—a kind of universal infant language—is left behind as their language adapts and enlarges to include the well-known sounds, words, expressions, phrases, and stories of the spoken and written language of their culture.

Throughout this language acquisition and learning process, children come to know certain properties of spoken and written language. At this point, we wish to introduce you to some of these, reserving a fuller discussion for later chapters. In particular, three properties seem to accompany the early phases of language and literacy learning.

One important property of language whether spoken or written that children soon become aware of is its **stability** (Wanner & Gleitman, 1982). In spoken language, for instance, there are chunks of sound or *words* that are consistently associated with particular objects, people and events: "Mama," "ball," "go bye-bye" and "Once upon a time" are just a few examples. Through their physical interactions children learn to relate certain chunks of sound to those who do (actors) and certain other chunks to what is done (actions). This differentiation of actor and action is the beginning of syntax or order in language (Lindfors, 1987).

Similarly in written language, words are ordered in a reliable way and a specific configuration of marks always says the same thing, for example, l-o-v-e always spells **love** (although we may not mean it). Realizing that particular features of language remain constant helps children to grasp the order and rules—the grammar if you will—of spoken and written language.

A contrasting property of language children grow to realize is its **versatility** (Goodman, 1986). In other words, language doesn't need to stay the same: it is changeable and many-sided. Language can be spoken and written; it can be in the form of sign language and Braille; it can be altered into nonsense and still make sense, as in, for example, the poem *Jabberwocky* by Lewis Carroll. And it can be transformed into a wide array of codes, as the "quick writing" of two preschoolers wonderfully illustrates in the following vignette (Quinn, 1991).

Darren and Paul are playing restaurant. To move things along, Darren suggests that Paul use a form of shorthand which he refers to as "quick writing" to take food orders.

Darren: You can do it like this. (Writes '2 p cr'.) Two 'p'—that means it says 'packets,' 'cause it's 'p,' 'cr' that . . .

Paul: That means 'cr' for 'crisps.' 2 p cr. (Writes.) Let's pretend you need two toffee apples. Two tof. a. (Writes.)

Darren: And two toffee bananas.

Paul (Writes.)

Indeed, language has differences. The more children participate in the world, the more they experience the diversity in language, discovering its rich potential for detailing their thoughts and feelings.

A third property of language that children learn about is its **predictability** (Pappas, Kiefer, & Levstik, 1990). The situations, events and contexts in which spoken and written language occur provide cues as to what words apply at the moment. For example, how we talk at a party will undoubtedly differ from how we speak in a classroom.

Language scripts that fit particular occasions or topics are referred to as linguistic **registers** or "special forms of language for use in special cir-

Figure 1.1

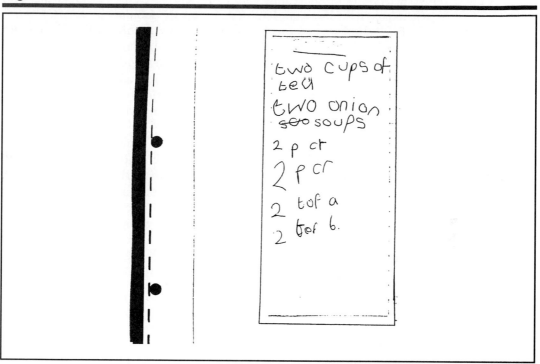

cumstances" (Goodman, 1986, p. 14). Children are introduced to such scripts early in life through simple, everyday routines: saying "bye-bye," going to bed (a script which seems to grow longer as babies grow older), eating out, reading bedtime storybooks, and meeting new friends. Notice how Sheona, a very busy 4-year-old, "sticks to the script" in her exchange with an adult friend in the following vignette.

Sheona (with pencil & pad): Are you signin' up for anything.?

Mrs. S: Am I signing up for anything? I don't know. Maybe I'll take ballet lessons. I would like to take ballet lessons.

Sheona (scribbling on her pad): The kids' size or the grown-up size?

Mrs. S: The grown-up size.

Sheona (talking softly to herself as she writes): Mrs. S . . . ballet lessons . . . the grown-up size . . .

Obviously Sheona has been involved in a good number of 'sign ups' or registrations in her short four years: she knows exactly what to say and do with spoken and written language to get the job done.

At first, children are very dependent on actual physical and concrete cues in a situation to prompt their use of appropriate spoken and written language. It's almost as if they have to see or do something to know what to say or *read*. But as they grow, their dependence shifts from a reliance on concrete cues alone in situations to linguistic ones as well (Menyuk, 1991). Like adults, they learn to *read* the situation and to adjust their language accordingly.

Although there are a number of properties of spoken and written language which we learn about over a lifetime, their stability, versatility and predictability seem fundamental. Combined with the human's intense need to make social contact with others, awareness of these properties supports and stimulates language and literacy use. As young children take notice of the likenesses and differences in spoken and written language, they use this information to make guesses about it. They test their guesses while in the process of "getting on" with others. In combination, these behaviors build a knowledge net that leads to language and literacy learning.

The Learning of Language and Literacy

We next turn our attention to the matter of how children learn to speak and listen, read and write, since it has much to do with conceptions of how language and literacy develop and grow. Up to this point, we have been touching more on the process of learning spoken and written language as a result of participation in real-life experiences than on the process of learning them as a consequence of teaching. Paraphrasing the sociolinguist, James Gee (1989), the following distinction can be made between learning as a product of real-life experience and learning as a product of teaching.

Commonly referred to as a "natural" process, learning as a result of living goes on rather unnoticed. It happens in everyday settings which are meaningful and functional for individuals, and it implies some sort of social interaction. Certain behaviors are "picked up" in these settings by repeated exposure to models and by trial and error. Learning to talk is an excellent example of this type of learning.

Learning to speak and listen, write and read, however, also includes "conscious knowledge gained through teaching" (Gee, 1989, p. 20). The process of learning as a result of teaching involves explication and analysis, where that which is to be learned is broken down into parts and explained by someone more informed. Furthermore, along with the content being taught, some degree of "meta-knowledge" about the content is also attained. In short, you not only know something, you also know what you know. Learning to read is an example of this type of learning.

In real life these two broad processes of learning intermix: much of our knowledge is learned as a result of living and being taught. Likewise, knowing how to speak and listen, write and read is an integration of these two types of learning. We make this point because it is central to our conceptualization of language and literacy development and growth.

"Learning" a language—to speak, listen to, write and read it—is a consequence of both learning processes. It is "natural" and it is taught. It is a whole, but it also has parts which warrant special attention. People model language *and* teach it. Children acquire language "naturally" *and* from instruction. Moreover, both types of learning are inextricably linked to environmental conditions and contexts of use, that is, what and how children learn about language is influenced by where they are, with whom and for what purpose.

In sum, our view of language and literacy development and growth reflects an ecological perspective: a point of view that there is a mutuality between people, their language, and their world. If children are to use spoken and written language in ways that endure and that empower them, their knowledge construction needs to encompass the processes of language (speaking, listening, reading, writing), through educative as well as "natural" forms of learning, and supportive environments of meaningful language use.

In the following section we provide a brief description of language and literacy learning from this perspective, followed by an equally brief overview of the principles of teaching that foster it. Both serve as an introduction to a program of language and literacy education in the early years.

A Brief Description of Language and Literacy Learning In the Early Years

The human quest to acquire and learn language could be described as a "whole series of little inventions and discoveries" (Luria, in Parker, 1983). We borrowed this phrase from the Russian psychologist, Alexander Luria, because we think it is an excellent way to frame a very complex matter and to synthesize ideas at the core of language and literacy learning and teaching. We'd like to explain these ideas more fully by taking the phrase apart and examining the words—almost one-by-one.

First . . . language learning is a "whole."

John Lennon sings in a wonderful song to his son, "Life is what happens while you're making other plans."

Language learning, spoken and written, is a bit like that. It happens in the midst of living; it is an inherently social process. Gesturing, speaking, listening, writing and reading take root, grow and thrive while we are busy with the whole of life. We do not learn to do these things apart from our lives. We learn them in the thick of it for three very important social reasons (Lindfors, 1987):

❑   to connect with others,

❑   to understand our world, and

❑   to reveal ourselves.

It is in "doing" for these intensely social reasons that we learn much of language (and life). Fortunately, social opportunities for learning language for these reasons abound in our day-to-day routines. Take snacking, for example. A lot of language learning goes on in this seemingly mundane activity (Dickinson, 1991). The snippet of conversation between 13-month-old Ricky and his mother in the following vignette illustrates this fact (Morisett, 1991). Notice, in particular, how the mother models verbal turn-taking and responds to Ricky as an active participant in the conversation.

[Note: Recorded during a snack of juice, cheese and crackers. XXX indicates an unintelligible word or phrase.]

Mother: Is that good cheese? Nummy cheese.
Ricky: (Offers Mother a piece of cheese.)
Mother: You eat it. Put it in your mouth.
Ricky: XXX (vocalizes and looks toward wall).
Mother: What you lookin' at?
Ricky: XXX (vocalizes and looks around the room).
Mother: Huh?
Ricky: (Reaches toward cheese in Mother's hand).
Mother: Want some more cheese? More cheese?

Here, Ricky is learning to 'talk.' We can see that this process involves more than mimicking sounds. It involves the orchestration of gesture (reaching for the cheese), watching and listening intently to Mom, and speaking in the flow of an important activity: eating.

There are a lot of things going on here at once! The baby is watching, listening, gesturing, eating, trying to form words. The mom is preparing a snack, listening, modeling, teaching "on the fly." In short, this is an instance of **integrated** language learning—the intersection of context, language function and form.

Second . . . language learning is a "whole series."

When we think of a whole series, we envision a number of things that are related, moving forward together over time or space. The television mini-series so common these days may come to mind. Or if you are mathematically-inclined, you may imagine a series of numbers, connected by a common rule, like 2, 4, 6, 8 . . .

Actually, a number of early childhood experts view spoken and written language development in a similar way. Robert Parker (1983, p. 39) suggests that "perhaps we are studying a single continuous process in development" not the separately developing processes of speaking, writing and reading.

In particular, the Soviet psychologist, Lev Vygotsky, believed that gesturing, speaking, playing, drawing and writing (and ultimately reading) are related language processes which are part of "a unified, historical line" (1962). They are interlinked, so that the development of one at some point impacts the development of the others. As a whole series, these processes attract and influence one another, spiraling forward in an interrelated way.

At various times, certain developmental strands are more apparent than others. For instance, in the earliest years of life, oral language development is more noticeable, while writing development is much less clear, as it is embedded in children's gesturing and make-believe play. Later in the primary school years, children's writing development becomes increasingly apparent as it approaches more conventional forms, while the subtleties of continuing oral language development are less easy to detect.

Kenneth Goodman (1986) describes this "unified, historical" view of language development and learning as "whole language," implying that these processes are co-occurring and interacting. Gordon Wells (1985) refers to it as "meaning-making," learning language and using it to learn. And M. A. K. Halliday says it is a process of "learning to mean" (1975). If we were to sketch a "unified, historical" view, it might look something like the graphic in Figure 1.2.

Although spoken and written language learning as a whole series of interacting strands may seem hard to imagine, it does make sense. Because of our great need to connect to one another, multiple pathways of language communication are developed. They stimulate and support each other. Over time they build a kind of communications "network," including spoken and written language.

One common activity where we can glimpse the mutuality of this network in action is children's play. As you enjoy the play excerpt in the next vignette, notice how the different developmental strands of language and literacy intersect to achieve communication.

Figure 1.2

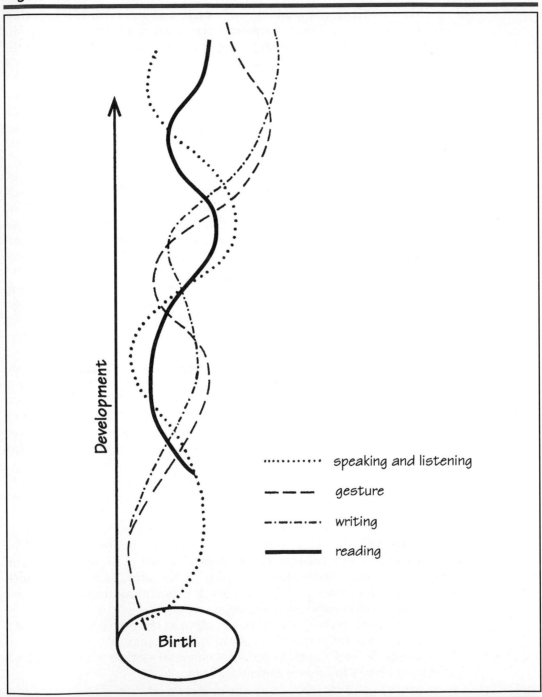

Jackie and Ericka (two 5-year-olds) are playing pharmacy in the Play Office. They are filling prescriptions for pretend customers.

Jackie (taking a phone-in prescription): Write this down, Ericka. 55 purple. No, no, 55 pink and 2 purple. 55 pink and 2 purple.

Ericka (scribbling this down on paper): There ya go. (She hands it to Jackie.)

Jackie (reading the paper): You forgot the name (she points and hands it back to Ericka).

(Ericka writes down a name copying from a child's name tag, then hands it and a small medicine bottle to Jackie).

Jackie: OK, a lady's comin' over now. Ding, ding, ding. Come in . . . (She talks to a pretend customer.) Hello! Here you are ma'am. She got it all ready. Your name is back and your medicine too . . . 55 pink and 2 purple.

In this play excerpt we can observe both oral and written language development. Through their efforts to initiate and sustain their play, the children use multiple language resources. They gesture. They talk. They even write and read. Some of these language resources are more developed than others, gesture for instance. But all are exercised in this one incident of play. Their integral use moves not only one, but all forward.

Third . . . language learning includes "little inventions."

Because it is so absolutely necessary to know and to make yourself known, babies, toddlers, and young children are wonderful inventors of, with and about language. For the most part, we are very fond of children's language inventions. We characterize them as cute, clever, humorous and ever so enjoyable.

Listening as intently as they do, young children use the language they hear to invent new words, rhymes, and seemingly never-ending stories. In the process, they learn more about how language works. We have all heard tell of these inventions in one way or another, like: "Rain Man" for Raymond, the language of Winnie-the-Pooh (for example, "Windsday") and young children's speech and word play (Cazden, 1974). In the next vignette, Claudia's magic chant for making sure she's always first and never last provides just another delightful example.

Hicka, vicka, sola, nicka,
Hicka, bicka, boo!
Alle manda, shoula backa,
Last on you!

—*Claudia, age 5*

Figure 1.3

Then, too, watching as intently as they do, young children also invent writing and reading. Take writing, for example. Children seem fascinated with it and eager to try out the tools that make it happen. Often (maybe too often), their earliest inventions are tried on the wrong material. A friend of ours related with much dismay how her son had etched his first scrawly "signature" permanently on the front of an antique cherry cupboard.

Although these early inventions of writing may be displayed in the wrong place, they nevertheless are the "right" thing to do. They reflect children's developing awareness of the features and functions of print.

For example, 3-year-old Tyler's Christmas List in Figure 1.3 suggests his awareness of a listing format as well as a budding understanding of alphabet letter formation in English. In Figure 1.4, 4-year-old Dana's efforts at letter writing indicate her understanding of how to format a letter and to address an envelope. She even demonstrates knowledge of the configuration of a favorite word of preschoolers, **love.**

Figure 1.4

As with writing, children also invent reading acts. Early on their inventions seem to be primarily physical depictions of reading. That is, they assume the position of the reader. They crawl up onto a chair—preferably a comfortable one—with book or magazine in tow (much like a favorite stuffed animal). They get situated after much wiggling about. The book is propped up in front of the face. There seems to be some fussing with the placement of the hands in order to hold it just right. Finally they look seriously at the page before them . . . which is often upside down.

After all, being a distinctly human in-the-head activity, it is difficult to conceive of what reading actually is beyond "holding" an object and staring at it. Nigel Hall (1987) shares amusing accounts of his interviews with very young children where he explores their beliefs as to what reading is. He asks: Can animals read? Some children respond: No, because animals don't have hands. But parrots can learn to read, because they can talk (p. 32).

Relying on visual evidence, young children tend to perceive reading only in its most physical sense—talking over, staring at and holding an object in a certain way. Their early inventions of reading activity reflect these perceptions.

Children do develop more accurate notions of what readers do and how they do it, but these emerge later in the preschool years. Through repeated storybook reading experiences, opportunities for book-handling and direct instruction, children begin to grasp the subtleties of the essentially cognitive nature of reading. They not only assume the position of the reader, they also begin to realize that readers interact with print and picture cues to bring about *reading*. Their demonstrations of reading as an activity—their inventions—reflect their growing understanding of these reader behaviors.

And Fourth . . . language learning involves "discoveries."

You are undoubtedly familiar with that old saying: "Nothing ventured, nothing gained." As a bit of folk wisdom, this is especially relevant to language and literacy learning. Because infants, toddlers and very young children are *active learners*, they are natural risk-takers. They are not sitting passively nor getting ready nor waiting for anything. They are doers; they venture forth undaunted into a verbal (and nonverbal) wilderness. And because they do, they make important discoveries about language. At this point, we would like to mention two big discoveries they make.

First and foremost, they discover that language is useful. Because children have thoughts to share and stories to tell, they quickly find out that language is a most practical means to do so (Halliday, 1975).

Second, they discover that language has different modes. Surprisingly for all its complexity and universality, language permits only three modes for communication. We refer to these as the 3 s's: speech, sign language, and script (Restack, 1988).

Children, barring a serious hearing or speech impairment, soon determine that speech gets you what you really want more consistently than gesture alone. For example, saying "chocolate chip cookies" is more likely to lead to the desired result than merely pointing to a row of cookie packages along a grocery store aisle. And as life gets more complicated, children also come to know the practicality of literacy. For instance, it comes in handy when you need to remember something, to issue a warning (like KEEP OUT!) or to say "I love you" to a grandmother far away.

From those two big discoveries, others surely follow. For example, there is the realization of the features of language, such as saying "went," not "goed." Also, there is an emerging awareness of language forms (for example, lists are not the same as stories). Also, children begin to recognize language functions—utilitarian, informational and pleasurable.

From our point of view, these four ideas provide a framework for understanding language and literacy knowledge construction: children coming to know and use spoken and written language in ways that connect them to the life around them. In so doing, they are engaged in learning **a language for life:** a communications network for knowing and being known in some enduring way.

Children are not engaged in this alone. As adults, it is our responsibility as well as our joy to participate in this effort. How do we assist spoken and written language development? How do we teach "a language for life"?

Active Learners With Active Teachers: Teaching A Language for Life

Once again we have deliberately chosen a phrase to synthesize our thoughts. The phrase, "a language for life" is actually the book title of the *Bullock Report* published in 1975 by the Department of Education and Science in England. In that time, it reflected "the richest distillation of practical knowledge about the teaching of reading" (Downing, 1979, p. 2). In our time, we use the phrase to "distill" how children's spoken and written language learning may be supported and stretched by others.

Earlier in our discussion of language as a whole series of little inventions and discoveries, we described in a very general way what children are doing to learn language and literacy. If we were to pursue that discussion, we would focus our attention on children's intentions, abilities, and knowledge pertinent to language. In short, we would examine **language and literacy development** and **what** is being learned.

But learning is not a solo act. It is embedded in social circumstances and events which impact individual language achievements. So, in learning a language for life, children are necessarily influenced by where they are and who they are with—their language "teachers." Spoken and written language learning, then, also include **teaching,** or **how** a language for life may be developed by others.

Developing a language for life in this more educational sense involves conditions that foster language discovery and use. By conditions, we mean the physical environment, social milieu, and adult behaviors which impact children's lives. Over the past twenty years, great strides have been made in describing practices that support and extend children's language acquisition and learning at home and in child care settings (Hymes, 1991). The 1988 publication of developmentally appropriate practices is one such example (Bredekamp, 1989). The Oxford Preschool Project in Britain is another (for example, Bruner, 1980).

Using these resources and others (for example, Holdaway, 1979; Wells, 1985), we have "distilled" certain teaching principles which we believe guide children's spoken and written language learning in early childhood classrooms. Our principles are necessarily general, since the details of individual children's language learning vary considerably. Our intent is not that these principles become prescriptions, but rather that they may serve as guideposts for informing those who assist young children on their language learning pathways. The essential point is this: just as children are active learners, they need *active teachers*—adults who participate vigorously in children's spoken and written language learning. In the remaining chapters, we provide information which elaborates this overarching idea and the principles which support it.

Principles of Teaching Language and Literacy

Active teachers become and remain knowledgeable about how language develops.

Although our life experiences may have provided us with a general sense of how language and literacy develop, this alone will not suffice. First, a basic understanding of language and literacy development is needed around which to organize personal experience and to cluster new information we encounter. This demands that we read and study.

Second, the manner in which language and literacy develop in human beings is not known. There is no one definitive explanation for these complex processes. Furthermore, new information is continually forthcoming. This demands that we read and study some more. So: If we are to genuinely assist children in their language and literacy learning efforts, if we are to be their "teachers," we need to become and remain learners *about* language ourselves. We need to read professional materials, attend conferences, watch children grow and listen to our colleagues to more fully understand this uniquely human aspect of development.

Active teachers design an environment that integrates language and literacy learning.

The quality of the physical environment is a powerful factor in language learning. The objects and opportunities it provides are the stuff out of which basic concepts are spun. What is available to label and to talk about, how accessible it is to touch and explore, and how it is organized influence both spoken and written language development.

If we are to encourage gesturing, speaking, playing, writing and reading in the early years, environments need to be created that support these communication processes in an integrated way. This cannot be left to chance; it is not simply "littering" the environment with toys and materials. In early childhood programs, the creation of a language and literacy rich environment requires an ongoing and conscientious consideration of space, materials and time. These become the building blocks of an environment rich in language use.

Active teachers provide experiences that illustrate language and literacy in use.

Of course, just having things lying about in the physical environment will not guarantee language and literacy learning. Children need experiences that stimulate them to use their language resources and challenge them to more sophisticated levels of expression.

It is our responsibility to plan and to engage children in a wealth of experiences that respect children's interests and how they learn. Gardens and gardening, making collections, water play, nature walks, cooking some favorite dishes and experiences like these become the curriculum where children meet and construct ideas, using language and literacy to express their ideas in diverse ways.

Active teachers bring the outside inside and take the inside outside.

Assuring reciprocity between the language and literacy learning going on outside the classroom doors with that going on inside of them takes considerable planning and effort. It means finding creative and effective ways to communicate with parents and others, to pull them into the classroom life. And it means developing curricular experiences that connect to the local community and larger world in lasting ways.

Fortunately there are an increasing number of technological and material resources available, making it easier to achieve these goals. Teachers in early childhood programs do not have to re-invent the wheel. But they do need to do at least these things:

❑ Find and read publications that suggest ways to connect home, school, and community;

❑ Select and use activities that build a sense of community in their own programs;

❑ Share and contribute successful ideas and projects for others to try.

Active teachers assist in developmentally appropriate ways.

We are supposed to teach children how to use language. That is one of our most important responsibilities as adults in early childhood settings. We are the language scaffolders, models and teachers (Cazden, 1974). But, we need to safeguard that there is a good fit between the help we are trying to give and the learning the child is striving to do. In other words, our assistance needs to dovetail with where children are developmentally.

Parent-child exchanges often exemplify this delicate meshing best. Because parents know their children so well, they assist their children's language learning appropriately by providing just enough, but not too many, language and literacy cues so that learning occurs.

The common "Peekaboo" game, the teaching of "Say bye bye," and parent-child storybook reading provide us with wonderful exemplars for our own practice. We can take our cue from these exchanges between young children and adults, learning how to share the language we know with what children need ever more appropriately. In these ways, our assistance leads to new language learning.

Active teachers learn to see.

Like us, you may enjoy Dr. Seuss' story, *Horton Hears A Who*. We like it for two reasons. First, it is a good story because of its memorable characters and plot. Second, it has a powerful message about observation. Because Horton pays attention to the unexpected, he learns to see and to understand the plight of the very small persons of Whoville. Similarly, we need to remain alert to the sounds and scribbles of children's language learning. In doing so, we learn to see what otherwise may have been overlooked.

To effectively observe and understand young children's spoken and written language development demands efforts on the part of early childhood educators in two areas. Early childhood programs need to be **built around** a strong curriculum which encompasses how young children learn, what learning is appropriate and when children learn best. Further, such programs need to **build in** the means and opportunities for all caregivers to watch and record what young children do in some systematic way over time (NAEYC, 1991). To do less is to risk losing the integration of language and literacy learning that children need.

Let's Review . . .

A number of ideas and themes fundamental to understanding language and literacy learning in the early years were introduced in this chapter. From birth, humans seem driven to learn language as they strive to connect and communicate with others. We described this process broadly as "a whole series of little inventions and discoveries," through which children acquire and learn the properties, functions and features of both language and literacy.

We then discussed briefly the adults' role in this process, viewing their responsibility as one of teaching children "a language for life." This requires that adults actively participate in young children's language and literacy learning, guiding and supporting children in their efforts to use language and literacy meaningfully in their own lives. We concluded this introductory chapter with six teaching principles which provide a framework for the remaining chapters and reflect many of the enduring themes in early childhood language and literacy education.

· ·

Let's Explore . . .

1. Make two vertical columns on a piece of paper and in one list what you think are the purposes for which you use talk and in the other the purposes for which you use print. Over the next two days, tally the extent to which you use talk and print for each purpose, adding any new purposes that emerge. Compare your findings with a colleague, considering what they reveal about the functions of language and literacy in daily life.

2. Observe some children in a day-care or preschool setting. Select one or two children and watch them for a sustained amount of time, e.g., during free play. Try to jot down:

   (a) situations in which you notice the children are conversing, writing and/or reading;

   (b) the sorts of things they are talking, writing and/or reading about;

   (c) any problems you notice in their attempts to use spoken and/or written language to communicate.

   Make these observations at the same time two or three more times and then make a summary of your observations, sharing it with the children's teachers.

3. Record yourself engaged with one or two children in a storybook reading situation. Listen to the recording, paying close attention to the questions the children ask. What do their questions reveal about what they already know about the topic? About books and reading? About words?

Language and Literacy Development

Language **Literacy**

acquisition *development* • listening to reading

constructive predictable • seeing contextualized and
decontextualized print

interactive incremental

functional conceptual • discovering the functions and
features of print

The Symbolic Function

language/literacy parallels language/literacy distinctions

Guidelines For Practice

CHAPTER 2

Understanding Language and Literacy Development

Meredith takes out a marker and writes on paper. To her friend
  Leah, she says:
"If you make these two lines—if you do this and this, it's an **M**
  for **Mom.** And there's an **M** and there's an **O**." (She writes
  the letters down.) I'll be ready for school in the fall 'cause
  I'll be ready to write my name."

*L*anguage learning is a synergistic, complementary process. From children's natural, ongoing encounters with oral language, they develop expectations of how language might operate in a different form, like written language. Children's independent attempts to "read" books, for example, enhance their understanding of how writing works. Initial playful attempts at writing also become the source of children's growth in reading and speaking. Current research (Clay, 1991; Teale & Sulzby, 1986) suggests that during infancy and the preschool years, children are actually acquiring a knowledge of both written language and oral language development. The two systems are intertwined and interconnected, changing and evolving during the process of child development.

While these language processes mutually reinforce one another in development, we are not suggesting that they are parallel processes, as some have claimed (Goodman & Goodman, 1979; Harste, Burke & Woodward, 1982). Rather, as we have mentioned in Chapter 1, there are important parallels between oral and written language which motivate language development and stimulate children's awareness of the language around them. But there are also some dissimilarities between these language systems that must be acknowledged and addressed through instructional practices. Especially for young children, meaning in conversational speech typically resides in an interaction between participants, their shared experiences and everyday knowledge, as well as the situation in which the communication takes place. In formal written language, however, meaning is conveyed to a much larger extent by the text itself. In fact, some experiences with written language require the child to disregard the immediate context in favor of moving beyond familiar events and situations. Like family relations, then, oral and written language share much in common and provide critical support to the other, yet they maintain their own unique character and form.

As teachers we need to know about the many aspects of language learning in order to provide experiences which can support children's language development. In this chapter, we first describe early language acquisition and early literacy development. Next, we will discuss both the parallels and dissimilarities between oral and written language. Finally, we'll consider the implications of what we have learned for those involved with children in the early years.

Early Language Acquisition

On walking our dog the other day, we met a mother and child strolling through town. The infant, clearly delighted with our golden retriever, pointed and said "Ga ga, Ga, ga." The mother smiled proudly and said, "Yes, that's right, Jenny. It's a *doggie, doggie*." And so, though seemingly inconsequential, such simple actions between mother and child actually belie a rather complex process of discovering that patterns of sound take on meaning and that language represents objects and events.

The challenging task of learning how to talk, though, is not purely imitative. Children don't simply parrot back the language they hear. Rather, they seem to use their natural ability to generate utterances even their parents didn't realize they knew. The insightful linguist, Noam Chomsky, in one of the most famous sentences of the 20th century, suggested that all human beings have an innate sense of the rules that govern language (1957). This sentence was, "Colorless green ideas sleep furiously." At first we may ask, "How can ideas be colorless and green?" or "exactly how do ideas sleep furiously?" And yet, as Chomsky noted, a certain sense can be derived from this proposition. For example, even a young child could respond to such questions as, "What slept furiously?" (ideas), and "What kind of ideas were sleeping?" (colorless green ideas). This demonstration reveals the child's native ability to use the structure of language without any formal guidance.

What Chomsky argued was that a speaker must possess, at some level, an intuitive set of rules indicating when different parts of speech can occur in given places in utterances. This set of rules is called grammar or syntax. His contributions have had an enormous impact on how we view children's language acquisition. Through their knowledge of a limited set of rules, children can produce virtually an infinite set of sentences. Thus, rather than purely imitative, language learning is **constructive**—through their own activity and thinking, children construct how language works.

The view that language may come just from the child, without any input from external forces, however, is too narrow. Following Chomsky's theory, there was a shift in emphasis, with a number of linguists beginning to focus on the communicative context for language learning. For example, Bloom (1970) described how an utterance, such as "Mommy sock," could take on many different meanings according to the particular context in which it was said. It might suggest, "Mommy get my sock," or "Mommy has a sock." In recognizing that sentences may take on different meanings in different situations, those interested in acquisition acknowledged the intimate relation between context and language.

It became clear that language is, in a sense, an instrument used for regulating joint activity and joint attention that has its beginnings in the parent-child relationship. Bruner (1975), for example, describes a peek-a-boo episode, where a mother is drying her 11-month-old child's hair with a towel, and says "boo" twice on uncovering. Ten minutes later, the child initiates the game in a different context, raising her skirt over her face and holding it until her mother says "boo."

Think about this interaction for a minute. Through interpreting the child's actions and expanding upon them, the parent used the opportunity to extend the child's language in an entirely new context. It represents a striking example of the way in which a rule may become elaborated. In this respect, the process of language acquisition is not only constructive but **interactive**—its roots lie in inborn abilities to formulate basic rules, and to interact with others in one's environment.

At about the same time, Michael Halliday (1975) began to explore the dynamics of this social interaction with his son Nigel who was nine months old at the time. He found that most of Nigel's interactions focused on his specific needs, such as demanding objects, or ordering people around. These utterances, not necessarily recognizable to anyone but his parents, were designed to carry specific meanings, suggesting to Halliday that the infant "learns to mean" long before he learns the correct form (how it is said) of the utterance. From his careful observations, Halliday found that there were seven main functions of language that children may learn throughout their development (Table 2.1).

Through social interaction, Nigel's language evolved, serving strictly the instrumental function at first ("Give me dat") and later, the more representational function of imagination ("Let's pretend"). With Halliday's

---

TABLE 2.1   FUNCTIONS OF LANGUAGE ACCORDING TO HALLIDAY (1975)

FUNCTION	MEANING	EXAMPLE
1. Instrumental	Used to satisfy needs; to get things done	"Give me dat" "I want"
2. Regulatory	Used as a means of persuasion; control	"Do as I tell you"
3. Interactional	Used to develop interpersonal relations	"Me and you"
4. Personal	Used to develop self-awareness, and to express feelings	"Here I come" "I don't like it"
5. Heuristic	Used to explore one's world	"Tell me why"
6. Imaginative	Used to build worlds separate from the world of reality	"Let's pretend"
7. Informative	Used to communicate information to others	"I've got something to tell you"

work, we began to understand the importance of purposefulness and meaningfulness in children's learning of language.

Taken together, these theories have dramatically shaped how we view early language acquisition. Rather than focusing on the syntax of language, or strictly on its meaning, many researchers of children's communication now refer to language acquisition as taking into account all these perspectives. Through their own activity and thinking, children construct knowledge about how language works and use it to serve their functional needs. Thus, the best explanation for what we call "knowing a language," is seen as:

- ❑ **Constructive**:   Children create language on the basis of an innate set of rules or underlying concepts.
- ❑ **Interactive:**   Language is mediated by adults through interactions designed to extend and elaborate its meaning
- ❑ **Functional:**   It is through the relevant use of language that children learn it.

Take 2 1/2-year-old Adam, for example. Bedtime every night is a struggle because of his fear of monsters. Right before bed, he says to his mother: "Want me to tell you about Timmy? To get to his house you go this way and this way." "Mmm," his mother answers, "I'm not sure I know Timmy. Tell me who he is." Adam says, "Oh, Timmy is my best friend. Actually he's my pretend friend. There's a monster in Timmy's bed."

Notice the sophisticated language play in this exchange. Fearful of bedtime and trying perhaps to delay the inevitable, Adam is attempting to engage his mother in conversation. His mother listens, and at the same time tries to understand her son's intended meaning (considering the situation and time of day), by asking him to elaborate a little bit more on his "friend". In doing so, she provides Adam with the opportunity to reflect on his fear in a manner that is far less disturbing to him. In this exchange, Adam uses the semantic/syntactic forms of language in the situational context of bedtime to explore and communicate his personal feelings.

Children's Growth in Language

Children acquire language through predictable stages of development. Interestingly, these stages are not marked by a steady trajectory of growth. Instead, it seems that language acquisition consists of overlapping phases of growth—spurts of growth, and then "regressions" to more simplified forms of communication.

During the first six months of life and after, infants vocalize by cooing and babbling, sounds that will eventually be combined into words. Then a few sequences of sounds begin to be used on a consistent basis in the same situations—"baba" for bottle, "wawa" for water—and it is these utterances that mark the real precursors of language. Even after they begin to speak their first words at about one year of age, children will still interject these babbling-type utterances that sound like actual words, but really aren't, leading Pflaum (1986) to speak of this form of expression as a kind of "pseudolanguage."

Children's first words, aside from the names of their caregivers, tend to be common objects in their immediate environment. Nelson (1973), for example, found that most of these words were like "sock" or "key"—something that was movable and handled by the children themselves. Following these beginning words, the growth of vocabulary increases tremendously. At age 1.0, children may be speaking and using meaningfully about three words; by age 2.0, the average number of words according to one researcher (Leopold, 1971) is 272!

But the language acquisition process is not merely incremental. As children begin to put words together, their vocabulary development and rules of grammar involve conceptual change. Linguists describe children's first combined utterances as not just one grammar, but a number of grammars, which are used in combination with their new learned words. An example is a conversation between 18-month Latoya and her mother:

Latoya (looking at a small toothbrush on a table in her room): Mommy brush. Mommy brush.
Mother: What? The brush? The toothbrush?
Latoya: Teethbrush.
Mother: You want to brush your teeth with that?
Latoya: Want to teethbrush.

Notice that Latoya uses two different forms of grammar to convey her interest in brushing her teeth ("Mommy brush" and "Want to teethbrush"). She begins the conversation with a "telegraphic" type request ("Mommy brush"), then with her mother's request for clarification, extends and changes the grammar of her utterance ("Want to teethbrush"). Notice also that Latoya revises her "brush" to "teethbrush" which may either denote "want to brush my teeth," or the over-generalization of a grammatical rule (in this instance, the joining of two nouns to form a compound word), which despite her mother's correction, to the singular "tooth" in "toothbrush," persists. Constructions like "teethbrush" are actually fascinating because they give us signs of the child's internal concepts and growth. Later, Latoya may use words like "goed," and "hided," suggesting that she has tacitly internalized particular rules (such as, in these examples, the addition of "-ed" to verbs to create past tense forms), yet has not yet fully recognized any exceptions. Therefore, what may look like regressions in her language patterns are signs of real growth.

While language acquisition research has generally focused on children under two years of age, there is still a great deal of development after the early stages. By about 3 1/2 years old, children's conversational skills are developing enormously. Early exchanges sometimes seem like parallel conversations, with talk not really related to the other partner, such as Brandon who asks Seth in his play group, "Can I use the truck, can I, can I" with Seth answering "let's play cops, let's play cops." Toward the end of the third year, however, children seem to make connections, linking their thinking and talking to their peers. Here the pretend play becomes intricately woven with talk, used to direct and negotiate the various roles in play.

(Adam, Sara and Sheona are playing together in the sandbox.)

Sheona: I'm makin' a cake

Adam: The cake goes in here (a big plastic bucket).

Sheona: I'm makin' whipped cream for your cake Sara.

Adam: Me too—I'm makin cream for your cake too. A lota cream in here!

Sara: We're cookers.

Adam: We're cookers.

Sara: Yeah, we cook.

Sheona: We cook recipes.

Notice how children tie together their actions and language, how they maintain the topic through several units of exchanges, extend their vocabulary and develop stories in concert with each other. These social exchanges with peers represent an important milestone in the development of language as a communication skill.

Language and Cognitive Development

Our young language learners, through constructing rules and interacting with others, are also engaged in actively structuring a system through which to understand the world around them. Two important thinkers, the Swiss psychologist, Jean Piaget, and the Russian psychologist, Lev Vygotsky, have influenced our understanding of how language and thinking intersect, and how adults may help to shape and structure the child's world to enhance learning. Though there are some differences, there are also a number of important commonalities in Piaget's and Vygotsky's theories which influence educational practices.

Both Piaget and Vygotsky believed in the central theme of activity: that children's thinking develops through active and largely unconscious structuring of input they perceive from their environment. But they differed in their views of what exactly constitutes "environment." For Piaget, environment included the objects that might be visually seen and physically manipulated with other objects; for Vygotsky, it was not only physical objects, or a society's "cultural tools," but the interactions with people—social interactions with more experienced members of society in which information regarding the tools and practices is transmitted in the "zone of proximal development." Vygotsky described the "zone" as the "distance between the actual development level as determined by independent problem solving and the level of potential development as determined through problem solving under adult guidance or in collaboration with more capable peers" (1978, p. 86). Essentially, the "zone" refers to what a child can do with the help of others and the support of the environment.

These differing definitions influenced the views of the role of language in children's thought. Piaget, in his book, *The Language and Thought of the Child* ([1926] 1955), believed in the prevalence of "egocentric speech" among preschool children, through about ages 7 or 8. Egocentric speech centers around the child's own actions, talking aloud, without concern of anyone else around. Sometimes we refer to them as soliloquies:

Tanya's in the kitchen playing with plastic dishes and fruit.

Tanya: "One day I was going home. One–two–three. And I saw some thing to eat. I bought those cupcakes for myself. Ahh, picadilly, picadilly, (her eyes get very big) Soooo—soon I'm gonna eat them all up! Oh—Picadilly likes that—and we'll all-l-l-l eat stuff together and have a birthday party."

Even though a little boy at one point comes into the kitchen and starts throwing packages around, Tanya is rather impervious to distraction as she continues to talk. In fact, sometimes it's quite hard to understand this language because it seems to be a bit "out of this world," leading one teacher to claim, "she talks, and talks, and says nothing!" Piaget argued that this type of egocentric speech is typical of children's behavior at this stage when they are all-consumed with themselves. He saw language as an attribute of development, rather than something that might push development further.

Vygotsky, on the other hand, in his book, *Thought and Language* (1962), felt that egocentric speech had a very definite and important place in the activity of children. Even this earliest speech of the child, referred to by him as "external speech," is essentially social. For Vygotsky, though, external speech had a far greater role in children's cognitive development than it did for Piaget. He believed that as children acquire names for objects and actions through involvement with adults and more capable peers, they begin to internalize these collaborative forms of social interactive behaviors. In this respect, what we hear when we listen to a child, like Tanya, talking to herself, is a planning or conceptualizing of ideas, sort of like "talking things out"—organizing, planning and working out solutions, rather than merely "talking for talking's sake". This external speech, according to Vygotsky, is the means through which thinking develops.

For Piaget and Vygotsky, no development takes place unless children are actively and thoughtfully engaged with the world around them. In Vygotsky's case, this world includes rich, meaningful, conversational exchanges between children and their peers, and adults by which language is internalized to more complex thinking. For both Piaget and Vygotsky, however, language serves an important representational function. Through language, children begin to detach particular words from objects, or actions. Words begin to stand for ideas. In doing so, thought begins to take on a symbolic function—children have begun to use the natural medium of **language** for representational thinking.

Early Literacy Development

Like language, literacy learning, defined as reading and writing development, begins in infancy. Even in the very first months of life, children come in contact with written language in the form of signs and labels, TV commercials, or toy-like books. These early contacts with print represent the beginnings of a life-long process of learning to read and write.

Reading

From its sheer ubiquity in our society, children begin to develop certain assumptions about how written language works. They see how their parents and other adults go about reading newspapers, filling out forms, and following recipes. They also participate in many informal literacy experiences, like following directions for putting a toy together, or helping their parents read instructions on how to pump gas. In many cases, they are fortunate enough to be read to regularly at bedtime. With such a variety of experiences, children begin to make meaning from print.

They do so on the basis of its functionality. That is, in these real-life settings, young children see reading and writing as being highly useful, serving to accomplish many different purposes. Even young children whose homes rarely include books have many opportunities to see and use written language. For example, young Adam's favorite foods are alphabet french fries, and Walter's Pizza—the telephone number he can immediately identify and distinguish from Good Fame Pizza (which is a lesser favorite) on the refrigerator door.

Children rely heavily on the context of the situation to determine the meaning of print. While chomping on his pizza, for example, we asked Adam to read us the words on his bib. "I think it says Red Sox (which it did), because my mom's friend Janet got it at a Red Sox game." Similarly, children begin to be able to identify print frequently seen in their environment. They know stop and exit signs, labels and the names of favorite foods like Burger King and Pepsi, and all sorts of food names in the grocery store. Rarely do children's phrases or names for things badly miss the mark. Rather, their knowledge of these words are examples of **contextualized literacy**—written language which is defined by its context. In this way, children relate words like "TV Guide," or signs like "Do Not Enter" to their actual function. Acquisition of these print–meaning associations usher children into the world of literacy as a purposeful activity.

But contextualized experiences with written language represent only one aspect of children's learning of literacy. Much of children's lives are spent listening to or reading stories told by others, whether they are simply anecdotes inserted in conversations, television comedies or dramas, or storybooks. Stories are an essential link to literacy. For the very young child, this world of stories can be as important and meaningful to them as anything else in their lives. A favorite story, full of fantasy characters (which are eventually recognized as make-believe), may give form to a child's worst fears—and in the process help to conquer them (Applebee, 1978; Bettleheim, 1975). In some cases, this means that the child needs to hear a story repeatedly, as in the case of one child who must have listened to *Velveteen Rabbit* about ten times to recall when all the toys got "fired."

Stories are examples of **decontextualized** print (Olson, 1977; Wells, 1985). Essentially, this means that unlike contextualized print experiences, written language has meaning apart from the particular situation or context of its use. The meaning of decontextualized print is derived from the language itself and from the conventions of the literary genre. For example, many of us who are mystery fans can pretty much identify what kinds of actions and events will take place over the course of a story—the particular details may not be known, but we could probably give a relatively good overview. Over time, we have developed a frame, or a sense of story, for how this particular genre works.

This same pattern is true for young children. Through listening to many stories, they begin to construct a mental model of the basic elements of a story. Story researchers refer to this as **story schema** (Bartlett, 1932) or story grammar (Mandler & Johnson, 1977; Stein & Glenn, 1979). Based on this internalized or idealized story, children develop expectations for the setting of a story, the attributes of certain characters, and the order in which events occur and how the story will eventually end up. Even very young children who have been read to regularly, when asked to tell a story will begin, "Once apona time . . ." and will end, "And they lived happily ever after." This understanding doesn't seem to come about simply by remembering certain stories, but is instead the result of an integration of memory and their internalized sense of how a story goes. Take 4-year-old Heather, for example, who could never seem to hear enough stories about the *Carebears*—little bears who protected others from evil spirits. One day while swinging in the park, she looked at the sky and said:

> That cloud—its a Care-a-lot cloud. The Carebears live there. The Carebears shaped me. I just jumped from the cloud. I helped take care of the teensie-weensies and kept them away from Dark Heart, who has red eyes and can turn anything he wants. He trapped the grown-ups and I have the key. More and more of the children were being hurt, and the adults were away, so me and my friend Lara, saved the Care-a-lots and flew home.

Story understanding, then, is a **constructive** process. In this case, Heather brings a rich blueprint of the *Carebear* story, its characters and plot, and builds a new story which essentially conforms to its basic structure. In other words, she integrates new information into her existing notions of how these events should come together to form a resolution for the story.

This sense of story comes about by hearing stories, and by being read to on a regular basis. Perhaps no other finding in research is as well documented as the simple fact that reading regularly to young children significantly influences their understanding of what reading is all about as well as their later proficiency in reading (Durkin, 1966; Feitelson, Kita & Goldstein, 1986; Heath, 1983; Wells, 1985). Reading to young children, then, actually *teaches* them about reading.

The book, however, is only one dimension of the storybook reading "event." Case studies of early readers attest to the importance of the informal conversational exchanges that occur between parent and child throughout the reading (Heath, 1983; Yaden, Smolken & Conlon, 1989). Ninio and Bruner, for example, provided one of the first systematic descriptions of adult–child interactions around books (1978). In their case study, they found that the mother supported the child's mastery of turn-taking rules and "scaffolded" the labelling that occurred through the reading, as in the following example.

Mother is reading Richard Scarry's *Egg in a Hole.*

Mother: Oh, look (points to a picture of a goat eating ice cream).

Anna: Ice cream that. Ice cream.
Mother: That's right. That's ice cream. Looks so yummy. Maybe
    we'll get some ice cream later, OK? (continues to read),
    "It rolled down . . ."
Anna: Ice cream good.
Mother: Right, that ice cream **is** good. You want to find the
    ice cream picture again?
Anna: (turning the pages back) That ice cream. Ice cream!
    (Anna's voice is triumphant.)

In this example, we see that Anna's mastery of the label "ice cream" is supported and extended through this interactional sequence. As these exchanges become more routinized, the mother will gently "up the ante" by providing a slightly more challenging task for Anna, which may require prediction or more sophisticated thinking about the printed material. It is these **interactive** processes that give storyreading its powerful influence on young children (see Chapter 3 for greater detail).

Over time, patterns that begin with a toddler labelling and commenting will progress to a preschooler's pretending to read books. They will demonstrate behaviors imitative of reading acts like holding a book in a certain way, using a particular body posture and eye movements, and turning the page as they use book-like language (Ferreiro & Teberosky, 1982).

With these behaviors, children are discovering what is in this activity that attracts and pleases them and they are showing us that they are

prepared to try it for themselves. Sulzby (1985) has documented these efforts, which she describes as "emergent storybook readings" or "independent reenactments." Often, children will choose books that have been read to them repeatedly, and using the narrative style and the approximate language of the book, they will "read"—preconventionally, that is. Soon they will begin to recite the text from pictures with such a degree of intonation that you might think they were really reading. Then after a while, without being directly taught, they will begin to notice some of the features of print, maybe first in the illustrations themselves, but then eventually in the larger sections of text on the page. In the final stages prior to reading, children will begin to actually *read* words and sentences with comprehension.

Notice the similarities between language learning and early reading development. Both oral and written language learning are motivated by the need to communicate, to interact with others, and to form a unique interpretation and response to the world around them. In both cases, language learning is **functional**, **interactive**, and **constructive.**

Writing

Children love to play with pencils, paper, crayons and markers. For them, these tools provide opportunities for spontaneous exploration—

Figure 2.1

for the sheer joy of movement and seeing marks appear on paper. Children's earliest attempt at this activity is generally described as scribbling. But just like babbling is to the beginning of talking, so is scribbling to the beginning of writing. Alongside oral language, writing has its roots in young children's growing ability to represent ideas and thoughts symbolically.

Scribbles can take many forms. Sometimes, a child's scribble will be in the form of circles; other times, they will look like approximations of writing. These forms are not at all stable in terms of development; rather there is tremendous variability between children and within children. Take for example, 2 1/2-year-old Lynira, who in one day at preschool plays with several different forms of scribble to represent clouds and circles for her teacher Ms. Lolita. Some of her actions look like "scribble writing" (2.1) while the others look more like "linear mock-like writing" (Clay, 1975).

In making these new discoveries about print, children are constructing their own ideas about writing that are not taught, are not modeled and are not conventional. They are attempting to represent what they see and what they know about real life. These first efforts, as suggested by Marie Clay, are "gross approximations" of what later will become more refined. For example, children will create their own alphabetic letters, invent all sorts of spellings for words and generate make-believe sentences. Such creative endeavors suggest that children are blending their own preconceptions of how things should be represented with the arbitrary conventions of our recorded language. Because these early efforts are both approximate and unstable, any new insights may change a

child's perceptions of these conventions altogether, leading to entirely new forms of writing. As Sulzby (1985) has suggested, children are building a repertoire of knowledges of written language that they may call upon later on.

Out of scribble, around ages 3 to 6, children begin to figure out that these marks on paper can be signs of meaning. They now attempt to discover strategies for conveying an idea, a thought, or something they like to others. And like reading at this age, their notions of print and pictures overlap; just like a picture is seen as conveying a narrative, so is a picture in writing thought of as symbolizing text. Children feel that their intentions are fulfilled through either medium (Dyson, 1982). Notice, in Figure 2.2, how Joshua's story is told through pictures and print, and in Figure 2.3, how Clare includes letter-like forms along with her pictures and scribbles in her story.

At this stage, children may hope that their printed pictures and symbols actually have some correspondence with what they are trying to convey. But there are no direct relations. In fact, Clay (1975) mentioned that

Figure 2.2

Figure 2.3

children at this age might hand their writing to an adult and ask, "What did I write?," assuming that the writing is interpretable to the adult, but not yet to them.

Their exploration continues as children begin to focus more on alphabet-like symbols and less on figure-like forms. Now they become truly inventive in the way they use signs; they turn letters around, decorate them, and add on a number of interesting nuances like dots. Notice, however, in Figures 2.4 and 2.5 that children are beginning to demonstrate more control in their hand movements as they explore the limitations within which a sign might vary.

These flexible forms are superseded by letter-like symbols, which in turn, are replaced by letters. You'll see in Figures 2.6 and 2.7 that children at ages 4 and 5 make a few symbols go a long way by repeating the patterns, which in turn, are replaced by writing a name, most often their own, or someone important in their lives, as in Elizabeth's case, "mom" or "dad."

Now a rather important shift occurs as children's writing becomes more interpretable to others. Lists of unrelated words are superseded by children's writing of phrases or sentences, with communicative intent,

Figure 2.4

Bunny the rabbit and his little sister rabbit.

Michael   age 4

Figure 2.5

My story is about a rabbit who hops.   Kyrie, age 3

Figure 2.6

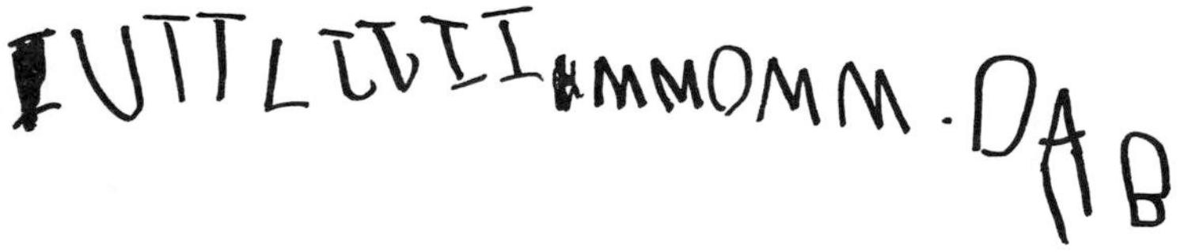

ᏆᏌᎢᎢᏞᏆᏆᏆᎢ ᴴᴹᴹᴼᴹᴹ · DAB

A story about a turtle.   Elizabeth, age 4

Figure 2.7

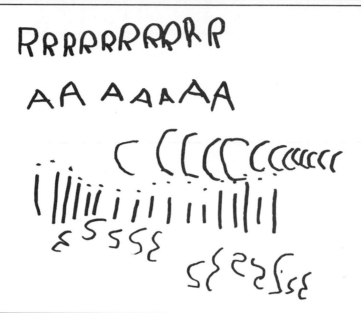

using the letters they know. The very beginnings of this effort may include a deliberate attempt to use an alphabetic symbol to stand for a word, like placing a letter "t" to stand for "truck." Shortly after, they begin to invent spellings—that is, they develop rather systematic ways to represent sounds in words they consider important. Charles Read's seminal work (1971) suggests that children place great reliance on their knowledge of English sounds, which they attempt to translate into alphabetic symbols. While appearing rather strange to adults, he argues that these spellings are, in fact, quite reasonable. Children are actively constructing a writing system which, with more experience and knowledge, will be modified many times, resulting in a fair approximation to traditional spelling. Still, as their writing develops, there will be patterns of variability. Children's paths of development in writing appear to reflect a shifting focus of attention from one aspect of the composing task (spelling) to another (sense of story), with refocusing efforts often resulting in a subsequent regression in one or another area. (Figure 2.8 gives an example of invented spelling at its more rudimentary stage. Figure 2.9 shows progression towards a more conventionalized form of spelling.)

Some children will arrive in kindergarten already writing their names and using invented spellings to communicate messages; others will be scribbling. Discoveries about print vary by interests and opportu-

Figure 2.8

4½
"ABCDEFG
HIJKLMN
OPQRSTUV
WXYZ"
"Heather Sullwan"
From
"Puerto Rico"

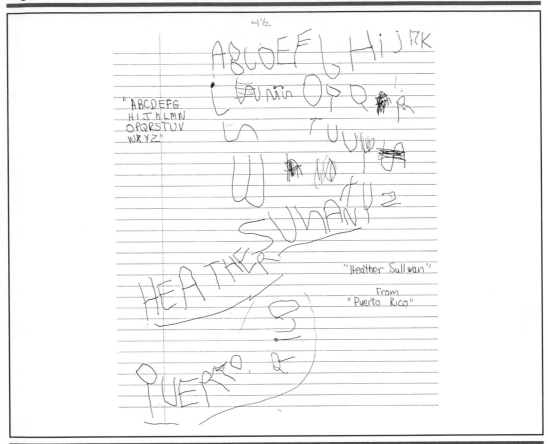

Figure 2.9

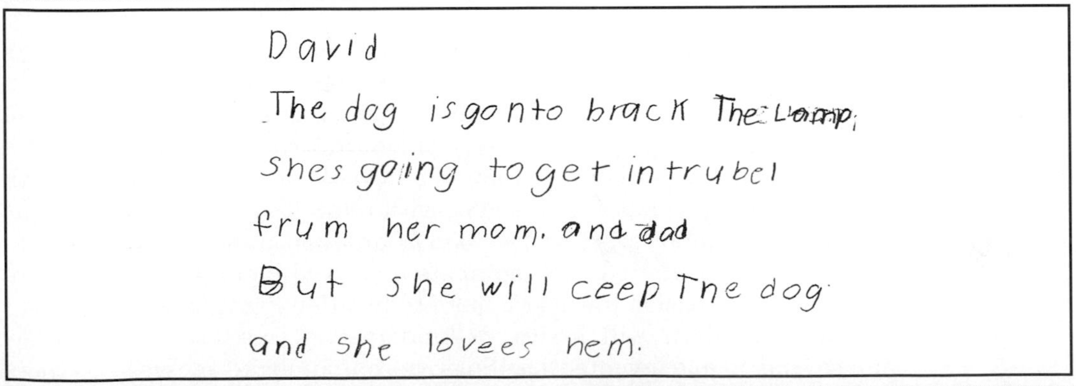

David
The dog isgonto brack The Lamp.
shes going toget intrubel
frum her mom. and dad
But she will ceep The dog
and she lovees hem.

nities. They are all learning about letters, words, and language simultaneously, but in different order and under different conditions. In our
office play center, for example, little 4-year-old Tasha who has been prac-
ticing writing her name in conventionalized form, uses a different kind of
writing to take an "important message." Sulzby's research of children's
writing also showed considerable variability, changing according to the
child's writing intent. When asked to "write everything you can," she
found that five-year-old children would write words in list-like fashion as
if inventorying their word knowledge. When asked to write "how grown-
ups do," they used scribble, like Tasha. (See Figure 2.10). Children's writing style reflected the particular task.

Just as **pretend reading** allows children to act like readers, they use
their emergent writing skills to act like writers. Through their play, they'll
indicate some of behaviors that writers do, like holding their markers or
pens in a certain way, and writing letters to each other. These writing
attempts seem to facilitate growth because they allow children to practice
what they have learned and to explore new dimensions of writing and its
functions. For example, three little girls are writing in the office play area:

Figure 2.10

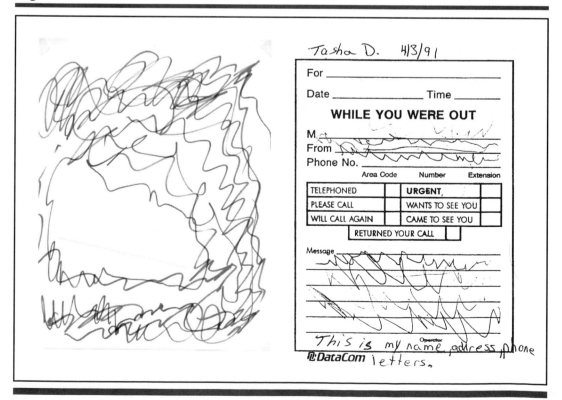

Megan: Bet you can't make this, Carol (she made a big "m" on her paper).

Carol: Betcha I can.

Jennifer: I can make something better than that.

Megan (to Jennifer): Do you know how to write?

Jennifer: Yup. You just hafta make lines.

Megan: We know how to make lines . . . lines is very easy. We don't need no help to make lines.

(They all continue writing and drawing on their papers.)

We see here that children as young as three years old make inferences about written language long before they have learned to formally read and write. They come to understand how written language works by experiencing it—by actively engaging in meaningful practice in child-centered ways. What is common to the uses of language, both written and oral, then, is that it is constructed, meaningful and in the broadest sense, social.

In summary, young children's literacy learning evolves out of many opportunities to observe, engage in, and practice language through a wide variety of experiences. Children construct their knowledge about print in fairly consistent ways from independent explorations of written language, interactions with adults and other children, and observations of others engaged in both functional and joyous literacy activities.

Parallels Between Language and Literacy in Development

We have seen the commonalities in the processes of early language acquisition and early literacy. Now we turn to how these processes in language learning compare in development.

Language Learning Begins as Play

Learning to talk and learning to read and write begin as a kind of play for children. As Bruner (1975) reminds us, play is an attitude—a way of approaching new experiences. Play is how children make connections between their immediate personal world and activities in the larger social context of family and community. They begin by playing with speech sounds in ways that resemble nonsense syllables, and by playing with the implements and materials of written language. They may even use characters and plots from their favorite stories in their pretend play. As Margaret Meek (1981) describes, "if reading looks like play to a child, it will be taken seriously."

The focus in the earliest form of play is on exploring particular sounds or features of literacy. There are really no set goals or accomplishments to be met, just the simple joy of manipulating materials and ideas in new, creative ways. Children's attentions lay in the **process** of the activity, and not the product of their explorations. When as caring adults, we might try to address these early explorations more seriously than intended, children will correct us, saying "that's not writing—it's just scribble." Goal-free in play, children discover that language is something they can use and control in a variety of ways and for a variety of purposes.

Play allows children to act "as if" they were accomplished readers and writers, nourishing their assumptions and expectations about becoming literate. Through oral and written language they may act as if they know how to read recipes, how to kill monsters, track down dangerous criminals, and to write stories. You can't simply tell a 4-year-old about the importance of learning about language—rather, through these encounters, the child discovers the pure fun of it. And it is through these early associations that children are later motivated to learn about the more formal rules and conventions of written language.

Language Learning is Partly Imitative

It is obvious that imitation plays a general role in language acquisition and literacy development. Children growing up in English-speaking homes, for example, learn to speak English with relative ease and speed, not some other language they haven't heard. Similarly, diary studies of toddlers simultaneously acquiring two languages suggest that children usually learn one language from one parent and the second from the other with little difficulty or interference between the two languages (Lindholm, 1980). Coinciding with their normal acquisition of spoken language, children often imitate the particular literacy tasks of their parents, like making shopping lists, and writing telephone messages. For example, in one of our preschool classrooms, we found groups of children pretending to do homework, imitating the school activities of their older brothers or sisters.

Imitation alone, however, is certainly not the whole answer. Rather, these imitative acts are used to learn *from*—not simply to learn. Not consciously, children pick up models of behavior from members of their home and community and try to make sense of them in their own unique ways. Take this scenario, for example, in the preschool:

(Four children are together in the kitchen writing at a table.)

Claire: Here, Elizabeth, this is your homework.

Elizabeth: I'm doing my homework (*She grabs a pencil to write on her paper*). These are for writing.

Claire (to a little boy who comes to the table): This is our homework. Don't bother us. All mine homework. I made my homework and I'm makin' my homework. (*She then puts a piece of her homework in the refrigerator*).

Certainly Claire and her friends don't regularly see their older siblings putting their homework away in quite this manner. Nevertheless, in this example, we are seeing the beginnings of communicative competence. The children are modelling some of the behaviors they associate with homework—the use of pencil and paper, the notion of not being disturbed—and constructing a new scenario. As young meaning seekers and meaning constructors, they use what has been shown or modeled to them, and through their interaction with people and things, play them out to suit their own particular purposes.

Clearly then, imitation and modeling are part of language learning development, even though they can only describe an aspect of the acquisition of these behaviors. A study by Ervin (1964) examining children's spontaneous language found relatively few direct imitations between parents and their children. What this suggests is that the rich language and literacy models that children pick up and imitate from their families and community become further articulated and enriched through their participation in many different social contexts. As Heath (1983) describes, different communities foster different "ways with words," indicating the powerful influence that these first imitative efforts and models exert on language and literacy development.

Language Serves Many Common Needs to its Learners

Investigators of oral language development suggest that knowledge about the functions of language is as much a part of becoming competent in oral language as acquiring the correct grammatical forms (Pflaum, 1986). As children learn language, they create impressions of what language is, what it is used for, and what language can do. Halliday (1975) argues that the recognition of the function of language, and the need for language, actually precedes and is a prerequisite for its acquisition.

What has often been overlooked is that a similar process holds true for literacy learning as well. Children's responses to tasks of reading messages or signs in their environment indicate that they have amassed numerous perceptions about the functions of written language prior to understanding some of its specific features. For example, when Hannah points to a sign and says "this means danger," she is attempting to capture the meaning of the sign (not the specific features of the words) and, in the process, is demonstrating her knowledge of the regulatory function of written language in daily life.

To examine children's developing conceptions, we observed fifty 3- and 4-year-olds during their spontaneous free play over a 3-month period (Neuman & Roskos, 1989). We found that preschoolers demonstrated a broad number of the uses of literacy on their own and with others, in ways that were meaningful to them. They used reading and writing for instrumental purposes, to claim ownership, to aid memory, and for authenticating actions. In play, children demonstrated their understanding that print carries a message while engaged in activities of their own volition. These findings provide evidence to suggest that very young children have developed conscious knowledge that print has meaningful functions, serving many of the common needs associated with oral language. Four of the functions that we identified, in fact, were comparable to Halliday's functions of oral language, as noted in Table 2.2.

The fact that language, whether oral or written, is recognized by children as fulfilling certain needs is an illustration of the nature of their language accomplishments prior to any kind of formal instruction in school.

Language Learning is Enhanced Through Opportunity

Learning to talk and learning to read and write evolve through a process of experiencing language. This suggests that young children come to understand how oral language works by participating in talk, using whatever linguistic resources they have at the time. The give and take of conversation allows them to extend their own language system and in the process, practice new forms. To do so, children need exposure to the context of conversation that is meaningful and sufficiently relevant to command their attention. Dinner conversations on subjects of academic politics are sure to arouse only distracted yawns. But tell children the story of when they were born and you will see their interests and questions come alive.

Similarly, children come to understand how written language works by having many opportunities to explore reading and writing in a variety of circumstances. By broadening the opportunities for engaging children with print, we make it possible for them to use what they already know to discover the predictability of print for themselves. Each situation creates new expectations for language usage; for example, children seem to intu-

TABLE 2.2   A TYPOLOGY OF CHILDREN'S UNDERSTANDINGS OF THE FUNCTIONS OF LITERACY AS EVIDENCED IN THEIR SPONTANEOUS PLAY (NEUMAN & ROSKOS, 1989)

DOMAIN	KINDS OF FUNCTIONS	EXAMPLES
Exploratory (the "how does it work?" function)	experiments with print handles literacy-related materials	Child writes letters Opens envelopes
Interactional* (the 'between you and me' function)	plays a rule-governed game communicates information about literacy to others	"let's play cards" "want me to show you how to write my name"
Personal* (the 'for me' function)	uses words to express personal ideas claims ownership	"I wrote I love you" "This is my picture— see it has my name"
Authenticating* (the 'regulatory' function)	uses literacy to verify information uses written language to act grown up	"This says Happy Valentine's Day" "I'm writin' up my taxes this year, cause you did 'em wrong last year"
Transactional* (the 'informative' function)	constructs meaning from text attempts to identify the meaning of print	"That word doesn't say 'dinosaur' "I'm on this page of the book"

*Similar to Halliday's language function.

itively lower their voices and quietly concentrate on the print and illustrations when at a library and learn to quickly scan labels to identify popular products when at the grocery store. Even at very early ages, they are using different reading strategies for different purposes, extending their repertoire of behaviors and accompanying social conventions associated with written language.

Language Learning is Extended Through Routines

Parents' responsiveness to the subtleties of children's conversations and attempts to extend their language uses has been recognized and described as facilitating language development (Snow, 1983). Another aspect of interaction that also contributes to language learning is the use of common routines. Neither rigid nor unexpandable, routines are highly predictable language events that condition children to anticipate what comes next, and to know how to act under such circumstances. Oral language routines may vary from the simple salutary "hi, how are you," "fine, thanks and how are you," to the more complex, multilayered set of interactions that typically accompany the bedtime routine.

Routinized contexts also contribute to children's literacy acquisition. Studies examining book reading routines (Ninio & Bruner, 1975; Snow & Goldfield, 1982) suggest the storybook reading event represents a powerful context for parent-child interaction in learning about vocabulary acquisition through labelling pictures and print, the development of a sense of story, as well as associating pleasure with print experiences. A prime example of the exploitation of a routine is the use of predictable books, like *Caps for Sale* (Slobodkin, 1947). After reading the book a number of times, 2 1/2-year-old Hannah can anticipate what will come next:

Mother (reads): Once there was a peddler who sold
   (pauses) . . . . what did he sell?
Hannah: A sale?
Mother: What did he sell, he sold (pauses) . . . . what's on his
   head?
Hannah: Caps.
Mother (reads): He walked up and down the streets walking
   very straight so as not to upset his caps and as he went
   along, he called . . . .
Hannah: Caps.
Mother (reads): But one morning he couldn't sell any caps. He
   walked up the street and he walked down the street,
   calling . . .
Hannah: Caps.

In the book reading routine, Hannah's mother's voice signals to her daughter that she is waiting for a response. Following an initial unsuccessful attempt, she then asks Hannah a direct query, providing informational cues to help her along. Once Hannah has learned the routine, the reading continues smoothly. These routinized events are said to ultimately contribute to increased word learning and reading comprehension (Snow & Goldfield, 1982).

Contexts formatted from common experiences involving literacy also constitute an ideal medium for language and literacy acquisition. Take Justin's and AJ's play in the kitchen for example:

(They are pretending to eat out.)

Justin: I would like dinner. I wanna eat outside.
AJ (pretending to be a waiter): Whatta ya wanna eat?
Justin: I'll have a burger.
AJ: What else?
J: I want pop.
AJ (goes to the kitchen and says): I wanna burger and a
    Sprite and a Pepsi for me to go . . ."

AJ and Justin are demonstrating their familiarity with the appropriate routines associated with eating at a fast food restaurant. Using a set of learned sequences, children begin to internalize the behaviors and actions associated with being literate.

Consequently, in the process of development, oral language and literacy share a number of important commonalities:

- ❑ the significance of play in their development
- ❑ the influence of imitation and models in helping children figure out the intricacies of language and communication
- ❑ the centrality of communicative needs to the early stages of acquisition
- ❑ the importance of having opportunities to practice and extend abilities
- ❑ the need to engage in highly predictable sequences of behaviors in contexts free from failure

Distinctions Between Language and Literacy in Development

While the parallels between spoken language and literacy acquisition are impressive, there are also important ways in which these two processes differ. We believe that it is critical for child care professionals to recognize these distinctions in creating integrated language and literacy experiences for young children. Let's look at some myths that have been advanced in recent years, and dispel them by evidence from studies of children's language and literacy development.

Myth #1: Learning to Read and Write is as Natural as Learning to Speak and Listen

Acquiring oral language is a natural process, but just how natural are the processes of learning to read and write? There are some who contend that written language, like oral language, is learned incidentally and vicariously through opportunities to observe and engage in literacy practices in everyday settings. Goodman (1984), for example, gives numerous examples of the ways in which preschool children pick up information about the nature and uses of written language in a society like ours. Others (Harste, Burke & Woodward, 1982), as well, posit that children learn written language naturally, because it gives them power "to construct, manipulate, and even erase entire worlds of experiences and ideas which otherwise would never exist for them" (Smith, 1984).

We wish it were so. But the undeniable fact is that while children acquire spoken language through incidental and informal learning, there are few who learn literacy without some form of instruction. It is true that Bissex (1980), Baghban (1984), and Torrey (1969) have written compelling accounts of children who have taught themselves to read early and easily. However, even in homes where literacy is prized, the majority of children do not.

We suspect that the view that learning to read is as natural as learning to speak is a reaction against practices that regard young children as knowing little, if anything, about print prior to formal instruction. Unfortunately, such practices may have discouraged children from accessing what they already know about language and applying this information to written language forms. Nevertheless, the pendulum may have swung too far in favor of natural learning (see Donaldson's 1984 argument, for example). Unlike with speech, there are children who may need to be directed in a more systematic fashion to written language and its conventions. Teachers do young children a disservice to ignore these individual differences.

Myth #2: Written Language Doesn't Need to be Taught

A corollary to natural learning is the view that written language, like its oral counterpart, need not be taught, at least in any formal way. According to Smith (1984), for example, written language, just like speech, is learned through rich demonstrations—opportunities to engage in an activity, with little or no awareness on the part of either the demonstrator or child that teaching or learning is actually taking place. From this view, written language learning is implicit; it is a concomitant, not a consequence, of demonstration.

Similarly, Schickedanz (1986) argues that environments rich with physical resources and social mediation bring about literacy learning in the same fashion as oral language. "The fact that more children master oral language without tutoring than is the case for written language may say more about differences between typical oral and written language environments than about differences in children's cognitive dispositions to learn one form of language versus another" (1986, p.4).

Again, however, we suspect an overreaction. Formal instruction of the kind that focuses on the abstract systems of language such as letters and individual sounds surely fragment and make meaningless written language for preschoolers. But, as subsequent chapters will show, arguing for implicit teaching only ignores the many explicit strategies that bring children to literacy through their oral language development. Learning through nursery rhymes, music, and jingles are just some examples of the rich language activities that impact later literacy learning (Jusczyk, 1977). The issue, then, relates more to the developmental appropriateness of the activity, rather than its form of conveyance.

While oral language is a universal phenomenon, literacy is not. Unlike oral language, which is acquired without an obvious direct instruction, few children will become literate without some form of explicit teaching.

Myth #3: Written Language is Essential for Communicating

Oral language is viewed as an essential means for communicating; obviously, it would be nearly impossible to function without it. Is written language as equally compelling? Why should children try to make sense of print? Some educators believe that the same dynamic holds true; literacy is seen as an indispensable activity which need not be extrinsically motivated, directed and reinforced. Like oral language, it is constantly taking place without the child's awareness.

Nevertheless, the fact of the matter is that unlike oral language, unless children are raised in a culture that requires it, written language is often not seen as an essential means for communicating. In her description of literacy practices in the Piedmont Carolinas, for example, Heath (1983) described differences in language socialization among cultures. In the community of Trackton, families relied more on the oral tradition, using storytelling to convey information; Roadville, on the other hand, communicated a great deal of information through written language. To assume, therefore, that all children are equally motivated to learn about written language as a means to make sense of their world, is to ignore important cultural and home environmental differences. For example, if oral and written language were seen as equally essential, why then do we have as many as 25 million fluent, yet illiterate adults in the U.S? Rather, unlike oral language, teachers must convey through their teaching practices and demonstrations the power of written language as a communication system.

Consequently, there are two important and rather obvious ways in which the acquisition of language and of literacy differ:

❑ Unlike oral language, written language is not a universal phenomenon, learned by all children without some form of teaching.

❑ Written language is highly susceptible to environmental influences and existing cultural norms, which suggests that it may not always be regarded as an essential means of communication.

Guidelines for Practice

We began by discussing some important aspects of early language acquisition and early literacy development, focusing on the similarities and differences of these processes in their development. Consider the distance that we have traveled in our understanding of the complexity and sophistication of young children's oral and written language. Contrary to the view of passive imitators, it has become abundantly clear that children have a complex repertoire of strategies which serve them well when it comes to learning about language. This theoretical understanding of language development (oral and written) carries with it significant implications for teaching language and literacy in the early childhood classroom. We'll focus here on identifying important guidelines for instruction. Specific practices and activities are described in subsequent chapters.

1. It's never too early to learn about language:

The single best vehicle for language development is language itself. Experiences with language, as we have noted in Chapters 1 and 2, are cumulative. Encounters with oral language allow us to interact with others, to create and extend language processes; similarly, oral language provides resources for generating written language.

We've learned to recognize the importance of children's rudimentary efforts in learning language and their awareness of the writing that surrounds them. Equally impressive, we've learned that children are able to create meaning themselves with pencil and paper long before their writing looks representational to our conventional eyes. But we also recognize that these processes don't just emerge naturally. What appears to be natural includes environmental influences, adult interactions, and opportunities which enhance language learning.

From this view, then, it is evident that it is never too early to teach language, reading and writing. In reality, all language learning begins in infancy. Consequently, we believe that language and literacy can and should be taught to all children in preschools, day-care facilities, child development centers, Head Start programs, and prekindergarten programs.

2. Activities and lessons must be developmentally appropriate:

An important caveat to our first guideline, the ways in which we approach language and literacy instruction in early childhood must be developmentally appropriate. We simply cannot use a trickled-down form of language arts curricula or phonics workbooks used in the primary school and expect them to work. Programs like these make language and literacy seem unnecessarily difficult and irrelevant; further, they ignore what children may bring on their own to these language experiences.

Rather, activities and learning experiences should be developed that draw on the particular needs, language uses and activities that are unique to children at this age level. Obviously, the most rigid definition of teaching, as in telling or giving information about language and literacy will surely be ineffective; instead, we must develop language strategies to be learned in the context of the child's experiences, through their play and interaction with others.

Priorities are out-of-step with the nature of young children as literacy learners when preschools and day-care centers resort to pre-primers and workbook instruction, focusing on sight words and sound/symbol relationships. In fact, in the long run, they may actually do more harm than good, by making more difficult and dull what can be so satisfying and useful to young children. In contrast to these practices, then, it is critical for early childhood programs to adopt as their foundation functional and meaningful activities that involve talking, reading and writing in a wide variety of ways.

3. Children learn language through active engagement:

All of the research we've examined indicates the essential nature of activity in young children's language learning. Part of becoming a proficient language user involves having opportunities to play with, to "mess around" with and to experiment with reading and writing. As teachers, we must prepare the environment, and give time for children to freely engage in such independent explorations of print.

The focus, however, should not be on a literacy curriculum, per se. Rather, language activities should flow throughout the curriculum; they should be an integral part of the very nature of the child's day. How can one legitimately know when it's time to go to the library without reading the time? How can we tell our friend Amy that we're really sorry she's out with chicken pox without writing a letter? How can we possibly remember what to bring for the party without making a list? Even before children can actually read and write they can, with our help, begin to demonstrate the practices and attitudes of the literate community. Language and literacy skills and conventions grow from these roots.

4. **Children learn language by being treated like serious apprentices:**

   Observations of early literacy development among precocious children offer important insights into how adults may best create effective language learning environments for young children. These studies (Durkin, 1966; Daghban, 1984) seem to indicate a model of teaching that more closely resembles that of a guide or facilitator than the more formal role of teacher. In this role, the adult's job is to interpret the child's meaning, respond favorably to efforts to grow, answer specific questions, and provide the materials for learning.

   These interactions, like that of an encouraging parent, do not take the form of sitting a child down, workbook in hand, and drilling the child on the ABCs or phonics. Rather, encouraging adults participate in activities *with* children, demonstrating and involving them in the uses of written language. They may even use opportunities to create routines that integrally involve written language. Perhaps most important, encouraging adults take these initial efforts by children seriously, confirming to them that they are readers and writers while they simultaneously extend their facility with language as well as their understanding of the world.

· ·

Let's Review . . .

   Children begin to acquire language and literacy abilities very early in life. In their development, these processes share a number of important similarities. Theories of early language acquisition suggest that language learning is a constructive, interactive, and functional process. Through their activities and explorations, young children construct an understanding of how language works, and then use these skills with increasing facility to serve their needs.

   Like oral language learning, literacy learning is also constructive, interactive, and functional for our young learners. Children construct their knowledge about print in fairly consistent ways. Their first efforts often involve independent explorations of written language, interactions with adults and other children, and observations of others engaged in both functional and enjoyable language activities.

   There are important parallels between language and literacy in development as well. Both oral and written language begin as a kind of play, allowing children the freedom of exploration without severe consequences. They first imitate forms from role models, and then extend these interpretations to make language their own. Their desire to make meaning is created from their needs to function in the environment. As a result, children's language learning, in both oral and written forms, is greatly enhanced by occasions to make use of their developing conceptions and skills. Through common routines in home and school environments, we give children safe opportunities to do so.

But there are also important ways in which oral and written language differ. Unlike oral language, written language is not necessarily naturally learned and thus needs to be taught. Without appropriate teaching, we cannot expect children to become literate.

Appropriate teaching strategies, however, are required for young language learners. Guidelines for practice suggest that activities must be developmentally appropriate, gauged to young children's interests and abilities, and involve a great deal of active learning and encouragement.

Let's Explore . . .

1. Collect a language sample from a young child (ideally 2 to 3 years old) and his or her mother or father (or care-giver) as they are engaged in various routines: night time storyhour, bath tub, or doing the chores. Tape-record these samples and transcribe them verbatim. Examine these transcripts for evidence of how a child:

    ❑   constructs how language works. Are there particular "unique" words or constructions in their vocabulary?

    ❑   attempts to engage others in conversation. How does the adult's response enhance the child's speech?

    ❑   tries to use language to get things. Are there instances of instrumental, regulatory, or personal uses of language?

2. Ask a child to "read" you a favorite story. Try to assess his or her emergent reading behavior, using an adapted form of a classification system developed by Elizabeth Sulzby (1985):

    ❑   Child reads by labelling pictures, but does not attempt to tell a story.

    ❑   Child reads by following the pictures and tells a story.

    ❑   Child attends to a mix of pictures, reading, and storytelling, using the oral intonation of a storyteller.

    ❑   Child reads using the pictures, with wording and intonation indicative of story reading.

    ❑   Child attends to print, using some of the aspects of print.

Through this activity, a teacher can broadly gauge a child's conception of storyreading.

3. Ask a young child, or a group of children, to write a story (encourage them to write it "their way."). Examine these stories for evidence of the following developmental patterns:

   ❑   The child views drawing *as* writing. Pictures are used to communicate words and thoughts.

   ❑   The child scribbles, intending to write.

   ❑   The child makes letter-like forms.

   ❑   The child uses letter sequences, sometimes producing letters in long strings or random order.

   ❑   The child uses invented spelling, creating his or her own spelling for a word.

   ❑   The child uses conventionalized spelling. Words resemble adult-like writing.

Language and Literacy

At Home

characteristics

situations

cultural influences

At Child Care

characteristics

comparison to home

Building Bridges

Guidelines For Teachers

CHAPTER 3

Bridging Home and Child Care Environments for Literacy Learning

Mother to son as they're walking to school:

Mom: *"Really, school will be fun, I promise."*

*P*arents are our children's first language teachers. Almost every event, whether trivial or profound, provides an occasion for meaningful communication. Conversations over practical, everyday activities, such as eating or watching television together, create opportunities for children to ask questions and for parents to relay information about language. And from these routine, collaborative experiences, children in all cultures build their ideas about the functions and uses of language, internalizing many of its rules and processes, long before coming to school.

But in moving from home to school, the child enters a different world. At school, language experiences may differ dramatically from those in the shared learning environment of the home. Now the child must adapt from a very small setting in which he or she was a central character to a much larger group setting. Language or topics which were once freely discussed may be "off-limits" in the more formal, public environment of the classroom. Whereas most of the language and literacy activities at home were situated within common, practical activities, a good deal of the language activity at school may be centered around relatively abstract tasks which may hold little interest for the child. Language learning strategies which had once served children so effectively at home, therefore, may seem less successful and sometimes even counterproductive in the child care context.

What do these observations advise for creating effective language learning environments in the classroom? They suggest that we need to provide for greater continuity between home and school practices. In this chapter, we will discuss bridging the gap between these two contexts. We will explore the special characteristics of the home learning environment to gain some insights from parents on early language learning . Then, we will investigate the classroom as a context for learning about oral and written language. Finally, we will consider the implications of what we have learned for teaching and the development of curriculum.

Characteristics of the Home Learning Environment

Four-year-old Katy is watching television with her mother.

Katy: Mom, is it warm in Princeton, New Jersey in February?
Mother: No, Katy, but why do you think so?
Katy: Everybody is wearing short sleeves on the program so I thought it must be warm.
Mom: I think it's probably because we're watching a rerun.

Typical of home learning, several important aspects of language development are revealed in this simple exchange between parent and child. Notice how Katy's mother first listens thoughtfully to her daughter's question before offering an alternative response. She then probes, attempting to interpret the reasoning behind her question. Finally, she offers her own understanding of the situation. Gordon Wells (1985) has described this parental pattern, as "leading from behind"; Katy is encouraged to take the initiative. Then she is supported and assisted in her language attempts.

None of these efforts are consciously "educational." In fact, much of what is learned is incidental to the ongoing activity. Such simple questions, expressions of interest on the part of the child, may often prompt spontaneous information-extending conversations. Like Heather, who asks her mother after watching "Wild Kingdom" on TV, " Mom, do them Africans eat dead animals?" Her mother responds, "I don't know much about Africans, but I suspect they eat meat just like we do." It is through these everyday exchanges that the child gradually takes on the adult way of interpreting the world, not through deliberate teaching, but through experiencing life's events together.

However, such an appreciation of the home as an educational context for learning about language is relatively new. Not long ago we used to believe that language and literacy development were better left to the schools to teach in some formal way. Even now, the emphasis in many child care programs is on "educating" the parents. Less often have we focused on what we can learn from the examples parents offer us.

Yet a number of recent observational studies of young children suggest that the home is a powerful learning environment (Heath, 1983; Tizard & Hughes, 1984; Wells, 1985). These researchers have found that before children come to school, their language development takes place largely through talk, or conversation. Generally, these conversations are compact—brief educational excerpts in the midst of active involvement in a task. The following conversation between Brett, 22 months, and her mother illustrates the interplay between adult and child. Brett is playing with her wooden rocking horse while her mother is sorting clothes.

> **Brett:** Mommy, I'm riding a horsey. That's, that's a . . .
> (indicates mother's activity). Put clothes in there.
> **Mother:** I'm putting your **socks** away in the **drawer.** See,
> there's some long tights?
> **Brett:** Tights?
> **Mother:** These are all tights that you can wear this winter,
> when it gets cold, colder, and colder.

Without intentionally trying to teach Brett, her mother emphasizes particular words, and describes a setting in which they might be used. Take note of the sheer amount of general knowledge that the child is given, especially in relation to such an ordinary routine. In most cases, a notable feature of these conversations are their brevity due to the close relation between what is said and the activity in which the speech is embedded. Since parent and child share the same world, a great deal of meaning can be conveyed with relatively little effort.

When more extended conversations do occur, they tend to be at odd times, when nothing in particular is going on—waiting at the doctor's office, or sitting around after dinner. Here are the times when a parent might engage in more discursive conversations which include talk about their social activities, family relations, and past events. These conversations provide not only general knowledge, but to a large extent, relevant social knowledge. In a sense, the parent establishes a conceptual framework in which to fit the child's experiences. Studies of communicative competence suggest that virtually all aspects of communication are strengthened through these types of conversational exchanges (Cazden, 1981; Genishi, 1987).

As active seekers of information, children's curiosity often leads to "passages of intellectual search"—long, seemingly endless "why" and "how" questions to their parents (Tizard & Hughes, 1984). Sometimes, it seems like a series of challenges, as we see in the case of Christopher and his mother:

Mother: What do you want a drink of?

Christopher: Apple juice

Mother: Ok, you can have one glass of apple juice but that's all for now.

Christopher: Why?

Mother: Because it's close to dinner and I don't want to spoil your appetite.

Christopher: Why would a drink spoil my appetite?

Mother: Because it is filling and it has a lot of sugar.

Christopher: Why can't I have sugar?

Mother: Because it will make you more thirsty.

And so, the conversation continues, as the parent attempts to satisfy the puzzled mind of the young child. But while frustrating at times, these questions illustrate the intense need of children to make sense of apparent anomalies in their limited knowledge base. Analyses of conversations have consistently revealed the rather persistent, though logical, ways in which children are attempting to make sense of their world. As Tizard and Hughes describe, "the mind of the four-year-old contains a large number of half-assembled scaffoldings which have yet to be integrated into a more coherent framework" (1984, p. 131).

These observations suggest that home learning may be characterized by the following features:

1) Learning is often embedded in contexts of great meaning to the child.

2) Learning is typically incidental, often involving brief "shorthand" excerpts in the context of ongoing activity.

3) Learning is commonly initiated by the child's persistence and curiosity in wanting to know "why" and "how."

4) The vast body of shared experiences helps parent and child to convey a great deal of learning through talk, helping the

child make sense of present experiences by relating them to their past.

Contexts for Learning

What are the most effective learning contexts in the home? A number of studies have examined parent-child interactions in family settings of imaginative play, games, TV viewing, lessons and stories (Tizard & Hughes, 1984; Wells, 1985). Two important conclusions have been reported: First, since learning appears to be implicit in many ongoing activities, these researchers suggest that all contexts have the potential to extend children's language through their talk and involvement in print. Children learn to relate oral and written language to their surrounding environment. Second, of these family contexts, storyreading, in particular, appears to be most powerfully associated with later literacy success. Let's turn now to an examination of each of these findings.

Exposure to Language in Context

The extensive range of activities that take place within the home provide children with opportunities to learn about a wide variety of topics. Much of what they learn, as we have seen, is through regular conversations with their parents. But through their involvement in ordinary activities, children are also continuously interacting with and attempting to figure out the meanings of visible language as well. They show their awareness of print by asking, "What does this say?" or by recognizing familiar signs and labels. Although most young children can not "read" print in any formal sense, a conscious awareness that print has particular meanings becomes quite well developed during the preschool years.

Seen as an important step in early literacy knowledge, the term **environment print** refers to print that is supported by a situational context. The context may include a familiar, predictable setting, as well as other cuing systems like a particular form of script, color, or shape to define its meaning. For example, children may use the unique form of script to identify Crest toothpaste or McDonald's signs. Regardless of the specific cuing system used, however, an intriguing study by Goodman and Altwerger (1981) reported that at least 60% of the 3-year-olds in their research were able to read environmental print when it was embedded in context.

But context is a tricky concept. For one, there are degrees of context. A Burger King sign, for example, represents a rather determinate context; if asked, a child might refer to the sign as McDonald's or perhaps indicate its function, like "it's where you go to eat." Rarely, however, would many children completely misrepresent the term. Together, the sign, the place, the smell, and the activity help to cue young children as to the word's identity. Now, take a very common sign, like EXIT.

In this case, the word is seen even more frequently than the Burger King sign; it is found in a common spot—over a door that leads out—and it is characteristically printed in capital letters. Yet, young children are less likely to be able to read this sign. In this case, though situationally based, the context is far more general. Thus, while certainly not denying the importance of environmental print, it is questionable whether children are actually reading or logically reacting to a number of clues from the environment.

Rather, as Masonheimer, Drum and Ehri (1984) have discovered, the task of extracting meaning from environmental print seems to focus on more obvious cues, like color or logos, and less on differentiating letters or words. For instance, noting that the color of a stop sign is red, a child might identify all words surrounded by the color red as the word "stop." In some very real sense then, children tend to read the environment instead of the print.

What this suggests is that while the world is filled with environmental print, children are not likely to begin reading printed words encountered in more decontextualized settings (like storybooks, for example) on the basis of their acquisition of these print-meaning associations. Rather, by pointing out labels and signs, parents can make children aware of the generalized notion that print carries meaning. This, in itself, is an important precursor to literacy development.

Storybook Reading

No other single experience features quite as prominently in case histories of early readers as storybook reading. Evidence of the importance of

reading aloud abound in the professional literature; correlational, (Wells, 1985) experimental (Elley, 1989) and ethnographic research (Heath, 1983) confirm that interactions with books provide children with a breadth of information about the processes and functions of written language.

Aside from the sheer intimacy of reading books together, what accounts for its powerful influence as a context for learning? One reason is that compared with conversation which arises out of shared activity, storybook reading cannot rely on the external world to determine the interpretation of the text. Rather, words must create the world of meaning. The child begins to discover the symbolic potential of language.

Gordon Wells suggests that in listening to stories, children also begin to gain experience in the organization of written language and its characteristic rhythms and structures. The simple and predictable text found in many picture books, along with repeated readings, lead children to hear patterns and to remember them. Further, stories communicate information, taking children away from their immediate environment, and vicariously extending the range of their experiences.

But perhaps one of its most important features, is that of a conversation starter. Parent–child exchanges over books often resemble the extended conversations that occur when parents are free from other tasks. A number of mother–child case studies of storybook readings have shown that a rather routinized exchange tends to take place between mother and child. For instance, Ninio and Bruner (1978), examining readings by a mother and her young son from when he was 8 months to 1 1/2 years old, found that the events consisted of a dialogue cycle, following a standard pattern:

Mother: Look. [attentional vocative]
Child: [attends to picture]
Mother: What's that? [query]
Child: A doggie. [label]
Mother: Yes that's it! [feedback]

This example describes how the adult–child dialogue may support or scaffold the labeling of items in picture books. Here, the adult maintains a very consistent routine, which over time the child responds to with increasing skill and decreasing variability. Notice that as the child gets older, the parent ups the ante, providing scaffolds for high-level learning, seen in the following example:

Mother is reading *Bear* by Don Freeman to 2 1/2-year-old Hannah:

Mother: One wondrous day, Thear, the little boy, went away and just when he'd be back he wouldn't say. He was all alone for the first time. Bete, the bear, amused himself by looking at a book, an ABC animal book. "Why hasn't anyone told me this before," said Bete sadly to himself. 'B' is for bear—an animal brave who lives in a . . ."
Hannah: I don't know.
Mother: Who's in a cave?
Hannah: Why?
Mother: That's where bears usually live—in caves. They have their babies in caves. (continues to read) I wonder if there could be a cave for me—way up in those hills—and taking a long shiny telescope he searched the side of the hill until he spied a . . .
Hannah: Hole
Mother: Right, a cave—it's a hole in the mountain.

In effect, Hannah is encouraged to be an active participant in the reading. Whatever she can't do is filled in or held up by her mother's scaffolding activities. Over time, as Snow and Goldfield (1982) have demonstrated in their case study, the child seems to pick up what she has heard her mother say on these occasions, and eventually uses these same utterances as her own. This is an example of Bruner's "voluntary hand-over and willing receipt" (1975) principle—the child accepts what the parent has to offer, and then initiates further learning on his/her own.

As a child's facility with language grows, these conversational exchanges become more extended and often more complex. Children engage in "passages of intellectual search," much like they do in conversations. One common type of verbal interaction is called "life-to-text" exchanges (Cochran-Smith, 1984; Heath, 1983). These interactions help story listeners use their knowledge of the world to make sense of the text. For example, Heather, age 4, has just finished reading a chapter of *Ramona the Pest* (Cleary, 1968) with her Dad:

Heather: Daddy, what's a pleat?
Dad: A pleat? I've never heard of "pleat." What do you think it is?
Heather: A skirt?
Dad: Oh, I think you mean it's her pleated skirt. Ramona talks about her pleated skirt.
Heather: Yeah, she was skipping in a pleated skirt.
Dad: Do you remember when you spin around and have on a pleated skirt, and the skirt rises up?
Heather: Yup.
Dad: That's what it means—pleated.
Heather: Oh, I get it.

Notice that her father is successful by bringing Heather's own life experiences to bear in attempting to understand the word, "pleated." In effect, Heather's father is demonstrating an important comprehension monitoring strategy of using one's prior knowledge to make sense of the text.

Another common verbal pattern is called "text-to-life" interactions. Here, the parent–child exchanges focus on the personal meaning of the story, connecting the storyreading with the child's everyday experiences. In this example, Heather and her Dad are reading *One Morning in Maine* by Robert McCloskey:

Heather: Are those the trees that they're talking about?
Father: Yeah, those are pine trees.
Heather: We have pine trees out back.
Father: We have some but not so many do we?

Heather: Yeah.

Father: Remember there were so many in Maine. Sometimes when the fog came up we couldn't see them, remember that? Real gray and foggy. Then when the fog went away we saw all little islands filled with trees just like that.

Here, the father is weaving together the text and the child's own personal history. These conversational exchanges help to extend the child's own thinking about things, couched in terms that she understands. In a sense here, father and daughter are using the book to construct knowledge together. According to Wells (1985), this constructing of stories, or **storying** is one of the fundamental means by which we, as humans, gain control over our world.

Storybook reading, therefore, may represent an ideal environment to learn about language and literacy for the following reasons:

1. It provides a situational context for extended conversations between parent and child.
2. In reading together, children begin to develop concepts of the form and structure of written language.
3. In their conversational exchanges, parents demonstrate and children internalize reading strategies which may be used in later literacy development.

Learning language and literacy in the home, then, occurs across two broad categories. First, there is the context of everyday living. A good deal of learning in this context occurs incidentally in the midst of ongoing activities as children participate in events with their families. Simply by being around family members, talking, playing, helping, and endlessly asking questions, children are provided with large amounts of information relevant to their language and literacy development. And, in their efforts to learn and to participate, they insert themselves in the adult world, and begin to display many of the behaviors and preconventional skills that are part of that world.

But a second, more child-centered context is that of storybook reading. Here, the parent must enter into the child's world. In this context, it is the mother or father who must adjust his or her behavior to the child's level of functioning. When the child cannot respond to the parent's request for a response, the parent accepts what is offered, then provides a response until such a time as the child can produce it on his or her own. Unlike everyday living, it is the match between the support system (that is, parent scaffolding) and the acquisition process that provides such a critical influence in storybook reading. This finely tuned interaction represents a key feature of why the storybook reading context, over and above all other contexts, is so strongly associated with later literacy development.

Differences among Cultures in Language Learning

Are these language and literacy processes socialized identically across different cultures and ethnic groups? Certainly not. Rather, we see wide variations in language styles, dialects, and uses practiced and maintained in home environments. And in many cases, these differences have created implicit assumptions about the child's learning potential. Some educators have perceived the nonstandard dialect of their students as signs of inadequacy. Unfortunately, this has led sometimes to the notion that difference is akin to deficit. Before making any such conclusions, however, let's explore the evidence currently available on how language and literacy development might be influenced by these differences.

The Deficit View

To a great extent, differences in language dialects (that is, variations with language distinguished by phonology, syntax, meaning, and use) in the early 60's were largely viewed as an explanation which might account for the underachievement among children of poverty. Going along with the beliefs of experts, President Johnson, for example, funded the Head Start program to help poor children overcome educational deficits in verbal abilities associated with general intelligence, and general school achievement. The assumption was that if we could only modify the kind of language these children brought to school, then along with changes in home practices, we might influence their later school success.

In fact, this explanation achieved great popularity because it provided educators with a solution to what seemed an incorrigible problem: the increasing achievement gap between middle- and lower-class children. Programs like DISTAR and FOCUS were specifically designed for the language deficiencies seen in these disadvantaged children. These programs engaged children in language, through repetition of structural patterns common to Standard English or "school dialect." For example, the interactions might conform to the following pattern (Bartlett, 1981):

Teacher: This ball is round. Now you say it.
Child: "This ball is round."
Teacher: What kind of ball is this?
Child: "This ball is round."

While somewhat effective, the advisability of such practices was seriously questioned for young learners. As Blank (1982) pointed out, these types of materials actually seemed to circumvent the natural language learning process, making it artificial and more difficult to learn. Further, they smacked of a bias toward any dialect variation. This reflected the heart of the problem with the deficit view.

The Difference View

An altogether different explanation was proposed by William Labov (1970). Far from inadequate verbal stimulation in the home, he argued that ghetto children participate in a highly verbal culture, possessing the same basic vocabulary, the same capacity for conceptual learning, and the same logic as any typical middle-class child who learns to speak and understands English. According to Labov, the view that these children were verbally deprived was "part of the modern mythology of educational psychology" (p. 154).

Rather than language deficiency, he suggested that it is the social situation that impacts on perceptions of children's linguistic capabilities. For example, in one of our studies, we found black preschoolers displaying very limited understanding of verbal routines in a test situation. Yet, when playing in the office play center, these children were far from reticent, demonstrating language structures and behaviors very typical of this age level:

Leslie, Daryl, and Delores are sitting in the Office. Leslie is writing.

Daryl takes the phone: The cops comin' to get you and your brother.

Leslie: No they ain't.

Daryl: Yes they is.

Delores: They ain't gonna come get me; they gonna come get you, cause you's bein' bad.

Daryl (to Delores): I'm callin' the cops on you again.

Delores: No you're not.

Daryl: Yes I am. (uses phone) "Cops, come get these girls."

Delores (starts singing): I just wanna be me old crazy, cause I'm me.

Daryl (who is talking to the cops on the phone): You ain't crazy, Delores.

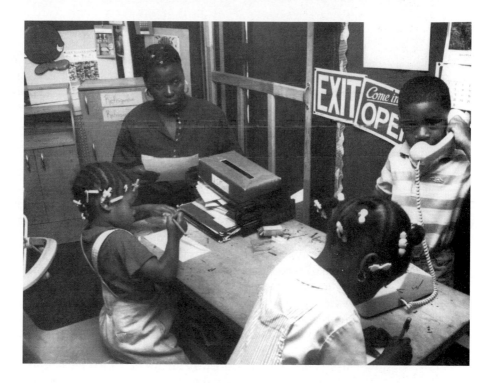

Note the lyrical quality of the children's language. You can almost "hear" the intonation and the inflections of their words. Unlike the "deficit view," then, we can see that these children are highly verbal. Programs that compensate for "language deficiency" are unfortunately misleading; black English is not easier or less capable of encoding complex ideas. It's just different. Consequently, Labov suggests that it is the teacher who must adapt to the child's dialect and value it, and not the child to the teacher's manner of speaking. Adults must try to enter into the child's world to enhance interaction and communication.

Such a view has contributed tremendously to a greater appreciation of language variations. It has also made people aware of the often, though largely unstated, assumption which suggests that middle-class Standard English represents the correct form of language usage. Nevertheless, the view that dialects are different and not deficit, has not really addressed important educational issues or instruction for children of poverty that might enhance the closing of the achievement gap. Essentially, their stance has remained noninterventionist. As Pflaum (1986) accurately points out, however, merely understanding the features of black English, and adjusting our attitudes toward those who speak it, still leaves unanswered a basic question: Why is there such a wide variation among linguistic groups in literacy development?

The Cultural Discontinuity View

A more plausible explanation relates to the cultural discontinuity view. Sociologist Basil Bernstein (1970) in Britain, studying working and middle-class children, suggested that differences in achievement were not related to differences in underlying linguistic abilities, but to children's language socialization. He argues that certain social settings generate particular forms of communication, which virtually shape the intellectual orientation of the child. Working-class families speak in what he calls a **restricted code,** one used in situations in which a speaker and a listener know each other and the topic well, and conversation is generally tied to the immediate, face-to-face situation. Middle-class families, on the other hand, are thought to speak in a more elaborated code, used to communicate across various groups, permitting more exact, more explicit communication.

These differences in codes become particularly salient when children enter the school context. Now, the child from the working-class family experiences a radically different system of communication—one that emphasizes the individual over the communal, and the abstract over the concrete. As a result, children from these families may not be as able to master the subtleties of the speech codes or expected norms as their middle-class peers, who learn these strategies with ease from their parents.

Bernstein's theory has, itself, become more elaborate over the years and some have disputed a number of his findings (Entwisle, 1970). But the fruitfulness of his argument lies in his sociological approach of examining how families very early in a child's life sensitize and, in a sense, prepare a child to use and become attuned to certain language styles and patterns in their environment. If these patterns later conflict with those in the mainstream culture, the child must develop code-switching strategies in order to bridge the gap.

The cultural discontinuity view was proposed by Heath (1983) in her extensive ethnographic study of language and literacy learning of cultural groups in the Piedmont Carolinas. She studied the interactions in communication of children in two working-class communities: one was black, and the other was white. In the black town, Trackton, children were highly verbal, storytelling, monologuing and playing songs. Their uses of literacy were contextualized in their everyday activities; few books or toys were available for children. In the other community, Roadville, however, children learned a different method of communication. Here, they were encouraged to "follow the rules," to do things the "right" way. During storybook reading, they were encouraged to sit and listen, and not to interrupt or ask any questions.

Children from both communities had difficulty in school. Heath argued that their ways of talking in the home were incongruous with that of the school. The verbal capacities of the Trackton children were generally not recognized by teachers; while initially serving them well, the rule-bound behaviors of the Roadville children eventually did not enable them to explore and extend their knowledge into new areas. In each case, there was a cultural discontinuity between what was practiced in the home and what actually occurred in the school context.

Note that these differences reflect a situational influence, and not a cognitive one. No one is suggesting that working-class children are any less competent at conceptual and logical thinking than middle class children. No one is suggesting either that these are immutable patterns that are resistant to any type of educational intervention. Rather, the cultural discontinuity view suggests that children may come to school exhibiting attitudes toward literacy and language styles which may either be compatible or not with that of the school.

Variations in Language and Literacy Practices

Let's take a few examples from studies examining these variations among advantaged and disadvantaged linguistic groups (Bernstein, 1970; Heath, 1983; Tizard & Hughes, 1984; Tough, 1982; Wells,1985). Here are some illustrations of culturally congruent practices between home and school:

❑ Parents make frequent use of language for complex purposes and use a wide vocabulary in talking to their children.

❑ Parents answer children's questions and encourage them to explore ideas on their own.

❑ Parents engage in a wide range of shared experiences with children and talk about them.

❑ Parents read to children regularly.

Now, some examples of practices that are not congruent:

❑ Parents use language to control others; children may rarely have questions answered or hear explanations.

❑ Parents use limited vocabulary with conversations focusing on the here-and-now. Children may not be encouraged toward abstract thinking.

❑ Language lacks explicitness.

❑ Parents have little interest in literacy themselves and rarely read to their child.

As we examine these differences, it becomes clear why for some children the activities of school seem like a natural extension of home practices, while for others, the connections are far more difficult. However, recognizing differences is not enough. Rather, the cultural discontinuity view compels us to do something about it: to adjust our teaching and curriculum activities to account for variations in linguistic styles and home literacy-related practices—practices which we'll explore in the upcoming chapters. Only then may we be successful in helping all children achieve in schooling.

Children with Limited English Proficiency (LEP)

Children learn the language and the styles of communication of their families. But what if the language learned at home is not English? Even so, many LEP children will have engaged in similar communication processes in their home environments as those children who speak English as their first language. They will have seen adults reading and writing for different purposes in stores, offices, and places of worship. They will have engaged in language and literacy experiences for culturally appropriate purposes in a variety of different contexts. And these same communicative competencies can quite naturally transfer to the learning of their second language in other settings.

Just like their native English-speaking counterparts, these LEP children will begin to acquire literacy at the same time as they continue to develop oral language. They will do so by selectively tuning into the language and literacy events around them, and from these experiences, they will creatively devise their own individual versions of language (Hough & Nurss, 1992). Not explicitly modeled or taught, this active process will be constructed by them, tried out, and confirmed in many different contexts as part of their involvement in the ongoing experiences with the everyday world. Many non-native English-speaking children will continue to acquire and use their native language and culture at home and in their community as they simultaneously acquire proficiency in English, without signs of interference. These children will become truly bilingual and bicultural.

By contrast, problems will often occur for those LEP children who come from an impoverished **first language** environment. Cummins argues, in fact, for an "interdependence" effect (1979). When young children have engaged in many of their native language and literacy events in the home, bilingualism genuinely has an **additive** influence: children seem to acquire high levels of vocabulary and concepts in both languages. But for those children who attain only a very low level of competence in their first language, bilingualism often has a negative effect, leading to low levels of ability in both languages.

These findings, therefore, demonstrate the critical importance of a rich language and literacy environment for all children, regardless of the specific native language spoken in the home. They highlight the basic

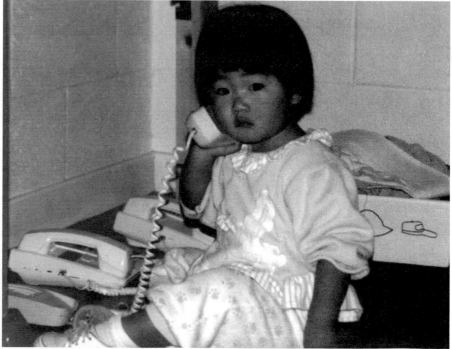

commonalities among first- and second-language learning processes. All children need opportunities to engage in meaningful oral and written language experiences, which enhance conceptual knowledge and linguistic understanding of language prior to formal schooling. All children need to engage in the meaningful use of language integrated throughout every aspect of daily activity. These understandings serve as the foundation for developing communicative competence in the child's second language.

Learning at Home

Our observations of the home suggest that it provides a very powerful learning environment for young children. The intimate parent-child relationship allows for many opportunities to engage in meaningful conversations, providing children with prior knowledge on a whole host of subjects before entering and throughout their schooling. The extensive range of activities that take place within the home give them models of adults actively engaged in a variety of literacy-related activities. As a result, children come to learn a great deal of language, oral and written, as it is embedded in the ordinary everyday events of living in a family. These experiences with print may be further broadened through conversations and interactions while listening to stories, where parents contextualize story events by shaping them around their children's lives. This task of linking present experiences to the past clearly facilitates children's uses of language as a medium for intellectual growth. Seen in a nutshell, then, learning in the home may be characterized as:

- ❑ highly individualized
- ❑ broad in scope
- ❑ personally relevant to the child.

Although these learning characteristics are common across families of different socioeconomic backgrounds (Schachter, 1979; Tizard & Hughes, 1984; Wells, 1985), certainly there are differences in language styles and uses relating to underlying family values and attitudes. While respecting children's dialectic variations, this suggests that not all communication styles in home learning environments may be equally as conducive to school learning as others. Unfamiliar with the expected forms of communication, some children may not be as ready or as able to adopt the language styles and group norms of schools that many of their peers learn from their parents at home. Without strategies to ease the mismatch between home and school language, these children may have difficulty adapting to the communication styles typical of school contexts.

Two Different Worlds

Home and school learning environments represent two very different worlds for young children. Just consider the adjustments that are required in making the transition between home and school. Perhaps the most critical one involves the sheer number of children that must compete for the teacher's time and attention. Whereas once the child may have had a good deal of individual time to engage in long passages of intellectual search, now he or she must share that time with 20 other children!

Also consider the differences in teacher practices and school curriculum. Unlike a parent who might spend extra time with a needy child, it is difficult for teachers to do so; rather they must try to be egalitarian to all the children in a classroom. In addition, although sensitive to individual differences, many teachers may know very little about their children's past or personal interests outside of the school context. As we will see later, this lack of shared past experiences places a great strain on communications between teachers and young preschoolers.

Further, teachers' educational aims and methods tend to be very different from those of parents. Most teachers see themselves as encouraging development by means of a planned environment, in which children learn through self-initiated play and an organized curriculum, with stated educational objectives, and structured activities. These programmatic qualities represent a far cry from the informal, highly contextualized, individualized type of teaching that goes on in the home environment.

We need, therefore, to become more sensitive to what skills and strategies children bring to the learning environment in the preschool, specifically, the way they learn language and expand upon its meanings. Rather than sharply break from this previous style, our task should be to extend and broaden their range of experiences, and to encourage more sustained and deliberate attention to topics of interest. Equally important in the preschool learning environment, then, are two major vehicles for language development that are experienced at home: engaging children in conversation, and listening to stories.

A Comparison of the Language of Home and School

As we've mentioned in chapters 1 and 2, children learn language by actively engaging in constructing meaning with others. Through their conversations, they test their new language constructions and receive feedback on their effectiveness in conveying meaning. Holding a conversation is an ideal mechanism for refining these expressive abilities. At minimum, a conversation may be defined as a three-element exchange on a single topic; thus, if A talks to B, B replies, and A then responds to B's reply, both partners have a pretty good indication they've been understood.

Studies of parent–child interactions underscore the tremendous natural ability that parents have in understanding their children, and in talking to them at an appropriate level. Here's a typical example:

Two-year-old Audrey is trying to open a box with little cars in it.

Audrey: Open, open, open.
Mother: You want to open the box?
Audrey: Other open.
Mother: You want to open it the other way?
Audrey: Uuuuuhhhh (getting frustrated).
Mother: That's right. You have to get it right on top. That's right. You're opening up the box all by yourself!

The context, as well as the vast body of shared experiences, helps the mother to interpret what Audrey is saying. In all likelihood, it would be difficult for an outsider to be quite as efficient or effective in understanding what Audrey was attempting to do. And this points to one of the key constraints in conversing with children in the preschool environment. As teachers, we rarely have the intimate knowledge of children's past experiences, or language uses, which can often impinge on our ability to sustain a conversation. Further, children's unique constructions of words can present roadblocks in communicating with outsiders. For example, one of our sons always used the word "angy"—saying to his teacher one day "I'm very angy" again and again. The teacher thought David was hungry, but in fact he was trying to express that he was very "angry" at his friend.

Studies which compare home and school language among adults and children indicate a rather chilling finding: Compared with homes, preschools do not appear to provide much time for adults and children to freely converse. Even those conversations that do occur tend to be brief, and much more adult-dominated than conversations at home. Summarizing findings from his study, Wells (1985) reports that:

❑ Children get fewer turns at speaking in school, express a narrower range of meanings and use grammatically less complex utterances than at home.

❑ Children ask fewer questions and make fewer requests.

❑ Teachers initiate a much higher proportion of conversations than parents do.

As a result, children are often placed in the position of a passive role in the preschool classroom, responding to teachers' queries rather than initiating talk on their own. Taken together, these findings suggest that preschools may not be providing an optimal environment for language development.

Why do preschools provide so little conversation time between adult and child? In truth, holding interesting and stimulating conversations with preschool children is no easy task for most teachers. Along with the issues that we've already mentioned (that is, transition from home to school and cultural discontinuity), some of the problems practitioners face relate to the children's conversational ability (Wood, McMahon & Cranston, 1980). For example, Wood and his colleagues describe that young children often neglect to "frame" their conversations, making it difficult to know exactly what they're talking about. Instead, they may "chain" one thought onto another. Here's a typical example:

Anna, Kate and Charlie are sitting at the art table.

Charlie: Do na na na BATMAN!
Anna: Look at this, Katie (holding her paper).
Katie: Oh its beautiful. Know what I heared on the radio . . .
snow is coming on the radio.
Anna: Oh my goodness! (Starts humming).
Charlie: Na, na, na BATMAN! Along came superman popped
him in a garbage can BATMAN!

Notice how this talk is only loosely connected. Only one exchange in fact, actually relates to another's comment. The chaining effect appears more like a stream-of-consciousness-like talk than that of a real conversation. No wonder that it is sometimes difficult to get a handle on what children are talking about.

Further, the somewhat impulsive quality of children's entry into conversations can prove to be a major obstacle to sustained conversations. It tends to foster disjointed, rather shallow conversations for both teacher and children. Here's a typical example from a classroom:

John: Ms. S., see what I got for my birthday? It's a baseball
mitt.
Ms S.: Oh that's terrific John. Won't it be fun to play?
Sheriff: I got a doll for my birthday.
Ms. S: You did. And what is its name?
Sheriff: Malief. It gots two dresses that comes with it.
Jennifer: Well I'm going to get a Barbie for my birthday.
John: My friend is going to come over after school to play
baseball with me.
Ms. S: Oh, that's great John.

Here, the teacher is forced to float between various conversational tidbits. These types of exchanges do not extend meaning-making for either partner. In fact, they represent a real dilemma for teachers. Should we attempt to sustain a conversation, or should we try to engage as many children as are interested in our interactions? Neither solution is entirely satisfying.

Perhaps as a consequence to these frustrations with child-generated attempts at conversations, most preschool teachers tend to rely on questioning techniques. In all the studies measuring adult–child talk, the chief characteristic shape of a school conversation was a question-answer session, with the child's role mainly confined to answering questions.

Teacher: What did you do this weekend?

Sarah: We went to the beach.

Teacher: Was it fun?

Sarah: Yeah.

Teacher: Did you make sand castles?

Sarah: Yeah.

Teacher: Did you go into the water?

Sarah: Yeah.

Teacher: Was it cold?

Sarah: Yeah.

We've probably all engaged in conversations like this at different times. As the conversation becomes more difficult to maintain, we try to fill the gap by asking even more questions. Inevitably, children's answers become more terse and monosyllabic. In some cases, they simply do not answer, no longer certain about how to respond. Notice that in our continuing effort to encourage talk through questions, we are actually taking *control* of the conversation. No longer is the child really contributing.

Characteristics of Good Teaching

Creating an Environment for Language Learning

How can we create a more effective language learning environment for preschoolers? Many studies seriously question the educational value of question and answer sessions with young children. Rather, we are reminded to recall what occurs more naturally in the home environment. At home, parents tend to create an environment in which children are partners in conversation. They are free to question and comment about whatever is going on. As teachers, we must ask relatively few questions and encourage children into conversation with us and with one another.

Typically, conversations between parents and children deal with practical, everyday activity, using the familiar to discover the unknown. As teachers, we must let children discover meaning through activities, which not only extends their facility with language, but gives them real purposes for talking. Parents tend to listen to the gist of their children's language efforts. Intuitively, they track children's meaning, and attempt to fill in only as required by the situation. As teachers, we must learn to listen more carefully and meaningfully to children's talk; we must learn to go beyond the specific words they use to interpret their intentions and help them find ways of saying what they want to say. And we, ourselves, must be willing to be questioned by children and to hear unsolicited ideas from them.

So in contrast to questions that often remind us of being interrogated, we need a more collaborative approach to interacting with children. This suggests techniques that encourage children to explore topics of their own interest and to ask questions without fear of reprisal. In this more child-centered focus, the adult's actions and talk now become **contingent** on the child's interests and efforts. Take this example from Wood et al (1980):

Simon is working on a jigsaw puzzle, with his teacher alongside him. Stephanie is nearby.

Simon: . . . missing here?

Teacher: You'll have to start the right way up. You have to get them all turned over the right way.

Stephanie: Can I do this?

Teacher: You can do that one, Stephanie, yes. I put that out for a little girl.

Stephanie: I'm a big girl.

Teacher: Oh, you're a big girl. I'm sorry.

Simon: Does this go at the top?

Teacher: Yes, Simon. Look at the top of that clock again and that's the one that comes right at the very top. Look the big hand's on it. Can you see? Right, start off with that, alright?

Simon: This at the top.

Teacher: No, that one comes next, doesn't it?

Simon: Then . . . then that one goes in there and that one goes in there!

Teacher: That's right. Now you've got the idea.

Simon: That goes there.

Teacher: Good boy.

Simon: I'm doing very much.

Teacher: You're doing very much. That must be because you're four now, mustn't it?

Simon: Yes.

Notice how much more interactive this conversation is than the previous one. Rather than provide isolated comments, here the teacher becomes involved in an extended interchange with the child. In this conversation, the teacher highlights what Simon should attend to and helps him to maintain his interest by breaking down the task when necessary. Throughout, she offers him praise and encouragement.

What Bruner and his colleagues (1980) found is that these conversations between an adult and a child are extremely important because they help to prolong the activity. Without teacher involvement, in the above example, Simon might have just gone off in frustration and played at some easier task. Similarly, teacher interaction in play activities is important. Bruner found, for example, that the average play episode was two times longer when there was elaborated dialogue between adult and child, as well as conversation among children. In fact, he suggests that the best inspiration to extended and connected conversation is a teacher joining a small group of children as a participant in play.

The way in which a teacher interacts with children in many ways represents the essence of his or her teaching and priorities. Children have far fewer resources than adults to call upon in their conversational styles. Therefore, they tend to reflect those of the surrounding adults. One episode, clearly demonstrating this influence, occurred in a classroom where the teacher always emphasized neatness and order with all the classroom materials. When we asked several children what they were playing with one day, they said, "a calculator." "And what do you do with it?" we asked. "You put it back," they answered.

In this respect, a child's conversational style tends to mirror that of his or her teacher's. When a teacher initiates contact with children for purposes of telling them what to do, or managing them, the children often respond to the teacher in a similar manner. Correspondingly, when a teacher promotes a collaborative approach, listening and reflecting, the children will more likely explore ideas, and try things out. In short, these observations suggest that adult styles of conversation exert a tremendous influence on children's participation in and contribution to verbal interaction. Further, how well children play their part as conversationalists may determine the quality and effect of adult instructional encounters.

Creating an Environment for Literacy Learning

As we've seen, storybook reading in the home environment is an intimate affair. It provides an opportunity for close physical contact and peaceful interaction between parents and children. Much of the benefit of storybook reading resides in the collaborative talk that actually surrounds the book reading event. This is when parents may carefully guide children in their interpretation of stories and relate this information to their own personal family histories.

Such a collaborative experience, however, is difficult to achieve in the school context when reading a story to 20 children at a time. In one case, for example, we watched a teacher read the favorite book *Alexander and the terrible, horrible, no good, very bad day* (Viorst, 1976). One child called out, "I got new sneakers," then another, "Mine have a great stripe on them." Soon, the teacher was virtually deluged with comments on the same and related theme. Finally, she had to call a halt to their contributions in order to continue reading. Unfortunately, the opportunity to create explicit links between children's own experiences and the story was inevitably lost.

What do our observations of parent–child interactions in storybook reading advise for creating more dynamic story sessions in the classroom? They suggest that we need to support a more interactive and participatory environment for listening to stories. The following techniques, described in greater detail in Chapter 7, are based to a large extent on insights from parent practices in the home.

Use predictable books:

Predictable materials seem to naturally encourage children's responsiveness. They have several key characteristics. They use repetitive language patterns (as in *Green Eggs and Ham* by Dr. Seuss), catch-phrases (for example, *Chicken Soup with Rice* by Maurice Sendak), or cumulative patterns (as in *Drummer Hoff* by Ed Emberly), which allow children to anticipate what is going to come next. They often have a rather short text, with a good match between the print and illustrations. This feature lends itself to independent pretend readings among preschoolers as they use the pictures to help them figure out what the text might be likely to say. And predictable books, as well as songs, nursery rhymes and poems, are designed to be read over and over again, just like a parent might do in the home. Soon these books become a very part of the classroom community, as children all join in repeating with delight "that Sam I am, that Sam I am, I do not like green eggs and ham."

Shared reading:

Shared book reading experiences (Holdaway, 1979) evolved as a strategy to recreate the intimate atmosphere of home storybook reading for the classroom environment. The most familiar form of shared reading involves the use of "big books." Big books *are* what they appear to be: favorite children's stories (unabridged) in enlarged type and illustration. Since children in a group are all able to see what's on the page, these enlarged books set the stage for involvement as they listen to and watch the teacher read. With simple and predictable text, along with the repeated readings that typically accompany the big book experience, children often learn the lines of several stories by heart. This oral rendering of the text provides a powerful scaffolding device when children become interested in figuring out how the print on each page actually works to represent the story they know how to say.

Small groups and one-to-one readings:

Most teachers typically read stories to a whole group. These sessions are, in many ways, intended to be a forerunner of the kind of experience children will meet when they move on to primary school. During these sessions, some children may listen intently, others may fidget and look bored. Still others may suck their thumbs, twiddle their hair, and clutch their teddy bears, using this time to sit back and recharge their batteries. In addition to its significance in literacy learning, storybook reading represents an important change of pace in the busy and often hectic preschool day.

In addition to whole class reading, a number of studies (Morrow, 1988; 1990) have indicated the important benefits of reading to young children in small groups and on a one-to-one basis. Clearly, reading in these settings most closely reflects the intimacy of storybook reading at home. Here, children may freely ask questions, make personal contributions, and predict story events without fear of interjecting too much, or ruining the story for others. At the same time, a teacher or an aide may be able to assess children's understanding of the story and adjust his or her reading on the basis of these responses. In such small group settings, many children even recognize some of the structural features of print, and begin to map speech to print.

In these settings, there is a spirit of collaboration as teachers and children work together in constructing meaning in stories. Rather than question–answer sessions, teachers (just like parents at home) engage children in conversations, where there is a give-and-take nature to the system. In a sense, it is a process of co-producing meaning, like in the following example, with the teacher Ms. J. and Jennifer:

Ms. J: Look at the book I have. This is called the title page, "The Mare on the Hill" by Thomas Parker. And look at the beautiful illustrations. Can you find the mare on the page? (Jennifer points). Right. Now this doesn't look like fall does it?

Jennifer: No, it kind of looks like summer.

Ms. J: (reads) Well, "it was spring when we saw the white mare. Grandpa had gone to a horse sale to buy a mate for us . . ."

Jennifer: What's mate?

Ms. J: Like a partner, a wife or a husband. So they must have a male somewhere. Remember the black one was the father horse and this would be the female horse. The mare is a female. Why do you think Grandpa did such a thing?

Jennifer: I don't know. He probably wanted to have another horse. A baby horse. You have to have a mare to have a baby horse.

Ms. J: (continues to read) "Grandpa told us that the mare had been mistreated . . ."

Jennifer: What does that mean?

Ms. J: It means that someone is very mean to her. What do you think they might do if they were very mean to her?

Jennifer: I don't know

Ms. J: Did they hit her or scare her?

Jennifer: I bet they hit her.

In this one-to-one setting, Jennifer is encouraged to closely attend to the details of the story. In a dialogic form, Ms. J. assesses Jennifer's knowledge of words and her comprehension of the story. In addition, she gives Jennifer numerous opportunities to practice and share her interpretations, making this storybook reading event a more collaborative effort.

While acknowledging the potential benefits of small group or one-to-one readings, some teachers might feel it lacks practicality in the school setting. We know it's really difficult to set aside specific times to read to individual children. Other adults, however, beside teachers, may become involved in story sessions; aides and adult volunteers often enjoy interacting with children through books. In addition, some schools offer cross-age paired reading, where older students may read to the younger ones, benefiting both participants. Small group reading also offers a pleasant option for children to spend time with an adult during the free play period. Considering the significant benefits for engaging children's interactive behaviors in reading stories together, it is well worth our efforts to encourage such practices.

Guidelines for Teachers

For Language Development:

Considering the vital role of conversation in language development, Bruner (1980) and his colleagues have suggested a number of practical guidelines for teachers. Certainly, they are not designed as prescriptions to be filled out at all times. Instead, they represent general rules of thumb, when working with young children.

- ❑ For preschoolers, actions often accompany language. Consequently, most sustained conversations between adults and children occur in the midst of ongoing play and structured activity. Interactions work best, therefore, when your questions and comments relate to the specific actions that the child has initiated.

- ❑ Try to give children challenging activities which require their problem-solving abilities. Step back and let them explore on their own; if frustration sets in, help them out, and then move to the background once again. Challenging activities encourage children to raise questions in their efforts to understand how things work.

- ❑ Don't ask questions to which you already know the answer. Children seem to have an intuitive sense of what is a real question versus one that encourages them to guess what's in the teacher's head. These types of interrogation questions only limit conversation rather than enhance it.

- ❑ Avoid many adult-oriented projects. Activities such as baking or sewing often demand a great deal of adult control and management. In a very real sense, these types of activities often limit children's initiative and their verbal interaction. For example, asking one of our children what he did at school that day, he said "I watched the teacher make jello." In contrast to these practices, the most interactive sequences tend to occur when children and teachers work together on a project that is a child-oriented, self-sponsored activity.

❑ Particularly for limited English proficient children (LEP), demonstrations with concrete objects or visual aids that illustrate vocabulary help to bridge familiar concepts with vocabulary labels. This allows children to build vocabulary in their second language (L2) by tapping their existing network of words and concepts in their first language (L1). Further, by combining speech with gestures, movements and facial expressions, you can help them to clarify the meaning of specific terms.

It is important to emphasize that, especially for young children, knowledge cannot simply be transmitted to them. Rather, it must be **constructed** by them, through their self-initiated actions and language. In order to help children learn through conversation, then, we must take their perceived concerns seriously, listen carefully, make sure we understand their intentions, and extend their thinking about ideas through comments, suggestions and praise.

For Literacy Learning:

We've seen throughout this chapter the importance of storyreading experiences for literacy development. How, then, can we support young children's access to good books and stories in preschool programs?

❑ Try to read high quality books that *you,* as well as the children, enjoy. Nothing is more fun than sharing a favorite book, like *An Anteater named Arthur* (Waber, 1967) or *Alexander and the Terrible, Horrible, No Good, Very Bad Day* (Viorst, 1976)—stories that you might especially enjoy reading. In fact, you'll find your facial expressions and voice take on a more animated tone when reading stories that are as special to you as they might be to the children.

❑ Create an attractive library corner. You'll discover that appealing displays of books entice young children to use this area. Think about the following features in considering your library corner: Are the books and props that might accompany these stories easily accessible to the children? Are the books rotated on a regular basis? Are the book covers colorful and attractive? Is the area comfortable, with pillows and a rug, so that children can relax and enjoy their reading?

In addition to favorite published books, try to include books made by the children themselves. By adding a special library envelope to the back of these books, children may check them out for the weekend. Also, photo albums of school celebrations with captions describing these events fascinate young children.

❑ Give children opportunities to practice their emerging reading abilities on their own. Many children enjoy the peace and quiet of the library corner, looking through books or reading "their way." Support these efforts by visiting the area on an intermittent basis, while at the same time, encouraging children to explore reading by themselves or with their peers.

❑ Offer children a variety of different types of books. Expose them to traditional nursery rhymes, folk and fairy tales— stories that are a part of our heritage, yet may not be familiar to many children who have not been read to on a regular basis, or who come from different cultures. In addition, you'll want to include realistic fiction dealing with real-life issues, and informational books to help children explore ideas and stimulate new interests.

❑ Include books that are predictable or have repeated refrains (see Appendix); these are especially effective for LEP children. The predictable language encourages LEP children to join in orally with the rest of the class, using chunks of story language that are meaningful to the particular context.

• •

Let's Review . . .

In this chapter, we first examined some of the special characteristics of home learning. We analyzed a number of factors that account for the home being a powerful learning environment. Among these factors are:

❑ An extensive range of activities that provide children with opportunities to learn about a wide variety of topics.

❑ The shared experiences among parents and children that facilitate language experiences, conversations, and meaning-making.

❑ The opportunities to learn that are embedded in contexts of great meaning to the child.

❑ Parents' attitudes toward and habits of reading stories to their children that help to extend their understanding of the uses of decontextualized print.

We also recognized that there are broad variations among families in language and literacy patterns. Some authorities have claimed that these language variations represent deficiencies to be ameliorated through extensive drill and practice. Others suggest that linguistic practices among ethnic and culturally diverse populations are merely different, and should be widely accepted by schools just like any dialect variation. Still others argue for cultural discontinuity, indicating that some linguistic variations and language styles may lend themselves more easily to school communication patterns than others. This approach appears to be most profitable because it offers important instructional implications for teachers and other helpers.

Finally, we examined the world that children encounter in moving from the very small setting of the home, to the much larger setting of the school. Compared with homes, we found that in many cases, schools are not providing an environment that fosters language development. Several reasons may account for the lack of language stimulation. First, it can be difficult to carry on conversations with young preschoolers. Second, constant interruptions and interjections involving management tasks and needs of other children may make sustained talk a complex task. And finally, teachers, at times, have over-relied on question-and-answer strategies which do not lend themselves easily to collaborative activity.

We can draw several important implications for classroom practice from these observations. Among them are:

- ❏ Dyadic encounters between adults and pairs or small numbers of children are critically important in language development and learning for young children. Put simply, the larger the adult–child ratio in a group, the more elaborated the conversations and involvement with story readings are likely to be.

- ❏ Less emphasis should be placed on programmatic teaching and greater emphasis on contingent teaching. Following children's leads encourages them to take more initiative and responsibility for their own learning.

- ❏ Teaching strategies should focus on encouraging children to participate actively in language and in negotiating meaning with others while listening to stories.

Let's Explore . . .

1. Tape-record 10-minute episodes of parent–child exchanges in at least two of these different contexts: a storybook reading

context, a playful context, and one in which a parent is engaged in chores (such as cooking). Transcribe these exchanges. Compare how the parent and the child attempt to make meaning together. Are there typical patterns in each context? Does the nature of the context impact the length and quality of the exchange?

2. Observe several children in a preschool. Count the number of exchanges they make with an adult over the course of one morning. Classify these exchanges into the following categories: instructional (for example, having to do with an activity), managerial (putting materials away, and so on), and conversational (discussing something together). On the basis of your brief observation, what preliminary conclusions can you make regarding the language environment of the preschool?

3. Visit a preschool classroom. Listen carefully to the speech of one child as he or she engages in play. If possible, record the language verbatim. Now, engage the child in a more structured task, similar to one that seems like a testing situation. Are there differences in the nature of the child's language in these contexts? What do these differences mean?

4. Read a story to children in three different contexts: one with a large group of children, one with a small group of children, and another with an individual child. What are some of the differences in the children's behaviors in these contexts? Do children ask more questions and make more comments in one context rather than another?

5. Visit a preschool classroom and focus on one particular child (this is easiest to do during free play time). Try to engage the child in a conversation. Tape-record this conversation, if possible. What do you notice about your own behavior in trying to carry out a conversation with a young child? What do you notice about the child's conversational skills? Based on your observations, what could you do to enhance these exchanges?

6. Read a predictable text to a classroom of children (see Lists of Predictable Books in Appendix A). Write down some of your observations of the children's behaviors. What are some of the factors that give predictable texts their powerful effects?

Designing the Physical Environment

Understanding the Human Behavior-environment Relationship

Humans demonstrate...

- different behaviors in different settings

- similar behaviors in the same setting

- behaviors consistent with a setting

Using Principles of Environmental Design

The environment should...

- inform & personalize

- support & extend curricular activities

- foster sustained work

- develop a sense of community

- be aesthetically pleasing

CHAPTER 4

Designing the Physical Environment for Language and Literacy Learning

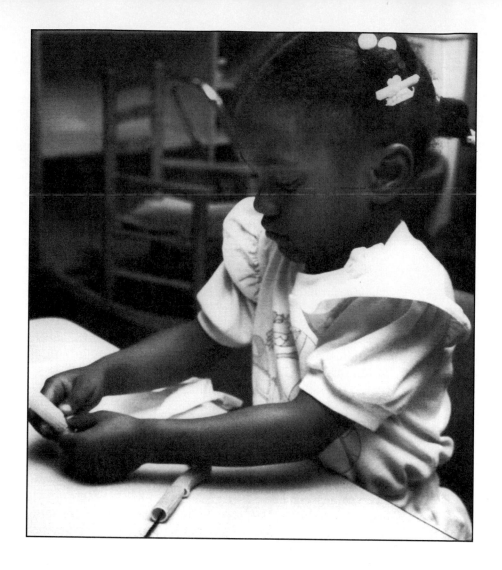

Sheona: Sara, she just fights over that tablecloth (on the table in the housekeeping play area) 'cause whoever has . . . she keeps pulling it off the table 'cause she thinks that I have more and I don't!

Teacher: How do you fix that problem?

Sheona: We take it off.

For young children, learning to talk and learning to write and read are, above all practical activities, undertaken primarily to connect with the world which surrounds them. As demonstrated in the previous chapters, children form, test and modify their hypotheses about language and literacy in the course of their daily lives. They learn spoken and written language *while* eating and playing, *while* shopping and conversing, *while* storybook reading and saying goodnight. Because the allure of language is in its use, learning to talk, read and write is intimately connected to the physical settings in which it naturally occurs. Consequently, what surrounds children becomes extremely important, since their surroundings provide them with opportunities to witness, practice and extend language and literacy as ways to construct meaning from experience.

Realizing that children's physical surroundings affect them substantially is not new. In fact, how they affect them has been a topic of inquiry since the late 19th century. Two German investigators from this period suggested that children from different "social addresses" (rural vs. city) may have been affected in different ways, accounting for variations in their knowledge of concepts upon entry into school (cited in Pellegrini, 1991). The influence of the physical environment on children's development has been a concern of educational theorists, researchers and teachers ever since, with a number of cultural–ecological theories advanced to explain the critical role of environment in human language functioning and growth (e.g., Barker, 1968; Bronfenbrenner, 1979; and Ogbu, 1981).

Although it has been generally accepted that environmental conditions impact children's language and literacy acquisition, exerting a strong influence on their quality, the powerful role of environment on human behavior is often overlooked in early childhood settings. Too much attention tends to be focused on *what children bring to the learning environment* and too little on *what the environment brings to children.*

Thus, at this point in our discussion of language and literacy learning, we are concerned with what surrounds children in early childhood programs, thereby supporting and stimulating their language and literacy use. We will talk a lot about **setting,** that is, where children physically are, examining how the physical environment can be organized to assist and extend children's language and literacy growth. Before we proceed, however, we need to examine several research-based generalizations that highlight the relationship between human behavior and the physical environment with implications for the environmental design of early childhood settings (Barker, 1968; Fernie, 1985; Gump, 1989; Kounin & Gump, 1974).

One of these is the rather obvious fact that children's behavior changes from physical setting to physical setting. What they do in the block area, for example, is typically different from what they do in the Book Corner. This is due in part to the fact that different settings *press* for different behaviors from them. The layout and objects in the block area urge one thing, and that of the Book Corner another. In other words, the organization and objects of physical settings tug at children, inviting them to behave in particular ways.

Awareness of this environment–behavior relationship has implications for the placement of activity and play settings in early childhood

environments. It would not make sense, for instance, to locate the block and book areas next to one another, because they are incompatible—one eliciting and supporting noisy behaviors and the other quiet ones. In one sense, placing them next to one another is to invite trouble, since these two settings each press for different behaviors to some extent unavoidable by young children.

Systematic observation of the environment–behavior relationship also indicates that different children behave in like ways in the same setting. For instance, when in the housekeeping area, most children will pretend to do as housekeepers do—cook, clean and take care of the family. The kitchen table and chairs, the small-scale appliances, the cupboards with utensils and dishes: these signal children to behave in ways that go along with a kitchen context.

Teachers can capitalize on this tendency, purposefully designing physical settings that promote and enhance language and literacy behaviors. A housekeeping play setting, for example, can include paper and pencils, children's cookbooks, grocery coupons and packages, all of which invite children to use writing and reading as well as conversation in their domestic play. In short, the physical setting in and of itself can be deliberately used to provide a common frame of reference for children's use of spoken and written language as means of negotiating meaning.

Finally, research suggests that children tend to behave in ways consistent with the intent of a physical setting. Although children may momentarily misbehave in a specific setting, the setting will coerce them to behave in ways that are consistent with it. That is to say, a physical setting seeks to have its way, inducing conforming behaviors on the part of its inhabitants. Naptime is a good example. The cots and their arrangement, the dim lighting and the quiet—all press the children to take a nap, even though some may desire to move about and talk loudly.

Teachers' awareness of this power of physical settings to influence what children will do affords them yet another means for eliciting and developing children's language and literacy behaviors. How and where children are seated and the use of props during sharing times, for example, can be engineered to enhance conversation and discussion.

Collectively, these generalizations are fundamental to an understanding of the environment–behavior relationship, providing the basis for designing physical environments that influence and support children's language and literacy development. Using them in conjunction with developmentally appropriate practices recommended by early childhood associations and exemplary programs (for example, NAEYC, ACEI, and Reggio Emilia preschools), we have derived five principles of environmental design that we believe influence language and literacy learning in early childhood environments. For us, these principles are one way of organizing a rather large and diverse body of information about the role of physical environment in children's language and literacy acquisition and learning. Moreover, they provide a framework for preparing physical settings where language and literacy may flourish while allowing for uniqueness in sites and situations. In the following section we discuss these principles, first explaining their significance and then illustrating how they may be applied to early childhood classrooms.

Principles of Environmental Design

#1. The Physical Environment Informs Children in Concrete and Personalized Ways.

That the physical environment conveys information and messages to children (and adults) goes without saying. But, how to make the environment an ongoing participant in the flow of young children's spoken and written language learning in early childhood programs is another matter. The chilling finding about the dearth of conversation in preschools, shared in the previous chapter, certainly underscores this challenge.

Scattered across research and practice, however, there are a number of suggestions for organizing and provisioning the physical environment in ways that inform children about the functions and features of spoken and written language. For the most part, those recommendations seem to cluster into three broad categories of environmental design: creating spatial boundaries, arranging and displaying provisions, and using personal touches.

Creating Spatial Boundaries

Recall from our earlier discussion that the physical environment presses for certain behaviors. Contributing to the power of this **press** is the organization of space which can influence children's movement and physical behavior, signalling them to move, to pause and look, to interact or pass on by, to talk, touch, read and write.

In general, research suggests that the physical space of an environment should be broken up into smaller play and activity settings so that boundaries are established in the environment. By partitioning space into a number of smaller, closed spaces as opposed to wide expanses, opportunities for social interaction and conversation among children and between children and adults are enhanced (Howes & Rubenstein 1978; Neill, 1982; Proshansky & Wolfe, 1975).

Furthermore, since smaller spaces accommodate fewer children, thus reducing noise levels and urging quiet, children tend to engage in more cooperative behaviors and to remain focused longer on specific activities (Preiser, 1972; Schoggen & Schoggen, 1985). In addition, smaller spaces and nooks afford children the privacy they need to integrate their experiences and collect their thoughts (Day, 1983).

When creating spatial boundaries to carve up wide expanses, it is important to ensure that the boundaries are clearly identifiable and evident *to children*. Two kinds of cues or signals can be used to indicate boundaries: (a) physical cues which employ semi-fixed architectural features (for example, book shelves), and (b) symbolic cues which utilize print and other symbols (for example, rebus writing).

To cordon off space using physical cues, low partitions (about 3' or so) will do. Furniture, book shelves, screens, mirrors, artificial trees, boxes, easels, and aquariums can be arranged to define spatial boundaries and set areas off from one another.

When using symbolic cues to define space, print can be combined with other symbols on mobiles or signs (hung low), identifying activity

and play areas. For example, a mobile comprised of shapes or the actual items commonly found in a post office (letters, envelopes, stamps) and the words "post office" is one way to use symbols to clearly designate a specific play area. When teachers deliberately use concrete semi-fixed architectural features and highly visible symbolic cues to organize space, they are providing children with the locational detail they so often need to signal and guide their behaviors.

Also important for spatial organization are information- and direction-giving signs, labels and inventories throughout the general environment. These should be authentic and functional, placed about for real reasons, encouraging children to *read* them and use them as environmental print sources.

For example, large directional signs (laminated and written with dark black print) can be posted throughout the environment, indicating where particular play settings are, where the child care office is, routes to the bathroom, and how to get outside. Storage bins can be labelled, similar to the bins in hardware stores and craft shops for reference purposes. Specific activity and play settings can be inventoried and their contents posted on the wall, as shown in Figure 4.1.

Using print *and* pictures to visually organize space helps children to see that written language is useful, making certain things easier to remember and do. More particularly, children discover that they can use these resources in their own attempts to gain control of the technical aspects of print, for example, letter formation and spelling. Take, for example, 4-year-old Steven's sign, "Stay out of here," which he taped in the block area (Figure 4.2). Borrowing letters from other signs around the Block Area, he practiced saying and writing letters to draft his warning which, when accompanied by a few shouts, got across his message.

Figure 4.1   Inventory of Art Area

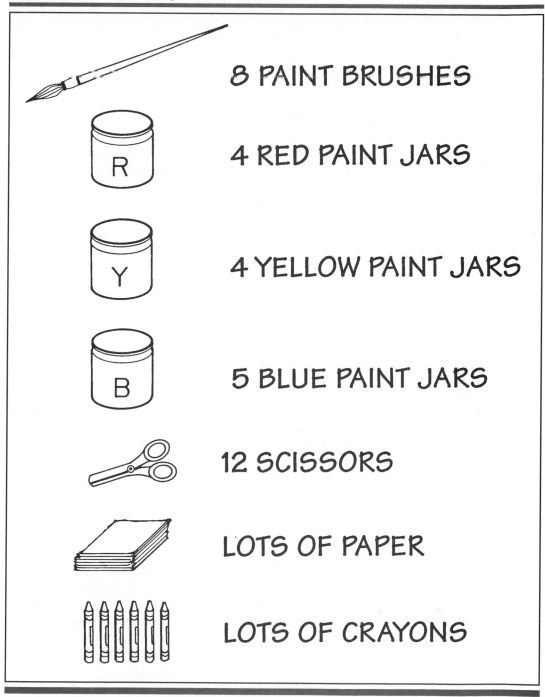

8 PAINT BRUSHES

4 RED PAINT JARS

4 YELLOW PAINT JARS

5 BLUE PAINT JARS

12 SCISSORS

LOTS OF PAPER

LOTS OF CRAYONS

Figure 4.2   Steven's Sign: "Stay out of here"

In Figures 4.3 and 4.4 on pages 109–110, we illustrate the use of physical and symbolic cues to create spatial boundaries in a physical environment. Figure 4.3 represents the "before" and Figure 4.4 the "after". In this preschool classroom, the physical space was organized into smaller, more intimate settings using existing moveable objects and mobiles with print and pictures to break up wide expanses. As you examine these "blueprints," note how the physical changes organized space so as to encourage the formation of small groups in well-defined play spaces. By creating spatial boundaries that inform and assist children in their attempts to work and play, the teachers in this classroom used the physical environment as a means of stimulating social interaction, thus enhancing children's language use.

We do need to point out, here, that creating spatial boundaries by partitioning and defining the physical environment does not need to happen all at once. Nor should it become a labelling nightmare. Nor should it remain the same for years. Rather it should be a natural outgrowth of efforts to use the physical environment to genuinely inform its inhabitants, providing locational detail and direction that facilitates classroom activities and guides behavior.

Arranging and Displaying Provisions

Child care programs generally include raw materials, toys, tools, books and common household objects for children to explore and manipulate. The house rule for provisions in the early childhood environment is twofold: They should be diverse, for example, of varying types and complexity (able to be used in more than one way) (Kritchevsky & Prescott, 1977). And they should match children's interests and development (Day, 1983). Provisions reflective of these factors stimulate young children to explore, observe, question and problem solve, using language and print to express their thinking.

When striving to use provisions as pivots for spoken and written language use, however, the issue is not so much one of having them as it is

Figure 4.3

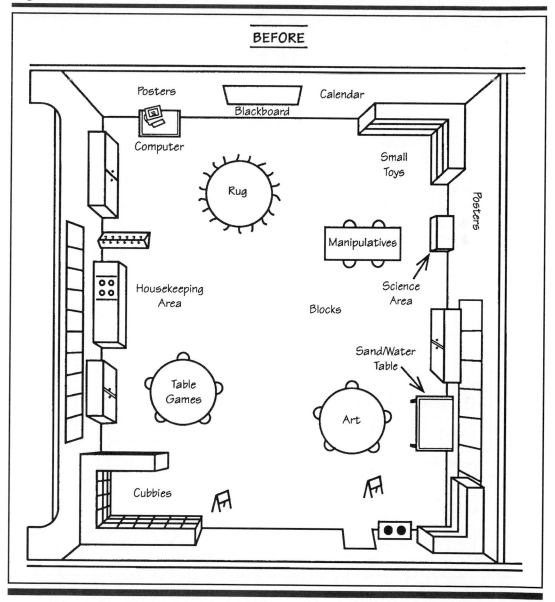

one of how they are arranged and displayed. Here we would do well to pay greater attention to the organization of museums, shops, and flea markets. Displays in these contexts are deliberately arranged to attract and to teach those who stroll about. We can learn much from them about

Figure 4.4

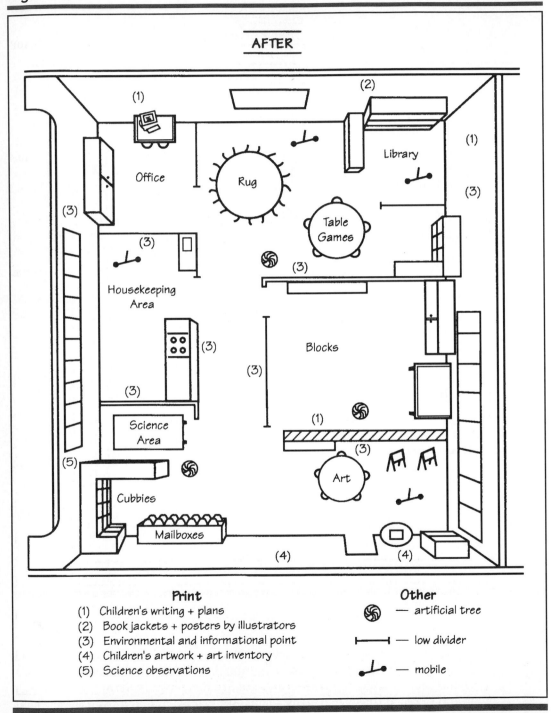

AFTER

(1) Office

(2) Library

(1)

(3)

Rug

Table Games

(3)

Housekeeping Area

(3)

(3)

Blocks

(3)

(1)

(3)

Science Area

Art

(5)

Cubbies

Mailboxes

(4)   (4)

Print

(1) Children's writing + plans
(2) Book jackets + posters by illustrators
(3) Environmental and informational point
(4) Children's artwork + art inventory
(5) Science observations

Other

— artificial tree

⊢——⊣ — low divider

— mobile

how to display "stuff" so that children may extend their language and literacy knowledge.

When it comes to arranging and displaying provisions, **aggregating** is the key. Aggregating is the collection of items into a network of related materials or objects. The list of items for post office play in Figure 4.5, for example, is an illustration of the deliberate aggregating of objects.

Thoughtfully collecting materials and objects into related networks creates rich, meaningful opportunities for children to name, categorize, describe and read and write. On a small scale, this can be as simple as ordering seashells along a shelf by pattern, something like Figure 4.6.

The seashells could just as easily have been ordered by color, feel or type with printed labels provided for these categories. Likewise, stones and pebbles could be arranged in small boxes by weight, by structure, by color or by feel, each appropriately labelled. Blocks can be arranged into labelled bins by size, by color, by shape or by material. Paper can be stacked in labelled trays by color, by size, by weight, by purpose. In fact, many of these arrangements can become sorting games in their own

Figure 4.5

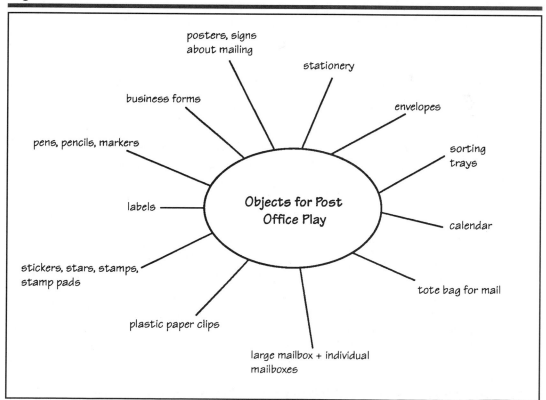

posters, signs about mailing

stationery

business forms

envelopes

pens, pencils, markers

sorting trays

labels

Objects for Post Office Play

calendar

stickers, stars, stamps, stamp pads

tote bag for mail

plastic paper clips

large mailbox + individual mailboxes

Figure 4.6

right, thus providing another opportunity for children to practice using language and print as a means of organizing information.

On a larger scale, themed displays may be organized to spark discussion, naming, writing and reading. As in museums, such displays should include some printed information which describes how the objects in the display are related. For example, a themed display entitled "Shiny Things" might be organized with related books and labelled items like utensils, pots and pans, ornaments, Christmas decorations, rocks and minerals, jewelry, mirrors, and some bubbles for blowing. Or a themed display of "Flying Things" might be developed, for example, sycamore, maple and ash seeds, a paper butterfly, a paper glider, a miniature airplane, a mini-parachute, and a kite. Or children might be invited to explore a collection of "Writing Tools": various markers, pencils (fat and thin, long and short), pens, crayons (all kinds), paintbrushes, and even their own fingers in soft clay.

Themed displays can also be organized into mini-museums, somewhat like the one about dinosaurs, shown in Figure 4.7.

Figure 4.7

As a guide for the dinosaur mini-museum, consider the book *100 Dinosaurs From A To Z* by Ron Wilson (1986, Grosset & Dunlap, NY).

They can also be transformed into see-through displays by putting particulars, like seeds (or treasures from a nature walk), into plastic bags which are then clustered in a window to be examined, counted, and compared in the light. Or a reflective display can be constructed by putting mirrors behind items, e.g., rows of colored water jars or bottles that hold different sorts of buttons (labelled, of course). Some displays can be changed into mobiles to show off collections of leaves, types of fabric, or colored tissue papers. Others can be arranged into galleries for children's drawings, constructions, and paintings.

No matter what form a themed display might take, however, it should serve as a springboard for discussion with an emphasis on naming, describing and relating objects, noting how things are alike and different as well as how they are connected to the broader theme. They also should include abundant print and related print sources: the name of the theme, some actual labelling of items, general comments about the theme, jotted down on chart paper nearby, books, brochures, and children's recorded comments. In many ways, creating connected clusters of objects, whether on a small scale or a large one, engages children in categorizing things and actions in relation to a given topic, supporting the development of schemata essential for expanded language use.

Finally, regularly used activity and play resources can be stored in a way that accentuates language and literacy as well. Equipment and materials in boxes, crates or bins can be arranged and labelled according to their purpose or size or the type of experience they offer. Notes (with pictures) about how to use specific materials can be jotted on box lids or bin labels. One example is illustrated in Figure 4.8, where resources for water play are organized in a way that teaches language and literacy through functional use (adapted from Richards, Collis & Kincaid, 1987, p. 41).

It is said that organization is the key to memory (Bruner & Goodnow, 1965). When teachers arrange and display provisions as networks of related items, they are purposefully using the physical environment to facilitate children's use of language to structure and recall their personal experiences. They are also helping them to organize ideas and information, building up stores of meaning interlinked by language.

Using Personal Touches

In new places, in strange places, children need a little bit of home to feel at home. We do not need research to confirm that! There are several simple ways to make the early childhood environment highly personal and a little like home. For instance:

Figure 4.8

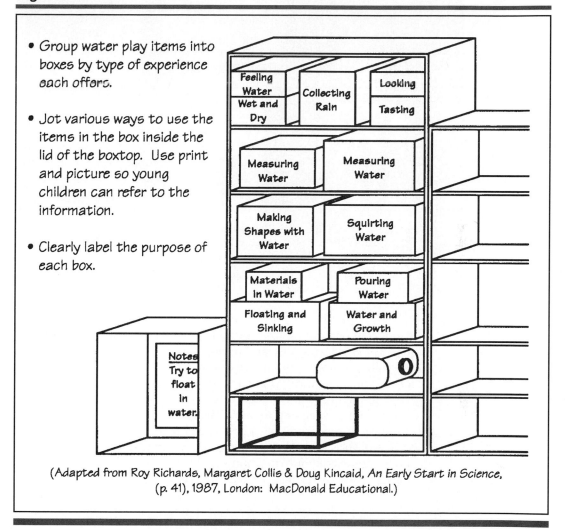

- Group water play items into boxes by type of experience each offers.

- Jot various ways to use the items in the box inside the lid of the boxtop. Use print and picture so young children can refer to the information.

- Clearly label the purpose of each box.

(Adapted from Roy Richards, Margaret Collis & Doug Kincaid, *An Early Start in Science*, (p. 41), 1987, London: MacDonald Educational.)

❑   Tokens from children's life experiences inside and outside the early childhood program can filter in and out of the environment through displays, share times, and collection-building activities. For example, children can contribute family photos for a photo essay about families and things they do together. The essay, in turn, can easily be transformed into a book for frequent sharing among the children.

☐ A sense of ownership and permanency can be attached to all forms of children's play and projects in a variety of ways. For example, photographs can be taken of block structures or lego inventions and compiled as displays or picture books for *reading* in the Book Corner. Notes can be sent home describing unique or special play activities or made-up play stories. Children can be regularly encouraged to sign their names on their artwork and other projects. They can also try to jot down remarks about their play or dictate their thoughts to a teacher for transcribing (Kuschner, 1989).

In these ways, displays of past work (paintings, drawings, collages, and photo essays) as well as works-in-progress can be developed for viewing in the environment.

As familiar images, such displays help to create a history of past experiences in the environment and serve as springboards to new ones. Eventually, these items can be included in children's folders or portfolios as indicators of growth—a matter we will take up more thoroughly in chapter seven.

☐ Personal messages and routine communications can be shared in various ways. Examples include:

(1) sign-up sheets for various play and activity areas;

(2) appointment sheets for scheduling conferences with the teacher;

(3) message boards for exchanging personal notes and ideas;

(4) small-scale kiosks (made out of cardboard boxes) for invitations, notifications, sketches and drawings;

(5) space dividers as bulletin boards for directions, pictures, posters, bulletins and reminders.

(6) mailboxes (constructed from shoeboxes, cylindrical cereal boxes or stackable junior crates) for children to send letters to each other, parents, teachers and other adults who are in the environment regularly.

(7) suggestion boxes for sharing good ideas, recommendations, and periodic complaints.

❑ Finally, familiar things can be tucked about in many places: along stairways, on cubbies, at snack tables, and in bathrooms, too. These areas can be personalized with plants, mirrors, picture galleries, mobiles, and books or small toys to touch and hold.

In summarizing this first principle of environmental design, it is clear that organization is at the heart of it. Creating spatial boundaries, arranging and displaying provisions, using personal touches: all of these techniques serve to organize the environment in ways that not only personalize the environment for children, but also inform them, compelling them to use language and literacy as modes of social negotiation and self-expression.

#2.   The Physical Environment Supports and Extends the Curriculum.

A solid and well-formed curriculum is the substance of any early childhood program. But the physical environment is the glue that holds that curriculum together. It provides the space and provisions which support the activities that address important and necessary curricular goals. In short, the curriculum comes to life within physical settings where children work and play, interacting with others and with materials. Within their boundaries, children, adults and the physical environment come together for the purposes of sharing and learning.

However, if activity and play settings are to sufficiently engage and motivate children to learn, they need to possess **high holding power** (Moore, et al., 1979). Rich with content and provisions that capture children's interest and attention for sustained periods of time, physical settings with high holding power invite children to explore, investigate and share information. They can be achieved in a few simple ways.

Creating resource-rich activity pockets that capitalize on what children already know is one way. For example, gathering together pots and pans, plastic tableware, various kinds of pretend fruits and vegetables, plastic jars containing a variety of edible food stuffs, grocery coupons and packages, children's cookbooks, shopping list pads, recipe cards, and a telephone into a housekeeping setting sets the stage for many domestic play stories. Because the context and props are well-known to children, there is greater opportunity for more complex play as well as elaborated and expanded language use which in effect "holds" children in the setting. Moreover, the children's familiarity with the setting invites innovation, prompting them to find new uses for objects and materials and to spin new stories.

Offering a variety of behaviors within the boundaries of the setting is another way to sustain children's task involvement in a setting (Kounin & Doyle, 1975). For example, the office is often a popular play setting for four- and five-year-olds because it offers opportunities to explore objects and materials (paper, pencils, a computer), to assume roles (policeman, secretary, captain), and to make up stories (create office-related themes and scenarios). When multiple options are afforded children in a single setting, they are enticed to stay there, subsequently focusing their attention, conversation and language use around a central topic or theme.

Settings that point out progress toward some end in a consistent way also keep children engaged for extended periods of time. In other words, concrete and continuous feedback is built into the activities of the setting. A science-oriented activity setting, for instance, may involve children in making a miniature garden in a large metal tray so that they may learn more about seeds and how they grow. The project consists of

specific steps illustrated on a large chart: planning out planting areas, setting down rocks and paths, planting the seeds, labelling the rows, watering gently each day, and watching the garden grow. With the completion of each step of the project, progress is pointed out, maintaining children's interest and attention. Utilizing print and other symbols to guide and confirm the completion of each step enhances the capability of a setting to point out progress and should frequently be used as a means of providing additional feedback, urging children to stay with the task.

Finally, activity settings where the interaction with materials results in an actual product have high holding power. In the art area, for example, a child may make a collage out of different textures of cloth, such as corduroy, silk, netting, or wool. Here it is the anticipated product which attracts and holds the child to the task for a sustained period of time. The inclusion of a sample, other children's work, or a picture of the product also bids the child to keep with the task until a product is obtained, and should be considered when developing settings for this purpose.

In sum, physical settings designed with high holding power in mind can contribute to the realization of broader curricular goals while simultaneously providing children with real reasons to use language and literacy. Not only do they attract children, they also teach them through their capability to hold children's attention to a particular enterprise, problem-solving task, project or product.

To help you visualize what an activity or play setting with high holding power might look like, we have sketched several in Figures 4.9–4.12. As you examine the organization and provisions of each, be thinking of

Figure 4.9   An example of a resource-rich activity pocket

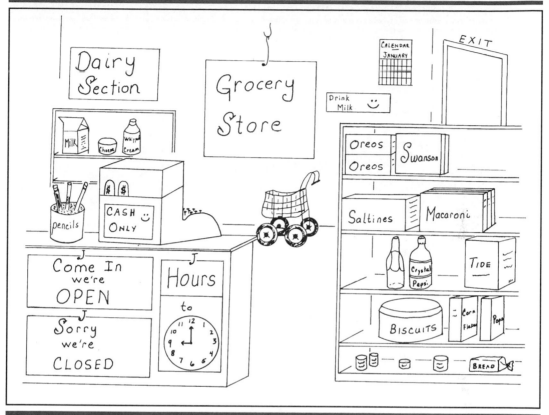

ways you can design similar settings supportive of the curricular goals in your own classroom.

#3. The physical environment fosters sustained work.

Although play is certainly essential in pre-kindergarten programs, it should not be the *only* business of children. Data on children's learning suggest that focusing children's activity around projects that are intellectually challenging is a viable and productive alternative to play (Katz, 1987). One of the key elements of project work is that it continues for some time, involving both academic and playful behaviors.

For the physical environment to accommodate sustained work, however, two environmental features need to be considered—one temporal and the other architectural.

Figure 4.10   An example of a generic setting that offers variety:
Exploring objects, assuming roles, and creating stories

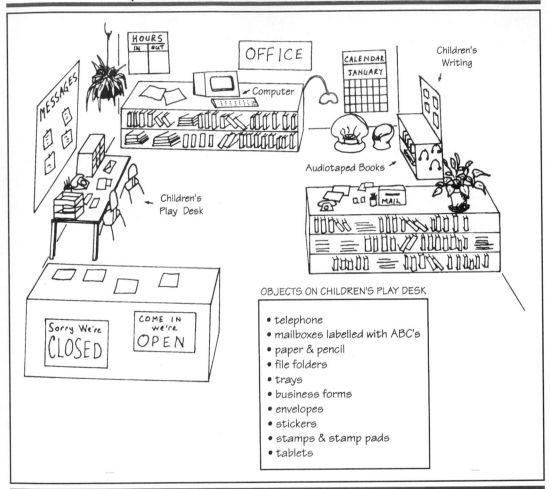

Temporal Features

Within the last decade, young children's natural capacity for sustained interest and work has met with a number of temporal stumbling blocks. One has been the tendency to adhere to rigid time schedules in child care programs, sometimes for very practical reasons, like food deliveries. Another is a pervasive misunderstanding of children's attention spans, these being misinterpreted as short, when in actuality children are simply not interested in some of the things adults want them to do.

Figure 4.11   An example of a setting that "points out" progress

You need: a pan, some pebbles, soil, clay for walls, a small dish for water, small plastic cups for rock garden, some herb seeds, some grass seed and some cress seed

Follow the steps...

(1)

- Use a large metal pan
- Plan gardening areas

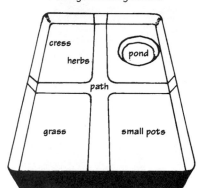

(2)

- Make paths
- Set out pots in rock garden

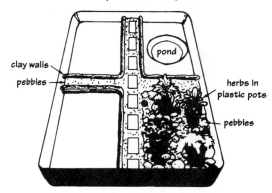

(3)

- Plant seeds in rows
- Put water in pond

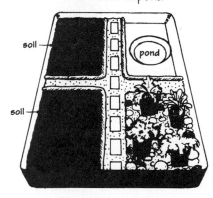

(4)

- Watch seeds grow
- Keep grass trimmed

(Adapted from Richards, Collis, & Kincaid (1987). *An Early Start in Science*, p. 17, London: McDonald Educational).

Figure 4.12   An example of a setting with an actual product

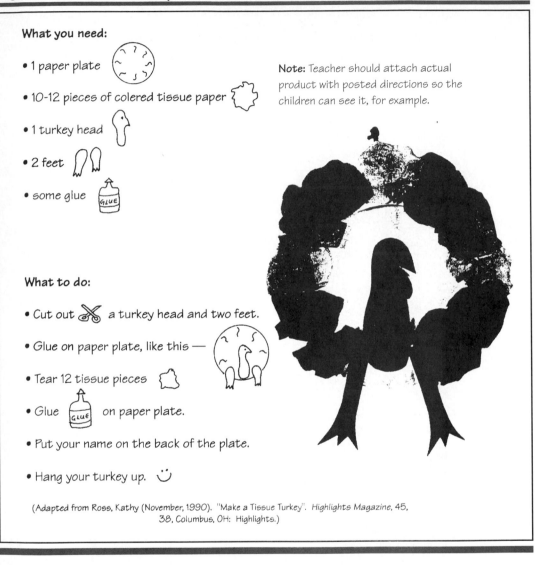

What you need:

• 1 paper plate

• 10-12 pieces of colered tissue paper

• 1 turkey head

• 2 feet

• some glue

Note: Teacher should attach actual product with posted directions so the children can see it, for example.

What to do:

• Cut out ✂ a turkey head and two feet.

• Glue on paper plate, like this —

• Tear 12 tissue pieces

• Glue GLUE on paper plate.

• Put your name on the back of the plate.

• Hang your turkey up. ☺

(Adapted from Ross, Kathy (November, 1990). "Make a Tissue Turkey". *Highlights Magazine*, 45, 38, Columbus, OH: Highlights.)

This strict adherence to time schedules coupled with misguided notions about children's short attention spans has led to frequent changes in activities scheduled throughout the day in an effort to keep children attentive and amused. However, these short bursts of doing (often exciting and fun) only undermine the development of children's interests and capabilities to attend (Katz, 1987). In short, for the sake of time, there is not enough time for young children to develop a disposition for sustained attention and interests.

One temporal feature, in particular, which has come under increasing scrutiny is clean-up time. A number of early childhood educators have begun to rethink this practice, suggesting that there is too much emphasis on it as a time and not enough on the meaningful activity which often precedes it (Gareau & Kennedy, 1991; Kuschner, 1989; New, 1990).

To adjust the focus of this practice, as well as the use of time in general, we recommend the following.

- ☐ Schedule large blocks of time for activities and play;
- ☐ Insert flexibility into the daily schedule by providing time cushions between major daily events;
- ☐ Focus on activities of the moment, not on what comes next.
- ☐ Avoid undue interruptions of play and work.

Clearly, if the curricula of child care programs are to be developmentally appropriate, greater consideration needs to be given to the young child's sense of time. As one very busy 3-year-old claimed, "I need two whole whiles." Young children need to experience many "two whole whiles" to develop the perseverance and enjoyment that stimulates lifelong interests and the motivation to pursue them.

Architectural Features

But then there are also building and structural features that impede sustained work. The most common is the perception that the physical environment of an early childhood program should be a multipurpose facility. Not only must the physical space accommodate activity and play settings, but also the same space may be used for snacks, naps and large group gatherings. In fact, in one preschool program familiar to us, each Friday the entire physical set-up must be torn down to make way for weekend activities and then rebuilt again on Monday morning.

Situations like these do not create the conditions for sustained work. If we are to give children the time they need to develop and complete projects in which they are interested, then we must allow them space to work on them for more than one activity or play period. Here we make two suggestions.

One, when young children start a large-scale project of obvious importance to them involving a number of materials within an activity/play setting, simply post a sign closing off the area until it is done. We know many teachers who have taken this common sense approach with considerable success.

Two, create a small area for long-term science, construction or art projects—a place where children can continue their efforts without having to put everything away. Such an area may be carved away from the rest of the room or perhaps a small space may be found in and around a closet, under a staircase, or by converting part of an office space.

Thus, where organization was at the heart of principle one, taking time and space is at the core of principle three. Although rarely easy, the utilization of these ideas is essential if teachers are to nurture children's interests and their predispositions to pursue specific topics in their work and play.

#4. The physical environment develops a sense of community.

Certainly, interacting with things in settings is an important means by which children come to know their world. But these interactions alone are not sufficient for meeting the great human need to know and become known that we discussed at the beginning of this book. It is when children's interactions become embedded in a social matrix that their linguistic reach penetrates new language and literacy possibilities.

What generates and maintains a modern social matrix is spoken and written language—people talking, listening, reading, writing to one another for all manner of real-life purposes and intentions. The physical environment can contribute to the development of a social matrix—a community, really—which expresses language and literacy through the ideas, values, attitudes, and cultures of the children and adults who comprise it.

Building a sense of community begins with an environment organized to promote pleasant relationships between people of different ages, to offer choices, and to provoke language and literacy learning. Extremely important are opportunities for verbal and written exchanges which can occur in natural ways—ways that are inviting and connected to the flow of events.

Spontaneous conversation and written exchange can occur on a regular basis if the physical environment is arranged to promote them. The thoughtful placement of compatible activity and play settings near one another is one way to encourage communication. Putting the housekeeping play setting next to a play post office to encourage literacy-related sociodramatic play is one example. Positioning the small manipulatives on tables in close proximity to block play to spark the negotiation of joint themes is another.

In conjunction with the strategic placement of activity and play settings is the inclusion of gathering places along well-traveled routes in the environment which allow for brief interchanges between children and between children and adults. Through the use of artificial trees, plants, chairs or benches, and mobiles, small niches for conversation can be etched into the environment, providing support for verbal exchanges.

Lightweight furniture can also be used to stimulate talk between children and should be included in the environment for their use. Teepees, small playhouses, large boxes, small desks, round tables, plastic crates, soft pillows, and old sheets are just a few objects with which children can make their own living arrangements and in the process engage in problem-solving conversations.

Places for activities and longer-term projects that induce conversation and writing can also be created. For example, double easels that accomodate 2 to 4 children can be provided. Kidney-shaped tables for building with small manipulatives can form one boundary of the small blocks area. Outdoor gardens can include low walls for setting things as well as sitting. And a breakfast-nook arrangement with easy access to print, paper and pencils can be considered as an alternative to the typical table and chair arrangement in housekeeping.

Lastly, throughout the physical environment, items that reflect the unique cultures of the adults and children who comprise the early childhood community can be included. Posters of annual events, local calendars, pictures of important local people and places, symbolic objects, and so forth can dot settings, promoting conversation and reflecting cultural heritage.

To develop a sense of community in a program, all the participants need to contribute to the shape and feel of the physical environment. Diversity should be celebrated, not cast aside in favor of commercial sameness. Through their play and work together, parents, teachers and children can create a lively and language-rich social matrix, reflective of their own particular community.

#5. The Physical Environment is Aesthetically Pleasing.

Our last principle is the most controversial because many will say that it is not practical. With limited funds, numerous environmental constraints and overworked teachers, beauty doesn't figure largely in the scheme of things. After all, if the environment is clean and safe, this should suffice.

We don't think so. We think that beauty must be a major consideration in our work, if the physical environment is to form a unifying thread that both relates and harmonizes people and their environment. To ignore the aesthetics of physical environment in the educational process is to risk the quality of our larger environment in the future.

According to Olds (1988), there are at least three factors that contribute to the development of a physical environment that is aesthetically pleasing—the quality of light, access to nature, and a variety of textures. Each factor affects children's behavior substantially.

The strategic use of lighting throughout the environment, for example, creates an ambiance, whether it be one of cheeriness, calm, serenity or joy. By skillfully locating wall lamps, windows, decorative screens and clip-on work lights , a preferred atmosphere may be achieved, contributing to the overall attractiveness of the physical environment.

A preponderance of natural things in a setting also contributes to an overall sense of beauty. Since there is an almost universal bias of humans to favor the natural environment over the man-made, attempts should be made to provide many types of natural objects within physical settings. Water, sand, trees, rocks, flowers, shells, butterflies, tadpoles, bugs: Children, especially young children, need to get in touch with natural things like these regularly.

Finally, texture is especially important to aesthetics because of its ability to arouse interest and curiosity. When the physical setting is characterized by different textures, variety and, at times, even surprise are introduced, both of which contribute to the general appeal of a setting. When considering texture in the environment, it seems easiest to think in opposites: hard things, like furniture, and soft ones, like pillows; rough surfaces, like sand, and smooth surfaces, like paper; dry settings—the library—and wetter ones—the water table; brightly colored areas and more muted ones; nubby wall hangings (wool and such) and silky ones and so on.

Although designing a "beautiful" physical environment certainly takes some forethought, it can be accomplished with relative ease in the pursuit of curricular goals. Children's drawing and writing, small-scale collections and themed displays, personal touches and well-planned settings: these combine not only to teach, but also to enhance the aesthetic feel of the total environment. In other words, the physical environment that informs and personalizes, supports and extends curriculum, fosters sustained work, and develops a sense of community is aesthetically pleasing. Moreover, it participates meaningfully in children's language learning, creating a special place where young children can thrive linguistically.

. . . .

Let's Review . . .

The focus of our attention in this chapter was on designing physical settings that support and enhance children's language and literacy learning. Following a brief discussion of generalizations basic to the human–environment relationship, five principles of environmental design which we believe influence children's language and literacy use in early childhood classrooms were presented and described.

So that the physical environment informs children in concrete and personalized ways, recommendations for environmental design were made in three areas: creating spatial boundaries, arranging and displaying provisions, and using personal touches.

To ensure that the physical environment supports and extends the curriculum, ways to design activity and play settings with high holding power were detailed, while the features of time and space to work were discussed as means for ensuring that the physical environment fosters sustained work.

Considerations of the strategic placement of settings to encourage communication and conversation, the use of appropriate furniture, and displays of local cultural items in the setting were highlighted as ways to use the physical environment in building a sense of community.

Finally, the importance of beauty in the environment was proposed with several ways to achieve this, for example, through the use of lighting, access to nature and textural variety in the setting. Throughout sketches of environments and design, techniques were illustrated to spark interest and ideas for use in your own classroom.

• •

Let's Explore . . .

1. Sketch the physical layout of a day care, preschool or prekindergarten classroom. Consider the spatial organization, drawing on principles one and four in your analysis. Make an appraisal of the environmental design, describing what you think are strengths and needs while keeping in mind the constraints of space and availability of furniture.

2. Survey the physical environment of a day care, preschool or early childhood classroom for the functional use of print in the following categories (adapted from Loughlin & Martin, 1987). Describe or sketch the specific print displays in each category.

   (a) Daily Routines

   (b) Labeling

   (c) Sign-on Charts

   (d) Directions

   (e) Record Keeping

   (f) General Information

3. Design a display around a theme of your choice. List books, supplementary print sources, and specific objects you would include. Share your idea with a colleague.

Planning Language and Literacy Experiences

Child-centered Activity Planning

possibilities   pitfalls

Considerations

Making Curricular Decisions

- about knowledge

- about skills

- about dispositions

Organizing Classroom Time

- Whole Group Focus Time

- Small Group Activity Time

- Sharing Time

- Reading Aloud Time

An Example & Illustration

A Topic Study of Seeds

CHAPTER 5

Planning for Integrated Language and Literacy Learning

Allison: Hi Becky.

Becky: Hi Allison.

Allison: Wanna play something *real easy?*

Becky: Everything's easy for us, right?

*I*n the previous chapter we examined how the physical environment can be purposefully designed to influence and enhance children's uses of language and literacy. In the discussion we sought to demonstrate how these processes flow throughout the whole environment, piquing children's interests and serving their purposes. We did not confine children's language and literacy encounters to sociodramatic play areas or book corners. Rather, we advocated design principles that permitted language and literacy to pervade all areas of the physical environment.

With respect to planning for language and literacy learning, we take a similar stance. From our point of view, language and literacy learning experiences should not be relegated to one corner of the curriculum, in the form of neatly packaged language and literacy programs. Recalling John Lennon's insight that life is what happens while we're busy making other plans, we believe that language and literacy are communication tools primarily used to do other things. It is in their use that children come to understand their features and forms and to discover their amazing functional range. Consequently, when it comes to planning language and literacy experiences for children's learning, we take the position that this planning should be **integrated** into more comprehensive curricular aims and intentions, not treated as an end unto itself.

In short, we believe that planning language and literacy learning must encompass more than reading storybooks to children, more than providing a writers' table, and more than teaching the ABCs through whatever approach. We think that language and literacy learning experiences must be embedded in some larger purpose, like learning more about oneself, about insects, the moon and stars, and fellow human beings. Planning for language and literacy learning, from our point of view, intersects with content area learning and those broader curricular goals which seek to develop children's knowledge, skills, dispositions and feelings (Katz, 1987). It is through their exploration of content in science, social studies, the fine arts and literature that children develop and grow as speakers and listeners, writers and readers. They learn language and literacy while pursuing themes and topics of interest which emanate from these essential domains of human knowing.

On the one hand, educators of young children have long agreed that the learning experiences they plan for children should be organized around children's need to know about their world, not abstract things disconnected from their lives (Morrison, 1988). Indeed, the curriculum specialist, Hilda Taba, argued quite some time ago that "children learn best those things that are attached to solving actual problems, that help them in meeting real needs or that connect with some active interest. Learning in its true sense is an active transaction" (1962, p. 401).

How to achieve learning "in its true sense," on the other hand, has met with much less consensus among educators. At issue is how to achieve learning "as an active transaction" in classroom-like settings where there are many children, finite resources, external curricular demands, and one teacher!

This is a challenge for two reasons. First, if learning is to be "an active transaction, "then instruction (planned learning and teaching outcomes) must take its organizational cues more from learners than from the content or skill to be learned. For instance, we would like to see teachers be responsive to the child's reading development timetable rather than any textbook notions of when and how reading should be taught. This suggests that teachers might plan their teaching on the basis of the children's ways of knowing, instead of prescribed program approaches.

Second, if the children's needs and interests become the instructional source, then to an extent, teaching cannot be totally *preplanned*. Again, what is to be taught must be responsive to what the children need and want to learn, not what curriculum developers or textbook publishers might suggest. Teachers working with children discover their joint interests and abilities, and together they establish realistic and relevant educational goals. Consequently, the organization and sequence of instruction cannot be rigidly structured for all children. It needs to change, depending on the particular group of children, the time, place, resources and, of course, the teacher.

For these two reasons primarily, planning for language and literacy learning around the needs, interests and preferences of young children is demanding. It requires that teachers be more than curriculum consumers. They must also be curriculum constructors. As curriculum constructors they must use what they know about children, language and literacy learning, teaching, and content to create relevant learning activities for particular groups and specific individuals.

But how to do this in the reality of classroom life is another challenge. In this chapter we specifically address the very practical matter of how to provide language and literacy learning experiences that appeal to young children's broader needs and interests yet guide them toward the language and literacy learning that the world requires and that adults know they must do. We refer to this process as **child-centered activity planning**, where topics and themes of interest to children are selected for exploration and through which language and literacy may be purposefully used. It is a practical planning process that **interlinks** curricular goals (what children should know and be able to do) and daily activities; **integrates** language and literacy into more comprehensive aims of early childhood education; and **interconnects** children's interests and needs with adults' teaching intents and responsibilities. Before describing and illustrating this process, however, it is valuable to be aware of its possibilities and its pitfalls.

Child-centered Activity Planning—Possibilities

Generally speaking, instructional planning that is sensitive and responsive to children's interests and needs while it promotes their language and literacy use has three characteristics (Goodman, 1991; Taba, 1962; Zais, 1976). Each characteristic opens up possibilities for teaching and learning that keep children at the center of instructional and curriculum planning.

☐ First, and probably foremost, planning for integrated language and literacy learning starts with children's needs and interests. By this we mean children's *expressed* or *observed* needs and interests, not what adults think these *ought* to be. Realizing this, two possibilities present themselves: (1) to discover what really does interest young children and (2) to assist them in selecting some of their interests for further exploration. From infants to preschoolers, giving eye and ear to what children express as their preferences is informative—the questions they ask, the books they like, the things they play with. Helping them to decide what to explore more closely and how to do so is our responsibility as teachers. It is the chief means by which we infuse language and literacy into the content they are striving to know and understand.

☐ Second, child-centered activity planning is a negotiation between adults and children. Together they plan experiences that solve actual problems, meet real needs, and connect to *active* interests. Out of these adult–child planning partnerships, new possibilities for spoken and written communication emerge which lead to shared understandings about what to do, how to do it, and how to judge its worth.

Minimal preplanning, however, does not imply a lack of preparation. The teacher does indeed engage in considerable advance planning by:

— discovering children's interests and needs (which does not preclude studying about them),
— assisting children in making decisions about what to do,
— helping children to plan and carry out learning activities,
— provisioning and arranging the environment, and
— including children as participants in the evaluation of accomplishments.

☐ Third, planning activities for integrated language and literacy experiences promotes interactive learning and problem-solving. In the pursuit of their interests, children interact with their environment, with materials and with others. Inevitably they encounter stumbling blocks in conjunction with these interactions. To overcome these stumbling blocks, they must engage in problem-solving, the very processes of which develop their communicative and social competence as well as understandings that are fruitful and enduring.

Child-centered Activity Planning—Pitfalls

As attractive and liberating as the possibilities of integrative instructional planning are, however, this process has its potential pitfalls. We need to be keenly aware of these pitfalls and take precautions so that the integrated language and literacy experiences we prepare and plan with children remain worthwhile.

☐ One pitfall is the tendency to focus too much on children's immediate interests and needs and to neglect the critical social goals of language and literacy learning, not to mention education. After all, as responsible adults we are striving to assist children in developing a language for life. Children's immediate interests, however, may not encompass the knowledge, skills, attitudes and values they will need to function in the modern world. For example, young children may not choose to accept the challenge of learning to read print over picture. But they must if they are to assume their rightful place in a literate community.

Adults' good sense must prevail. Planning for integrated language and literacy learning must include experiences which lead children into the future. Children's immediate choices need to be balanced with adult intentions that teach them what they will need to know if they are to grow.

☐ A second difficulty is the propensity for disorganization in this approach to planning. Because the teacher waits to include children's ideas, essential preparation may suffer. Often at the root of the difficulty is the lack of an organizing principle or idea which connects various experiences together into a comprehensible whole. The result is a flurry of activities that may be fun to do, but are neither coherent nor enduring.

What must be assured in instructional planning is connectedness. To safeguard that experiences and their related activities do connect with one another, teachers must deliberately and thoughtfully select organizers that frame activities they prepare *and* those that children decide to do. These organizers, whether topics or themes, serve adults' intentions to teach and children's need to learn, providing rich opportunities for language and literacy use.

☐ A third danger is the inherent lack of continuity in this form of planning. Its central aim of being responsive to children's unique interests can become its biggest drawback. Because children's interests depend so much on environmental conditions, pursuing these and these alone may be dangerously repetitive, narrow and one-sided. For example, planning language and literacy activities solely around young children's interests and preferences in rural Kansas could seriously mislead their growing understanding of the culturally diverse world within which we live.

To avoid this pitfall, adults must deliberately use children's specific interests as springboards to broader interests in and understandings of the world and the people who populate it. Adults consistently need to emphasize the generative nature of knowledge, showing children how to use what they know to go beyond what they currently think. There are many ways of doing this—playing with children, reading storybooks to them, and conversing with them—just to mention a few.

❑   Finally, there is the very practical issue of teacher competence. Planning "around" children places high demands on teachers' knowledge and skills. Not only must they possess a solid liberal arts education (generalists), but they must be well-versed in the intricacies of developmentally appropriate practice. Moreover, because of the heavy reliance on "interaction," teachers need to perform at high levels most of the time. This may be unrealistic. But it becomes more realistic when teachers are afforded ample opportunities for planning and ongoing staff development within parameters of their work and when they are provided support systems that sustain their effort and energy, for example, through parent volunteers and teaching assistants.

These pitfalls notwithstanding, commitment to the humane and liberating principles of child-centered instructional planning seems to create, more so than other curricular planning approaches, those learning conditions wherein both children and adults prosper. Acknowledging this, we next examine general guidelines teachers may use when making curricular decisions about children's language and literacy learning, ensuring that both are developed in ways that promote children's language and literacy growth while respecting their interests, preferences and needs.

Making Curricular Decisions For Integrated Language and Literacy Learning

Deciding on the specific knowledge, processes, and dispositions that simultaneously enhance and further young children's language and literacy learning can appear at times like an overwhelming task. Many early childhood books include long lists of teaching objectives, ranging from basic conceptual skills (for example, classification) to content knowledge in math, social studies, and science. These lists often seem to make our job even more complex: No matter how well we do, we still seem to have more objectives to accomplish!

Consequently, in this section we describe general guidelines for developing goals with respect to children's knowledge, processes, and dispositions, placing special emphasis on how these may incorporate language and literacy learning outcomes. Our discussion is purposefully broad for several reasons:

❏ Different groups of learners have different needs and
interests;

❏ Aims that are developmentally appropriate for one group of
learners may not be equally appropriate for others;

❏ As our values and knowledge of young children's learning
may change or become enhanced, so too will our aims and
objectives.

Here, then, are some key points which we regard as important in
making curricular decisions that influence language and literacy learning. They are certainly not designed to be carved in marble. Rather, we
offer them as considerations or springboards for thinking about how you
might want to go about deciding on language and literacy learning outcomes for the integrated experiences you plan.

Knowledge

The question of what knowledge to teach to our young learners has
become a perennial challenge to educators. Some curriculum developers
believe that a specific body of knowledge should be taught to young children, including such content as weather, literary genres, and magnetism.
Others, however, focus more on the processes of learning, or *how* to
acquire this knowledge through experiences, language and other forms of
representation.

We believe this is a false dichotomy. Rather, in choosing topics that
focus on children's interests and needs, we should help children acquire
knowledge *and* construct processes for future reasoning and critical
thinking. A body of knowledge, according to this view, contains both
information and a specialized method of inquiry.

How do we decide on a particular body of knowledge? We believe that
the knowledge selected should be related to some basic concepts that are
of sufficient importance and complexity to serve as threads throughout
your entire program. Concepts like cooperation and interdependence can
be taught through many different bodies of knowledge and may accommodate a broad range of individual differences and interests among children while extending their language and literacy use and abilities. For
example, later in this chapter you will meet Beth, who selects seeds as a
topic for learning about living things, because the 4- and 5-year-olds in
her class are involved in the spring planting of their farming community.
But her colleague, James, uses ants as a topic on living things, prompted
by his toddlers' smashing of ants on an urban playground. Consequently,
though each topic might focus on different facts, the underlying concepts
acquired, as in caring for others, and potential meaningful language and
literacy use will be the same.

This view allows you to adjust topics to meet needs and interests of your learners and to infuse relevant language and literacy learning into content-rich experiences. At the same time, it may encourage you to try many different topics to see which ones are most effective in achieving your broader curricular goals as well as those specific to language and literacy growth. Take for example, the important concept of interdependence. How might it be taught in various classrooms? Let's take a look at the array of topics in one early childhood program:

- ❑ Me and My Family
- ❑ Inventing Machines
- ❑ Helping Keep Our Environment Clean
- ❑ Learning About Bees

Notice that, while the specific facts under each topic may vary dramatically, each topic may engage children in knowing related to the concept of interdependence, such as the need to work together. Moreover, each topic offers rich opportunities for children to use language and literacy and for teachers to embellish these processes in situations of meaning to children.

While we are wary of creating any rigid set of concepts for all children, we present our personal view of some key concepts which can be appropriately addressed with children in the early years and around which bodies of knowledge and related language and literacy use can be developed (Table 5.1).

Processes Specific to Language and Literacy

An integrated view of language and literacy naturally requires a holistic approach to our instructional intentions for young children. Sometimes teachers may work on developmentally inappropriate activities because they aren't really sure what language and literacy processes to emphasize at pre-primary school ages. This raises the following questions:

1. What learning outcomes are we really trying to achieve in language and literacy for young children?
2. Are there skills and strategies that all of our young children should achieve by the primary grades?
3. With respect to literacy in particular, are there specific behaviors that indicate growth in literacy development?

In answer to these questions, we believe that school practices should attempt to closely mirror and extend the developmental patterns we described in Chapter 2. In other words, we must build on what children

TABLE 5.1	SELECTING CONCEPTS FOR THEME OR TOPIC EXPLORATIONS

CONCEPTS	EXAMPLES OF TOPICS
Causality	"What's That?": Exploring our world
	Keeping healthy
	Cause and effect
Change	Special seasons
	Growing things
	Predicting
Cooperation	About me and my friends
	Teamwork
	Relationships
Differences	More than one way
	Discovering beauty
	Free to be you and me
Interdependence	The Family
	Creating communities
	Sharing
Power	Machine magic
	How things work
	Dealing with conflicts
Traditions	Favorite holidays
	Cultural traditions
	Rites of spring
Values	A peaceful world
	Ecology
	Tender, loving care

already know about language and literacy. Broadly defined, our teaching intents should focus on three domains:

Helping learners become aware of and understand how language and literacy can be useful to them.

Children need language to give and get information, to express emotions and to control and direct others' behaviors (Halliday, 1975). Since oral language has memory limitations, literacy allows children to record their activities and experiences through pictures and/or words for instrumental purposes.

Helping learners use language and literacy creatively to construct new knowledge.

Language and literacy have the potential to develop learning and thinking. As children playfully use sounds and words and then put these words into stories, songs, and poetry, they use language and its written form to create new ideas that are unique to their own ways of thinking.

Helping learners use language and literacy to facilitate interaction with others.

Language and literacy are social processes which we use to communicate what we know, think and feel. Through interaction with others, children not only explore their own thinking, but modify and extend their ideas beyond their own personal experiences.

These are, of course, very general aims that apply throughout the whole program. In a sense, they represent the philosophy which ties together the varied language and literacy experiences in our classroom. Typically, they lead to more specific learning outcomes that address the language and literacy processes we seek to develop. In Table 5.2, we describe performance indicators of the processes embraced by these three language and literacy domains.

Dispositions

Broadly defined, dispositions are attitudes and values or "habits of mind" (Katz & Chard, 1989). These are behaviors that encourage children's motivations to learn long after formal instruction has ended. The probability that knowledge and processes will endure are vastly increased if our young learners feel positive about them. Effective learning can only be facilitated if children have positive attitudes toward what they are learning.

Sometimes teachers take these dispositions for granted. They may say, "Of course, we want to ensure children's feelings of success in learning." But do we provide ample opportunities for their manifestation? Often not. It is for this reason that the dispositions to be emphasized in the topics or themes selected for exploration should be carefully articulated and written out in planning instruction. Clearly, they are unlikely to be learned through direct methods. Rather, dispositions are more likely to be strengthened when children are engaged in meaningful learning that feels good. In Table 5.3, we refer to two broad categories of dispositions that are particularly relevant to young learners: attitudes toward learning and attitudes toward others (Katz & Chard, 1989; Taba, 1962).

Virtually all knowledge and all aspects of communication are more fully developed when children regard themselves as successful learners and as important members of a learning community.

With these broad guidelines for curricular decision-making in mind, we turn next to an equally challenging topic: organizing classroom time for ample language and literacy experiences. Recall from Chapter 4 how the use of time can influence the development of children's disposition for

TABLE 5.2   LANGUAGE AND LITERACY PERFORMANCE INDICATORS: THE EARLY YEARS

PROCESSES	PERFORMANCE INDICATORS
Social uses of language	Shows ability to use language as a tool for functional purposes: to get objects, give and get information.
	Develops skills in using language to engage others in conversation.
	Displays facility to use language purposefully, and specifically to convey meaning.
	Understands the social conventions associated with language: for example, not interrupting others while they are speaking.
	Speaks with increased confidence and clarity of pronunciation so that others can understand.
Spoken vocabulary and meaning	Increases ability to understand and use words in meaningful and appropriate contexts.
	Displays ability to discover meanings of words and sentences through their use in practical applications.
	Attends to and follows oral directions.
Rudimentary writing processes	Grasps and manipulates writing implements.
	Records ideas through pictures, words, and/or sentences his/her "own way."
	Writes and recognizes own name.
Concepts about print	Shows awareness of print permanency (that is, words in print remain the same from one reading to the next).
	Shows awareness that text is read from left to right, and from top to bottom.
	Shows development of print—meaning associations, such as environmental print, and assigns verbal labels to letter symbols or words.
	Uses pictures and print to label, and to tell a story.
Literature and sense of story	Enjoys listening to and engaging in rhyme, rhythm, songs, poetry, and storytelling.
	Plays with rhyming sounds and words, with increasing ability to discriminate and identify sounds.
	Expresses interest and attends to stories and informational text.
	Displays ability to retell a story, including characters and actions, demonstrating a basic understanding of story sequence (for example, beginning introduction, middle, and end).

TABLE 5.3   DEVELOPING DISPOSITIONS IN THEME OR TOPIC EXPLORATIONS

DISPOSITIONS TOWARD LEARNING	DISPOSITIONS TOWARD OTHERS
Curiosity	Generosity
Resourcefulness	Helpfulness
Creativity	Empathy
Independence	Open-mindedness
Responsibility	Appreciation of others' efforts
Challenge-seeking	Cooperativeness
Responsiveness to new ideas	Acceptance

interest, such as their capability of becoming deeply absorbed in something enough to pursue it over time. To give children the time they need to get lost in an activity, we recommended the scheduling of large blocks of time with some measure of flexibility. In the following section we pursue this notion further, discussing how to organize time in chunks which allow for sustained conversations and literacy-related interactions that meet children's interests and needs.

Organizing Classroom Time

Young children need a great deal of variety and diversity in their day. Consequently, when we think about how to organize chunks of time, we need to consider learning experiences that give children an opportunity to use language and literacy while working together as a whole classroom group, in a small group, and by themselves.

Here's how one teacher organized the 3 hours of his program day, integrating language and literacy learning experiences into the sustained exploration of a topic. Notice in Table 5.4 that time has been organized by the teacher to account for:

❑   Whole Group Focus Time
❑   Small Group Activity Time
❑   Sharing Time
❑   Storybook Reading Time

In the following section we'll briefly describe how language and literacy learning experiences and activities can be integrated into each of these chunks of time, borrowing from the daily plans of James who

TABLE 5.4   EXAMPLE OF A DAILY SCHEDULE

TIME	ACTIVITY
7:30–8.45	Arrival
8:45–9:00	Greeting
9:00–9:30	Whole Group Focus Time
	(1) Read If You Were An Ant by Barbara Brenner
	(2) Record what we know about ants and anthills
9:30–10:30	Small Group Activity Time
	(1) Blocks—Build Anthills
	(2) Sandtable—Make ant tunnels
	(3) Art—Make thumbprint pictures
	(4) Science—Make an ant farm
	(5) Book Corner—Read assorted books about ants
10:30–11.20	Snack & Outdoor Play
11:00–11:20	Sharing Time
	(1) Record what we know about ants
	(2) Reread poem about ants using choral reading techniques
	(3) Explain ant farms
11:20–11:45	Storybook Reading Time
11:45–12:00	Dismissal

teaches toddlers in an urban early childhood program. The excerpts we use are drawn from the children's study of ants through which James acquainted them with the concept of caring for others.

Whole Group Focus Time

Often called group time or circle time, this is essentially a time when the teacher brings the children together as a classroom community. Typically, the time is used for making general announcements, taking roll, and discussing the upcoming events of the day. In addition to these necessary "housekeeping" issues, whole group focus time is designed for teachers to:

❑   introduce a new topic, theme or unit, using literature and/or other media and materials;

OR

❑ focus children's attention on exploring ideas central to an ongoing topic or theme, using questions, dramatic techniques, demonstrations, and so on;

OR

❑ engage children in talking about and recording ideas and questions that lead to a greater understanding of the topic or theme.

Taking place first thing, Whole Group Focus Time generally ranges from ten to twenty minutes, depending on the developmental level of the group. Activities during this time are designed to serve as catalysts for children's explorations, investigations and activities for the day. Teachers we've observed use Whole Group Focus Time to:

(1) Nurture children's curiosity by posing a problem that needs to be solved. For instance, James says to the children, "We've been talking about living creatures during the past several days. Yesterday I found an anthill on the playground. What do you think might be inside an anthill? How can we find out?" He then goes on to record many of their ideas on large chart paper, writing each child's name by his or her idea.

OR

(2) Display real objects and encourage inquiry. Another time, James says, "Let's study an ant colony. We can watch what ants do everyday. We can draw pictures of what they do. Some of you may want to write about what they do. Let's become ant experts." Following this, he introduces the children to an established ant colony in a large plastic display case and invites children's observations, some of which he may record on a large piece of chart paper with the heading, *What We See.*

OR

(3) Demonstrate how to do a new activity. Here James begins by saying, "Today we are going to do an experiment with our ants to find out what sorts of food our ant friends prefer." He then proceeds to briefly describe what an experiment is (including the need to record and sketch observations) and how the children will conduct an experiment to observe what ants like to eat. Directions (print and picture) for the experiment are posted on the wall, and materials for conducting observations are readily available (for example, hand magnifiers, drawing paper and pencils).

Specific activities, of course, will vary according to the particular topic or theme of interest and the needs of your age group. The intent of these activities, however, will be the same: to encourage children as a group to actively engage in thinking and talking, reading and writing about ideas related to a topic of interest. Notice again that the focus of the activity is not on the direct teaching of language and literacy. Rather, language and literacy are seen and used as **tools** of inquiry.

Whole Group Focus Time should end with an effort by the teacher to help children summarize the ideas they've just explored, encouraging their use of spoken language and specific vocabulary to express their understandings. Sometimes this can be done by simply talking back and forth about what had preceded. Or it may take a more representational form, as in a printed list of ideas or a sketch of what the children observed. In these instances, certain concepts about print can be developed at this time, for example, using print to label items in a sketch or developing awareness that text is read from left to right and from top to bottom.

Small Group Activity Time

Now that you've piqued children's interest and aroused their curiosity, this is the time when they may want to explore and discover ideas on their own, trying out the language and literacy associated with the topic or theme. And here, in particular, is where you may utilize the environment as a teaching assistant, purposefully arranging activity and play settings to sustain and extend children's interests in the topic or theme. During small group activity time children may:

❑ practice and employ their developing language and literacy skills in pursuit of their interests;

❑ try to "take on" some of the activities and behaviors that have been demonstrated to the whole group;

❑ interact with their peers while clarifying and verifying their "hypotheses" and "theories";

❑ support their learning through conversations with each other and with adults.

During this time, children are free to select a setting of interest. For example, in the block building areas of James' classroom, children were encouraged in their study of ants to construct an anthill, with tunnels, obstacles and climbing structures (Klein, 1991). In the sandbox, they created mazes, similar to the one in the established ant colony. In the science area, the children made an ant farm by filling a ventilated jar with soil, sprinkling it with some sugar and putting ants in the jar. (Print and picture directions were posted in the area.) And in the art area, they made thumbprint pictures to represent their observations of ants in action. In short, activity time gives children an opportunity to use what they've learned or what they already know to create and extend their understandings on their own terms. And the teacher's careful, thoughtful use of the physical environment supports them in these learning efforts.

Small Group Activity Time is a busy, but special, time for teachers. It affords them the time to observe indicators of children's developing language and literacy behaviors, as described in Table 5.2, to engage in more intimate, extended conversations with individuals or small groups, and to monitor children's use of the environment as an aid to learning. Unfortunately, some teachers get caught up during this less-structured time into cleaning or doing some other administrative tasks. But really this time is quite precious, offering teachers an ideal opportunity to engage in many of the language and literacy activities that are often so difficult to do in a larger group setting—the intimate sharing of a good storybook, scribing children's ideas and stories, helping a child to print her name, conversing, and watching the communicative competence of specific individuals.

While the length of this period will vary due to special events, we believe that Small Group Activity Time is especially important and should last about an hour. This allows children the time to explore, investigate and immerse themselves in a range of independent activities. This is also an excellent opportunity for parent volunteers and others to interact with small groups of children on projects that may need more supervision.

Sharing Time

This is the final segment of time that is devoted to the exploration of a topic or theme, before Snack Time, music or large-muscle activities. In a sense, Sharing Time is designed to bring "closure" to what has been learned for the day. Now children have an opportunity to recall their experiences and share something special about the topic. Perhaps they'd like to show everyone a construction they made during Small Group Activity Time, a picture they made, a storybook they read or a demonstration of something they've learned that might be of interest to the larger group.

In James' group, some children tried to discover how ants ate by placing bread crumbs and crusts in the ant colony and observing their actions with hand-held magnifying glasses. They drew sketches of what they saw which James helped them to label. During Sharing Time they reported their findings to the whole group, who were just amazed to see how strong ants could be. Two other children had spent time in the Cozy Corner Library looking at *If You Were An Ant* (Brenner, 1973). They "read" the book to the entire group, encouraging others to read it, too.

It is important that Sharing Time be a voluntary activity. Everyone can benefit, including the teacher. Those children who do share get the opportunity to talk about their exploratory, investigative and play activity in front of an audience. Those who don't share get the chance to listen and to respond to their peers, obtaining some good ideas for future things to do and play during Small Group Activity Time. Finally, the teacher can use this time to share or bring to conscious awareness the key concepts and facts children are learning in association with a topic or theme and to highlight specific language and literacy processes, for example, how language and literacy can be useful to them.

Since listening to their peers in front of a group is still a relatively new experience for young children, it is important to set appropriate standards for Sharing Time. Children must be taught to act respectful of those holding the floor. Further, comments about each other's art work, demonstrations or writing must be designed to be helpful and not hurtful in any way. Teachers can help by modeling comments, somewhat like James . . .

- ❑ I *like* the detail of your drawing of the ant colony.
- ❑ I *learned* a lot about the way ants eat, thanks to your experiments.
- ❑ I would like *to learn more* about ants. Do you have some ideas about how I might do that?

Especially in the beginning of the year, it is best to keep Sharing Time relatively brief so that it remains a fun, positive activity, culminating the day's topic- or theme-related work and play.

Reading Aloud Time

The three hours end reflectively with a shared book experience. Here, your community of learners sits together to enjoy a story which may be related to your topic or theme of study. Sometimes, teachers may read predictable books which seem to just lure children into whole group participation. For example, at one point in the ant study, James selected for his group, *"I Can't," Said the Ant* (Cameron, 1961). At other times, teachers may use favorites, like *Ants Have Pets* (Darling, 1977), to spark new ideas, such as a parent-child project at home.

A shared book experience for young children should focus on the language and meaning of the story. Especially at this age level, it is not really appropriate to dwell too much on the conventions of written language (for example, punctuation and letter names) or to reconfigure the book experience into a reading lesson. Rather, the Reading Aloud Time should encourage children to listen carefully, to make good predictions about what may come next, to recall parts of the story, and to link the story with their own experiences.

At a few points in the storybook reading, teachers may want to stop and briefly "recap" the story. Some teachers do this by sharing their feelings about the story. For example, when reading *The Three Billy Goats Gruff* (Galdone, 1973), a teacher might say, "I wonder what may happen next. The large Billy Goat got eaten up. I'm really scared about what might happen to the next one!" In this manner, teachers may draw their young audience into the story, as parents do with their children.

Typically, at the conclusion of Reading Aloud Time, there may be a brief discussion of the story. We have found the simple question, "What did you like best about the story?", helps focus young listeners' responses to what they've just heard and the meanings it held for them. From here, we can make important text-to-life connections, bridging what they have learned from the text to personal interests and experiences in everyday life.

Having now described one way to organize time as well as broad guidelines for curricular decision-making, we are ready to share a detailed example of child-centered activity planning, where content knowledge, language and literacy processes, and learning dispositions are woven into activities that support and extend language and literacy growth. Although there is no single best approach for planning such activities, organizing them around a theme or topic has often proved practical and effective. In the following section we describe how this can be done in a way that infuses language and literacy learning into content which addresses children's broader interests, preferences and needs. Further, we hope to demonstrate throughout the example how the organization of time and the physical environment assist the teacher in achieving intended language and literacy learning outcomes, providing ample opportunity for spoken and written language transactions.

An Example of Child-Centered Activity Planning for Integrated Language and Literacy Learning

Purposeful activity is at the heart of experiences which develop children's abilities to speak and listen, write and read. Consequently, to guide our teaching and safeguard children's learning of language and literacy, the activities we plan for developing these language processes need to cohere and make sense. What's more, they need to make children think—which is to say that the activities need some element of challenge.

These qualities of coherence, meaningfulness and challenge are evident in the planning described below. As we lead you through its steps, we provide you with specific examples drawn from practice, namely a topic study developed by Beth, the prekindergarten teacher we mentioned earlier. We then gather the separate examples together into an **illustration** of integrative and child-centered activity planning which promotes children's language and literacy learning *as a result of* their using these tools to make sense of experience.

• •

To begin . . .

☐ Decide on an **organizer** (a theme or topic) for children's exploration.

This is enjoyable to do. Use what you know about children's development and their interests. Read what others have done. And most importantly, watch what children like to do.

For example, through her careful attention to children's words and deeds, Vivian Paley (1986) observed three recurring themes in her children's classroom play: friendship, fantasy and fear. She used these as organizers for children's exploration of their own play-stories as well as her language and literacy teaching goals.

Following is a more detailed example of how one teacher selected an organizer that had meaning for young children.

Beth teaches at a preschool class in a public school system located in a small community in the southern part of the United States. There are 15 children in her class, nine boys and six girls. It is springtime, and all around the community people are busy planting. Many of the children in her class are involved in this activity with their parents. So, naturally, they have much to say about it and many questions as well. Beth decides to capitalize on the children's immediate interest and to organize a study of seeds and how they grow. She realizes that the children can bring existing experiences to the topic and that she can use their current knowledge to generate new understandings about plants as living things and their ecological importance beyond the community. She also recognizes that important language and literacy processes can be developed through an exploration of seeds and how they grow, for example, recording observations of plant growth using picture and print, following oral and written directions, reading environmental print, and exploring related literature—stories, informational books, poems and songs.

Note here that a potential organizer for activity came from the culture, immediate environments, and families of the children themselves. In listening to what they were talking about, Beth made connections between their interests and the broader curriculum for which she is responsible. Furthermore, their interests provide a built-in motivation for the teaching she knows she must do. Because the children are interested, it is easy to guide them along pathways that result in learning.

• •

Next . . .

❑   Jot down what children can learn by exploring the organizer.

It is *essential* to note what children will gain by exploring the ideas and objects associated with a specific organizer, whether it be a topic, theme or unit of study. It is an early opportunity to assess the worth of the organizer with respect to children's interest and their learning, language and literacy included.

Simply jot down your immediate impressions in three areas of learning:

❑   **Knowledge**—What children may come to know as a result of exploring the organizing topic or theme;

❑   **Processes**—Language and literacy behaviors children may demonstrate, practice and extend;

❑   **Dispositions**—Attitudes and values children may develop about the topic or theme.

When finished, your jotting may look something like Beth's:

As Beth thought about the potential of seeds as a topic study that may further concept development and broad content goals, she began to write down what children could learn through their inquiry. She first considered main ideas, for example:

(1)   There are many different kinds of seeds.

(2)   Seeds grow into plants with roots, stems, leaves and flowers.

(3)   Most seeds need warmth, light, minerals, water and air to grow.

(4) Many foods we eat are seeds.

(5) Seeds need care if they are to grow.

She also thought about language and literacy processes the children could experience and practice, such as:

(1) using oral and written language to obtain and share information;

(2) discovering meanings of words and sentences in practical situations;

(3) recording experiences in different ways, for example, writing and sketching;

(4) doing simple experiments, following directions given in print and picture;

(5) developing concepts about print–meaning associations, for example, environmental print.

And she considered, too, the dispositions she could foster throughout the study, such as:

(1) a caring interest in the environment;

(2) a willingness to observe and make comparisons;

(3) a willingness to "wait" for results;

(4) enjoying using one's senses and handling living things.

Some of these were understandings, processes and dispositions Beth had urged before in the children's activities, and because they "fit" in this particular inquiry, she now chose to reemphasize them once again.

• •

Now . . .

❑ Brainstorm and select several activities children can do.

To pursue their interests in ways that both satisfy and stimulate learning, young children need structure. Teachers can provide the structure children need by selecting activities which complement children's choices yet assure an integrated system of exploration. Several things should be kept in mind when selecting these activities:

❑ They should be related to the topic, theme or unit serving as the organizer.

❑ They should be related to one another.

❑ They should build on one another so that knowledge, processes, and dispositions are developed.

❑ They should provide chunks of time for whole group, small group and individual activity.

❑ They should include a balanced range of media related to the topic or theme; for example, children's literature (stories, informational books, poems, songs, and rhymes), audiovisual resources (including computer software), and related play objects and props.

It is helpful to visualize this integrated system of activities as a spiral-like construction (Figure 5.1).

The topic or theme as the organizer defines and guides the activities we choose to do as well as those children suggest. Whether planning activities for a few days or several weeks, the organizer assures that the activities we do with children are related to one another.

But the fact that activities are related is not a sufficient condition for learning language and literacy. If the learning process is to occur, then the organizer itself must be held together by the knowledge, processes, and dispositions children need to meet, to practice and to internalize. To

Figure 5.1

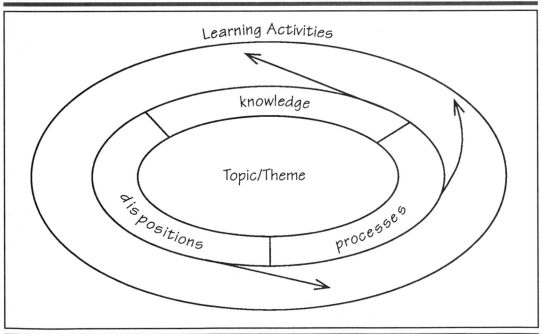

omit these learning essentials is to rob the activity of purpose and ultimately of meaning.

Furthermore, activities should be deliberately interrelated, each developing knowledge, processes and dispositions needed for the next. In this way, an organized, integrated and responsive system for developing language and literacy is created, uniting children's interests and adults' teaching intentions. As children's interests broaden and deepen, their learning (knowledge, processes and dispositions), including language and literacy, can be challenged and stretched in association with a particular theme, topic or unit of study.

Look again at Beth's work to observe how teachers select activities with these criteria in mind.

When she prepares for an exploration that children will do, Beth likes to select several activities *for* them so that the exploration coheres and maintains direction. She says it helps to keep the exploration "on track." So, she brainstorms and then selects certain activities for inclusion in the exploration. Some of her activity ideas for the seed study include the following:[1]

(1) Collect seeds (peas, beans, corn, watermelon, wheat, pumpkin, sunflower) into paper cups, plastic bags, or paper plates. To observe the seeds, sort them in some way, for example according to size or shape. (Caution: Avoid seeds which have been treated with fungicide.)

(2) Sprout seeds in domes for observation purposes. Make sprouters (Pace, 1990).*

(3) Make Silly Bird Seed Gardens (Allison, 1975).

(4) Make translucent window hangings.*

(5) Read literature about seeds and how they grow (stories, poems, informational books and songs). Some sources that come immediately to mind:

Seeds and More Seeds (Selsam, 1959)	*The Popcorn Book* (de Paola, 1978)
The Carrot Seed (Kraus, 1945)	*The Tiny Seed* (Carle, 1990)
Frog and Toad Together (Lobel, 1972)	*Ten Apples Up On Top* (LeSieg, 1961)
A Crack In the Pavement (Howell, 1970)	*A Reason for Seasons* (Allison, 1975)
The Apricot ABC (Miles, 1969)	*Seeds and Weeds* (Westley, 1988)

*Note 1: Descriptions of starred items are provided at the end of the chapter.

Growing Vegetable Soup   *The Little Red Hen*
   (Ehlert, 1987)   (Galdone, 1973)

More activities . . .

(6) Make and care for miniature gardens. (See Figure 4.11 in Chapter 4.) Record observations.*

(7) Observe seeds in fruits and vegetables. Chart and compare.* Organize these seeds in some way. Consider a Seed Mini-Museum (Williams, Rockwell, & Sherwood, 1987).

(8) Make seed candy (Butzow & Butzow, 1989, p. 56; Harlan, 1988, p. 55).*

(9) Draw black and white pictures of seeds and miniature gardens for display.

(10) Make music with seeds (Harlan, 1988, p. 55) and sing songs, for example, "The Garden Song" by Arlo Guthrie (RCA Records, 1990).

• •

Next . . .

☐   Prepare those activities the children will do.

Select several activities that go together and do some advance planning to ensure their success. Consider the **settings and props** you will need for each activity, for example, how you will bring the physical environment to bear on the activities the children will do. Outline the teaching **procedures** you will follow for the more complicated activities and the **learning** you will foster and observe through various activities. We are not suggesting that you go into great detail when doing this. Rather we urge you to think in a general way, mapping out what will likely occur, somewhat like this:

Beth's advance planning for making Silly Bird Seed Gardens (Allison, 1975).

Settings & Props: In the Science Area have sponges, bird seed, paper and pencils for labelling and sketching.

Procedures:

(1) Prepare the children by previewing what they will do. Post a chart similar to Figure 5.2.

(2) Pre-soak the bird seed overnight.

(3) On the next day, explain that the gardens will be made in the "Greenhouse" Area (the science area) during Small Group Activity Time.

Figure 5.2   Directions for silly bird seed gardens

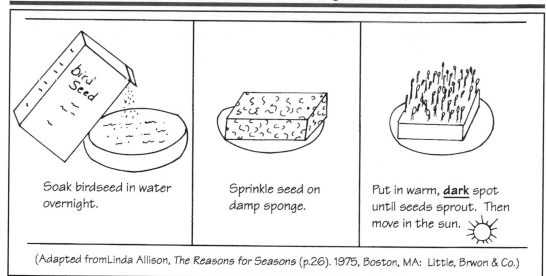

Soak birdseed in water overnight.

Sprinkle seed on damp sponge.

Put in warm, **dark** spot until seeds sprout. Then move in the sun.

(Adapted from Linda Allison, *The Reasons for Seasons* (p.26). 1975, Boston, MA: Little, Brwon & Co.)

(4) Cycle small groups of children (no more than 4) into the Greenhouse Area over the next few days. Encourage the children's prediction-making about what will they will see in their gardens. Record some of their predictions on large chart paper, putting each child's name by his/her prediction. Post the predictions for all to see and read.

(5) Have children label their gardens and put them in a dark cupboard in the Greenhouse until germinated. After several days, have the children sketch what they see in their gardens. Remind them of the predictions they made earlier, noting their accuracy.

(6) Following germination, place in the Windowsill Garden Area to grow.

(7) Make marking sticks and hand magnifiers available for children to examine and record the growth of the Bird Seed Gardens.

Learning To Foster & Observe:

(1) Knowledge that there are many different kinds of seeds and that they grow into plants.

(2) Ability to use language as a tool for functional purposes.

(3) Using print to record predictions and observations and to claim ownership.

(4) A willingness to wait for results.

(5) Enjoyment in using one's senses and caring for living things.

• •

Later . . .

❑   *Invite and respect young children's ideas and questions.*

After introducing the organizing theme or topic to children and after completing one or two activities, pause to ask children for their ideas and questions.

It is sometimes helpful to use a K–W–L (what you *know,* what you *want* to learn, what you have *learned*) frame like the one provided in Figure 5.3 to record children's thinking at this time (Ogle, 1986). While recording, feel free to use a combination of picture and print. When finished, post the children's "thinking" paper conspicuously in the room so that it may serve as a reference throughout the exploration. Occasionally, return to it during Sharing Time, asking children to express what they have learned and recording their comments in the appropriate column.

Figure 5.3

K-W-L Chart

What We Know Already	What We Would Like to Know & Do	What We Have Learned

(Adapted from Ogle, D. (1986). K-W-L: A teaching model that develops active reading of expository text. *The Reading Teacher, 39,* 564-570.)

Integrate children's questions and suggestions into the system of activities by (a) developing a new activity; (b) modifying a prepared activity; or (c) embedding the suggestion or question in an existing activity.

For example, Beth's prekindergarteners were quite fascinated by the germination process, so she developed two more activities related to seed sprouting. One involved observing which direction roots and stems grow. Here she gently turned one seedling in a sprouting dome so that its stem pointed down and its roots up. Daily the children observed the dome, noting changes in stem and root direction. The other was an experiment called the Problem of the Mixed Up Seeds, where children predicted what was growing in various domes by matching actual seed sprouts with those depicted on assorted seed packages.

• •

And finally . . .

❑   Decide on a culminating activity with children.

One exploration must inevitably give way to another. In other words, teachers need to recognize when children have had their fill, so to speak, and then guide them to a satisfying ending.

We rather like the idea of endings being viewed as celebrations of learning or what Linda Crafton calls "public observations of a job well done" (1991, p. 150).

She suggests that learning celebrations serve one or two functions:

(a) They applaud children's thinking.

(b) They provide a forum for children to present their discoveries.

What are some possibilities?

There are simple ones, like completing the K–W–L chart described in Figure 5.3 and listing all the children now know, or having the children share books they have written themselves, or representing new learnings in art or singing and dancing.

And there are more elaborate ones, like dramas, parties, field trips, teas, cooking, conferences, fairs, and so on that connect the in-classroom experience with the family and community.

For Beth and her class, the end went something like this:

To close their study of seeds, the children in Beth's class decided to have a Garden Party for their parents and all the adults in the school. They made and hand-delivered invitations. On the day of the party they served seed candy, made music with seeds, displayed their seed art, and showed off their beautiful gardens. In doing all of these things, they talked about what seeds are, how they grow and what people need to do to take care of plants. In this way they demonstrated what they had come to know about seeds, plants, and their care as well as the language and literacy processes they can use to express their ideas and understandings.

To recap, then, planning for integrated language and literacy learning is a process with the following steps:

- ❑ deciding on a broad **organizer** for children's exploration;
- ❑ jotting down what children can learn by exploring the organizer, including language and literacy processes;
- ❑ brainstorming and selecting some activities children can do;
- ❑ preparing activities children will do;
- ❑ inviting and respecting young children's contributions, and
- ❑ deciding on a culminating activity.

Through this planning process, the teacher **interlinks** content-rich curricular goals (what children should know and be able to do) with daily activities, **integrates** language and literacy learning into the more comprehensive aims of early childhood education and **interconnects** children's interests and needs with adults' teaching intents and responsibilities.

Before leaving this chapter and moving into the classroom for a closer look at the implementation of this process, we have consolidated Beth's planning in its entirety in Figure 5.4. It is an illustration of child-centered activity planning where language and literacy learning have been incorporated into a topic of interest to children. Using the topic as a means, Beth developed children's knowledge, language and literacy processes, and dispositions around the fundamental concept of caring. Moreover, she was able to use the topic as a real reason for children to talk and listen, write and read, providing them with multiple opportunities to practice and extend these essential communication tools. Beth created a plan responsive to children's interests and ideas, yet appropriate to meet their developmental needs.

Let's Review . . .

Based on the belief that language and literacy are best learned when used in the pursuit of broader interests and needs, an integrative and child-centered activity planning process was presented. Following a brief discussion of some of its possibilities and pitfalls, general guidelines with respect to curricular decisions and the allocation of classroom time were described in their relation to this process.

Specifically, broad suggestions were provided as to knowledge, language and literacy processes, and dispositions that might be developed when planning for the integration of language and literacy learning experiences with content areas. And one way of organizing chunks of time

Figure 5.4

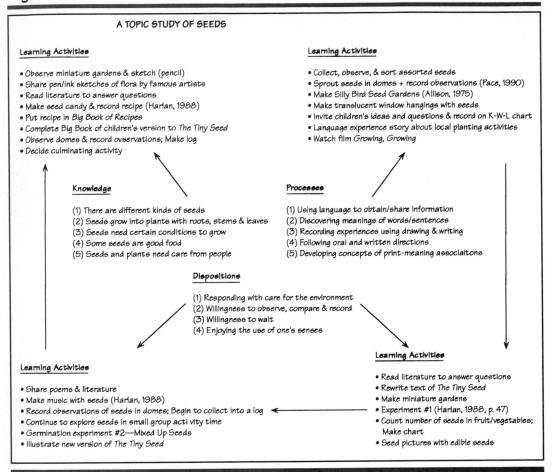

A TOPIC STUDY OF SEEDS

Learning Activities

- Observe miniature gardens & sketch (pencil)
- Share pen/ink sketches of flora by famous artists
- Read literature to answer questions
- Make seed candy & record recipe (Harlan, 1988)
- Put recipe in Big Book of Recipes
- Complete Big Book of children's version to The Tiny Seed
- Observe domes & record observations; Make log
- Decide culminating activity

Learning Activities

- Collect, observe, & sort assorted seeds
- Sprout seeds in domes + record observations (Pace, 1990)
- Make Silly Bird Seed Gardens (Allison, 1975)
- Make translucent window hangings with seeds
- Invite children's ideas and questions & record on K-W-L chart
- Language experience story about local planting activities
- Watch film Growing, Growing

Knowledge

(1) There are different kinds of seeds
(2) Seeds grow into plants with roots, stems & leaves
(3) Seeds need certain conditions to grow
(4) Some seeds are good food
(5) Seeds and plants need care from people

Processes

(1) Using language to obtain/share information
(2) Discovering meanings of words/sentences
(3) Recording experiences using drawing & writing
(4) Following oral and written directions
(5) Developing concepts of print-meaning associaitons

Dispositions

(1) Responding with care for the environment
(2) Willingness to observe, compare & record
(3) Willingness to wait
(4) Enjoying the use of one's senses

Learning Activities

- Share poems & literature
- Make music with seeds (Harlan, 1988)
- Record observations of seeds in domes; Begin to collect into a log
- Continue to explore seeds in small group acti vity time
- Germination experiment #2—Mixed Up Seeds
- Illustrate new version of The Tiny Seed

Learning Activities

- Read literature to answer questions
- Rewrite text of The Tiny Seed
- Make miniature gardens
- Experiment #1 (Harlan, 1988, p. 47)
- Count number of seeds in fruit/vegetables; Make chart
- Seed pictures with edible seeds

was offered and explained, namely the use of Whole Group Focus Time, Small Group Activity Time, Sharing Time and Storybook Reading Time. Finally, a detailed example of planning for integrated language and literacy learning was described and illustrated, portraying how language and literacy processes can be embedded in comprehensive curricular goals.

Let's Explore . . .

1. Generate a list of potential themes and/or topics you think appropriate for use with children in the following age ranges:

Figure 5.4 (continued)

RESOURCES:

Literature to browse & read...
- *Seeds and More Seeds* (Millicent Selsam)
- *Frog & Toad Together* (Arnold Lobel)
- *The Apricot ABC* (Mishka Miles)
- *A Crack In the Pavement* (Ruth Howell)
- *The Popcorn Book* (Tomie de Paola)
- *The Carrot Seed* (Ruth Kraus)
- *The Little Red Hen* (Paul Galdone)
- *Growing Vegetable Soup* (L. Enlert)
- *The Tiny Seed* (Eric Carle)
- *The Amazing Seed* (Ross E. Hutchins)
- *Seeds and Weeds* (Joan Westley)

Poems to say...
- "The Little Plant" (Kate Brown)
- "The Seed" (Aileen Fisher)
- "Seeds (Walter de la Mare)
  in *Poems to Grow On*, compiled
  by Jean McKee Thompson)

Films & Videos to watch...
- *Growing, Growing* (Churchill Films, 1987)
- *Plants Are Different & Alike* (Coronet/MTI Film & Video, 1990)

Songs to sing...
- *The Garden Song* (Arlo Guthrie)
- *Edelweiss*
- *Oats & Beans & Barley Grow*
- *The Paw, Paw Patch*

Fingerplays to do...
The Apple Tree[1]
My Garden

Note 1: Text of the fingerplays provided at the end of this chapter.

18-24 months, 30 months through age 3, 4- and 5-year-olds. Select your top two ideas for each age range and tell why you think they are especially relevant.

2. Using the way to organize time suggested in this chapter, develop a half-day plan around a topic of your choice. List the children's literature you would include and briefly describe the key activities you would use. Indicate the skills specific to language and literacy you would observe and develop.

3. Discuss the process of planning for integrated language and literacy learning with one or two veteran early childhood teachers. Solicit from them what they see as strengths of this

curricular approach and what they see as drawbacks. Have them describe how they would implement it and what a typical day in their classrooms might look like if this approach were used.

4. Outline a topic study following the steps suggested on pages 151–162. To have the benefit of children's input, visit an early childhood program and ask some children what activities they might like to do associated with your topic. Include their ideas in your planning.

Descriptions of starred items on pages 155–156.

(1) **Making a sprouter** (adapted from Pace, 1990).

You will need the following materials:

☐ 2 plastic cups (same size)   ☐ rubber cement
☐ soil   ☐ clear tape
☐ water   ☐ a nail or pin
☐ seeds

What to do:

(a) Half-fill one cup with soil and plant the seeds.

(b) Water the soil.

(c) Punch several holes in the bottom of the other cup.

(d) Put clear tape over the holes.

(e) Place a light coat of rubber cement on the rims of both cups.

(f) Fit the rims together. Allow the cement to dry.

(g) Place your sprouter in a sunny window.

(h) Periodically remove the tape from the holes to allow fresh air in. Replace the tape after a day or so.

(i) When the plants outgrow the sprouter, transplant them into a garden or a larger flower pot and watch them grow!

(2) **Making translucent window hangings**

(a) Select samples, for example, seed types, pods, cones, etc.

(b) Put one type of each seed in small plastic bags.

(c) Label each bag with the name of the seed, using a black marker.

(d) Punch hole in the top of each plastic bag.

(e) Arrange hooks attractively on window area. Use suction type plastic hooks available at most hardware stores.

(f) Attach plastic bags to hooks. Stand back and enjoy.

(3) Recording observations (adapted from Doris, 1991, p. 24)

Make the following form on manila paper.

OBSERVATION

Name _____

I am looking at_____

_____

A picture of what I see.

I noticed_____

_____

(4) Seed candy recipes

(a) *Seed Candy* (Harlan, 1988, p. 55)

Use blender to grate: 1 cup of coconut

1 cup of hulled sunflower seeds

Mix with: 2 tablespoons peanut butter

2 tablespoons honey,
confectioners sugar
or maple syrup

Form into a log, slice thinly and enjoy.

(b) *Crunchy Seed Candy* (Butzow & Butzow, 1989, p. 56)

Mix together the following ingredients:

1 cup sunflower seeds

1 cup honey

1 cup peanut butter

1 cup cocoa powder

Shape into one inch balls.

Spread one cup of sesame seeds on a sheet of waxed paper.

Roll each piece of candy in sesame seeds.

(c) Put the recipes on large chart paper and post for all to read.

Figure 5.5   Seed counting chart

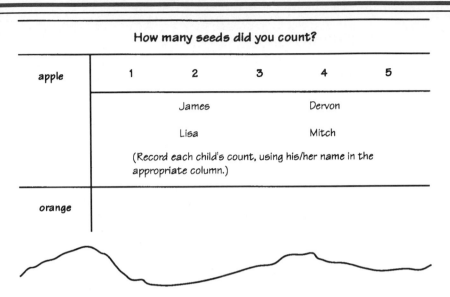

How many seeds did you count?

apple	1	2	3	4	5
		James		Dervon	
		Lisa		Mitch	
	(Record each child's count, using his/her name in the appropriate column.)				
orange					

Note: Each fruit/vegetable count can be separated from the others to examine it individually. For example, the "apple" count can be cut away from the other fruit counts. Point out the differences in the apple seed counts between the children, but also highlight similarities. Note the most frequently occurring number(s). Compare findings by re-counting apple seeds once again. Mention that this is often how scientists work: they observe, note differences and similarities, and re-check their findings before drawing a conclusion. Next compare the fruit/vegetable graphs to one another by positioning them next to one another and making comparisons. Highlight similarities and differences in seed counts across the various fruits/vegetables.

Later include in a *Big Book of Recipes* for future cooking activities.

(5) **Seed counting chart**

(6) **Fingerplays** (Harlan, 1988, p. 58)

The Apple Tree

Way up high in the apple tree	(Stretch arms up)
Two red apples, I did see	(Make circle with hands)
I shook that tree as hard as I could	(Shake "trunk")
Mmmmmm those apples tasted good!	(Pat tummy)

Author unknown

My Garden

This is my garden.	(Hold one palm upward)
I'll rake it with care.	("Rake" with curled fingers of other hand)
Here are the seeds	
I'll plant in there.	(Pantomime planting, seed by seed)
The sun will shine.	(Circle above head with arms)
The rain will fall.	(Fingers flutter down)
The seeds will sprout	(Spread fingers of one hand. Push up other fingers between them.)
And grow up tall.	(Bring hands and forearms together. Move up, spreading palms outward as arms move up)

Author unknown

Children's Literature cited in "Topic Study of Seeds"

ALLISON, L. (1975). The reasons for seasons. Boston, MA: Little, Brown & Co.

BRENNER, B. (1973). *If you were an ant: A second book of nonsense.* NY: Harper & Row.

CAMERON, P. (1961). *"I can't," said the ant.* NY: Coward-McCann.

CARLE, E. (1990). *The tiny seed.* Saxonville, MA: Picture Book Studio.

DARLING, K. (1977). *Ants have pets.* Champaign, ILL: Garrard Publishing Co.

DEPAOLA, T. (1978). *The popcorn book.* NY: Holiday House.

EHLERT, L. (1987). *Growing vegetable soup.* San Diego, CA: Harcourt, Brace, Jovanovich.

GALDONE, P. (1973). *The three billy goats gruff.* NY: Houghton-Mifflin/Clarion Books.

GALDONE, P. (1973). *The little red hen.* NY: Houghton-Mifflin/Clarion Books.

HOWELL, R. (1970). *A crack in the pavement.* NY: Atheneum.

KRAUS, R. (1945). *The carrot seed.* NY: Harper & Row.

LESIEG, T. (1961). *Ten apples up on top.* NY: Beginner Books.

LOBEL, A. (1972). *Frog and toad together.* NY: Harper & Row.

MILES, M. (1969). *Apricot ABC.* Boston, MA: Little, Brown & Co.

SELSAM, M. (1959). *Seeds and more seeds.* NY: Harper & Row.

WESTLEY, J. (1988). *Seeds and weeds.* Sunnyvale, CA: Creative Publications

One Day in a Topic Study of "ME AND MY FRIENDS"

Whole Group Focus Time

Small Group Activity Time

Sharing Time

Reading Aloud Time

Planning Considerations

Making Weekly Plans

Making Daily Plans

CHAPTER 6

Bringing Integrated Language and Literacy Learning into the Classroom

A number of children are in the post office area:

John: Mailman! Mailman!

Joseph: Oh good, is it cranky mail? Daddy likes it cranky.

John: Your Daddy like 'em cranky?

Joseph: Yeah, once my Daddy was sleeping and someone woke him up with some mail and my Mom said he got real cranky. So I'm gonna give 'em cranky mail!

And now, we join a classroom in progress, weaving knowledge, language and literacy processes and dispositions into practice. Here we attempt to capture, at the descriptive level, what a typical classroom actually does in a child-centered exploration of a topic. In this chapter, we will first describe the teacher's overall plan: the topic of study and the knowledge, processes, and dispositions that children will gain by exploring a topic, and then some examples of teacher and learner interactions throughout the day. At a number of points, we'll stop to reflect on the strategies used to enhance language and literacy, bringing to life basic guidelines from our previous chapters. Finally, we'll focus on creating lesson plans to guide teachers in the implementation of these activities.

A Topic Study on "ME AND MY FRIENDS"

Wanting the children to bond together as a community of learners, Denise has decided on a topic study of friendship for the beginning of the year. She is interested in developing a unit which will allow her 4- and 5-year-olds to explore their relationships with others. She feels that good friendships are influenced by an individual child's self-esteem. First, children must feel good about themselves; only then may they be good friends to others. By focusing on the theme, "Me and my friends," she intends to develop, at a very concrete level, the concepts of interdependence and cooperation.

This topic will provide Denise with many opportunities to engage children in integrated language and literacy activities. It will allow her to build on the prior experiences that children bring to this important topic in their lives. Consequently, it will likely serve as a good conversation starter. In addition to focusing on rich language usage, she plans to work with the children as a group to become an appreciative audience, encouraging them to not interrupt while others are speaking. These skills will lead to their use of new vocabulary which she intends to record in an ongoing language experience story, emphasizing concepts about print along the way.

Denise begins by collecting activities and books which encourage children to explore themselves; their images, their feelings, and other characteristics. These feelings of self-worth are designed to provide the foundation for exploring the importance of friendship and need for others. Activities will be planned to give children occasions to examine the characteristics of good friendships. Denise is hoping this will eventually lead to establishing new friendships among her diverse group of children in the classroom.

Table 6.1 describes Denise's plan for her topic study. She intends to spend about a week on each subtopic, ending with a culminating activity at the end of the third week. Notice how these subtopics build on the learning that precedes it.

The concepts of interdependence are first developed by children noting how different parts of their body work together; then they begin to experience interdependence through engaging with other people. Finally, they explore their understanding of interdependence and cooperation through establishing new friendships in the classroom community. Let's now take a glimpse at one day's activities.

The Day Begins . . .

It is 8:15 A.M., and the children and their parents enter Denise's bright and cheerful classroom. After removing their coats, and putting away their snacks in their cubbies, the children move to the open floor space in the room, reserved for group time, and sit on the floor. Today Denise has prepared a whole-group focus activity to encourage the children to explore different body parts and how they work together, and to

TABLE 6.1 AN OVERVIEW OF THE TOPIC STUDY, "ME AND MY FRIENDS"

SUBTOPIC	KNOWLEDGE	SKILLS	DISPOSITIONS
All about me	Learn about different body parts	Speak confidently	Encourage self esteem
	Each of us is special	Explore and discover meanings of words	Appreciation of rhyme, rhythm, meter of stories, songs & poetry
	Children have various likes and dislikes	Listen attentively to stories, songs, and poetry	
People need people	Cooperation means working together	Use language to engage others in conversation	Help children realize how people help each other
	We are all interdependent	Use language as a tool to get services and objects, to express emotions, get and give information	Encourage security in belonging to a group of people
	Different people have the same capabilities	Play with rhyming words and sounds	Encourage cooperative behavior
My friends	Friendship is built on trust	Listen for turn-taking cues in conversation	Sharing
	Friends show caring for each other		Gain a sense of the needs of others
	Friends work together	Record ideas through pictures and/or words	Show empathy

begin to explore their relations with other children. Her lesson plan looks like Table 6.2.

Once the children get all settled down, Denise greets them with a "good morning," and takes roll. Then she says:

> "We've been exploring a lot of different things about ourselves for the last couple of days. And we've also learned a lot about each other. Remember yesterday when we played 'Guess who I am?' We had to tell something special about ourselves that we especially liked. Can anyone remember some of the things that were mentioned?"

A number of children respond, and the group listens as they recount some of the children's favorite food or favorite activity. Then Denise says:

TABLE 6.2   A WHOLE GROUP FOCUS ACTIVITY LESSON

GROUP PATTERN	WHAT	WHERE	HOW PROPS	PROCEDURES	WHY
Whole group	"Shadow play"	Circle area	Big butcher paper	Review	Directional words
			flashlight	Encourage children to make shadows with fingers and hands	Motor coordination
				Place children in pairs	Cooperation Ability to interact with others Large motor coordination
				Discussion	Language use Explore and discover meanings of words

"Today, we are going to explore something more about ourselves. I'm going to turn off all the overhead lights now. Watch for the special light to shine on this white paper."

Denise shines a flashlight onto a large sheet of butcher block paper on the board. She invites the children to move their hands and fingers between the light and the paper.

"What are we making with our fingers? What do you notice about a shadow?"

Paul asks why the shadow is always black and not in different colors. Luis tries to figure out why the shadow always seems so far away, and tries to make it come closer. Other children begin to try to shape their hands into animal-like shadows. As they play, Chrissy remarks that the shadow is really a "copycat," because it does everything that she does. Denise says, "You know, that's a good description of a shadow. How would you all like to pretend to be a shadow?"

Denise pairs two children together and asks them to stand face to face. She then asks one of the children in each pair to be the other's shadow. "That means every motion you make has to be copied by the other." To encourage them, Denise asks, "What kinds of ways can you move your head, your arms, and other parts of your body?" She then names "left" leg, "right" arm and other body parts. After a few minutes,

Denise asks the children to change places, and let the former shadow become the leader.

Once both children have had a chance to be the leader, Denise asks them to return to the circle. "What have we learned about ourselves today?" She asks the children. Latoya responds: "It's hard to be a shadow!"

Denise follows up Latoya's comment with a probe:

"What do you mean? Why was it hard?"

Latoya thinks for a couple of seconds, then says, " Because everything Michelle does, I have to do too! And sometimes the stuff she does is too hard for me."

Denise comments, "You're right. Sometimes it's hard to get your body parts to work together. It's also kind of hard to guess what your partner might do next. You really have to anticipate what may happen . . . you have to think ahead about what they are going to do next. And your partner, too, has to figure out what you may or may not be able to do. So, in a sense, you really have to work together—you have to cooperate. And that's what good friends do—they work together and cooperate together."

As the discussion progresses for the next five minutes, the children begin to describe some of their favorite friends, and the activities they enjoy doing together. Throughout the discussion, Denise attempts to make explicit the concepts of cooperation and interdependence that underlie good friendships. She emphasizes "equal time" among her young participants, encouraging as many as possible to join in the discussion while not interrupting others. Throughout the activity, a good deal of new vocabulary is used in meaningful and appropriate ways. Even though the children still have much to say, Denise brings the whole group focus time to a close by about 8:50 A.M.

Commentary

From our observations, it was evident that the children were highly engaged in the Shadow Play. The activity encouraged active exploration and inquiry through social interaction and involved them in problem solving rather than focusing on the right answers or the right ways to complete a task.

But we were especially intrigued with the strategies Denise used in talking with the children. Rather than constantly asking questions, she seemed to pick up on the children's contributions, and appeared genuinely willing to listen to their ideas. In fact, she asked relatively few questions. Her style seemed to provide an enabling framework for the children. These behaviors, reminiscent of those we discussed in Chapter 3, included several key features, such as:

❑ reviewing, and connecting past experiences to present activities

❑ righlighting things children should attend to in order to maintain the right frame of mind

❑ emphasizing children's triumphs and successes

❑ asking relatively few questions, and making frequent contributions from their own perspective

❑ reflecting back, and helping to cast children's experiences into relief, bringing language and literacy alive

❑ making actions and talk more contingent on the children's efforts and interests

Letting the children engage in conversations of this nature tended to lead toward far more elaborated talk than the highly predictable question and answer session that often occurs between teacher and groups of children. How teachers engage children's participation in and contribution to conversations seems to represent one of the key factors in determining how well children play their part as conversationalists and language learners.

Independent and Small Group investigations

As the whole group focus time comes to an end, Denise shares with children some special options for activity time. In keeping with the theme of friendship, she has developed one structured activity for each day that relates to the theme. Some are mandatory, meaning that she wants all the children at some point to do the activity, and some are optional—children can decide to participate or not during their free choice time. Her plans for the day look like Table 6.3.

Today at the activity table, the children will be making "I can do" cards, with pictures, and writing to describe their special "talent." A parent volunteer is sitting in this area, ready to record and assist children in getting all their ideas down on large flashcards.

But there are other, less structured activities in areas throughout the room for children to interact with each other on the theme of friendship as well.

For example, Denise has provided a child-proof mirror on the wall in the science area. Next to it is a digital scale and a large measure so that the children may weigh each other, and note how tall they are. A large chart is there for them to record their findings. Denise plans to leave this chart up, so that comparisons can be made throughout the year.

In the housekeeping area, a small area has been set up for makeup and cosmetic exploration for the children to play with "who they are." Special dress-up clothes are beside the area, along with a hat rack, and a box filled with different, smaller articles, including gloves, boots, sweater, sandals, briefcase, and so on. As one child reaches in and pulls out an article, puts on an outfit, and a hat, the other children try to guess who she is trying to be.

TABLE 6.3   SMALL GROUP ACTIVITIES LESSON

GROUP PATTERN	WHAT	WHERE	HOW PROPS	PROCEDURES	WHY
Small group	"I can do" cards	Structured activity table	Flashcards	Adult to ask children to draw something they can do. Caption drawing	Self image
	Measuring	Science center	Chart Measure Scale		Self image Emergent writing Letters and numbers
	Make-up	House-keeping corner	Make-up Dress-up clothes Mirror		Features noted Fine motor coordination Self image
	Cut-up magazines	Art table	Magazines		Fine motor coordination Favorites Cooperation

The art area has stacks of many different magazines, including those related to sports, cars, travel, food and home. The children are cutting out pictures that they especially like and that remind them of themselves or their interests. Denise's aide, Mary, is helping the children who are having a bit of difficulty manipulating their small scissors. As she helps in their cutting, she tries to encourage them to articulate why they chose their particular pictures. Once the children have found their favorites, they will paste the pictures onto a larger piece of mural paper, and with Mary's help, write down their names on their section. This mural will eventually be hung up so that others may see all of the children's varying interests.

A small number of children are in the block and manipulatives area. Denise has encouraged them to use the blocks in creative ways to build airports, railroads, shopping centers, rocket ships, or whatever else they choose to bring to life with their rich imaginations. She suggests that they create a special space that they might name and use for a certain function.

With the use of these constructive materials, Denise hopes to encourage children to join together in expressing themselves through pattern and design toward dramatic play around the block structures.

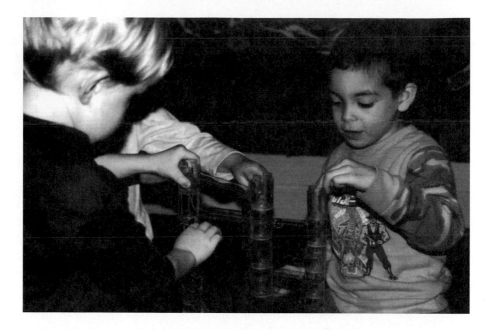

And finally, seated around the listening post are four children listening to "Free to be, you and me," by Marlo Thomas. One is looking at a booklet with pictures which accompanies the album, and the others are singing and dancing along.

After getting them settled, Denise roams around the room, interacting with children both individually and in small groups. These interactions, sometimes as short as ten or fifteen seconds, are designed to get an overall "feel" of what is going on during activity time. Are the children quickly getting involved in activities, or are they looking for something to do? Are the spaces adequate for the activity, or should they be reorganized to encourage more dramatic play? Are the children engaged in anything that might represent a potential safety hazard? She will review these notes with her aide, Mary, along with comments from the parent volunteers who are also encouraged to be observers of children's behaviors in play.

Denise begins to observe the activities of particular children. She frequently stops and makes notes in her small, spiral notepad. She observes with interest some of the children's literacy activities, making note that Latoya has attempted to write her own name next to the pictures that she has selected in the art area. She also records that the science area could use a parent volunteer to help children weigh themselves and record their weight on the chart. Denise also looks to see whether the children are incorporating the concepts of friendship and cooperation in these free time activities. She tries to take note of some sample activities for children to share during sharing time.

There is a constant buzz of conversation as the children seem to be genuinely engaged in a range of individual and small group activities. Feeling comfortable, Denise decides to enter into the science area, where she finds James and Michael playing with the scale and the large measure.

Denise: How are you doing here?

James: I'm the Doctor, and I'm seeing how much Michael weighs, but this thing is broke.

Denise: Show me what you mean. (James points to the digital scale that changes as Michael moves). Oh yes, Dr. James. I see what you mean. Can I pretend to be the nurse?

James: Ok, but I'm still the Doctor.

Denise: Of course, Doctor, can you have your patient stand on the scale? He must stand very still—he cannot move at all. (Michael stands on the scale). Look at the numbers. Can you see? Right, you look right there! It says "4" and "6". Together, these numbers mean that Michael weighs 46 pounds.

James: Hey Michael, now you gotta weigh me. (James gets on the scale).

Michael (to Denise): What does that say?

Denise: It says that James weighs 40 pounds. That means that you weigh a little bit more than he does. I'm going to write this down on the chart. Can you show me where your name is? How about you James? That's great guys. Are you pleased about learning that?

James: Mmmm.

Within about five minutes, Denise enabled the children to use the materials to extend their understanding of themselves. She knows that some teachers might regard this activity as beyond the children's level of competence. However, she finds that children are capable of making things and doing things with the help of an adult that they cannot yet manage alone. By providing a scaffolding for children, and filling in the gaps, she feels that teachers can supply the framework for children to succeed at activities that are a little bit beyond them, without their losing interest in the activity or confidence in their abilities. This is essentially the "zone of proximal development" as defined by Vygotsky (1978).

Following this exchange, Denise moves back to her observer role. She slips into the housekeeping area to watch as the children are giggling and trying on different clothes. One of the children has on a chef's hat and apron. Denise asks:

Denise: Hey Jennifer, are you a chef? Are you making today's lunch?

Jennifer: I'm making pizza.

Denise: Sounds good. I like pizza. What's on it?

Jennifer: Cheese, pepperoni, lots of stuff.

Denise: Olives? Mushrooms? Anchovies?

Jennifer: What's anchovy?

Denise: Long, skinny fish.

Jennifer: Yuck. This pizza's got no fish. (She sets the plates out for the others to eat.)

Sensing that the children are highly involved and not wishing to inhibit their play, Denise exits the play scene. She moves to the activity table, where children are making their "I Can Do" cards with the parent volunteer. Sitting down at the table and watching the children, she hears some stories about the children's outside lives, their families' activities, and their neighborhood friends. She makes some last minute informal notes as the activity time draws to a close.

Commentary

As we watched Denise, it was evident that she played many different roles during activity time. At first, she seemed to take on the role of manager, making sure the children were busily engaged in some activity. Her interactions were of a monitoring nature—quick comments designed to keep the wheels of adult–child interactions in motion. Once the children were obviously involved in their tasks or activities, she began to observe the classroom more critically. Now, she seemed to move about the room looking more closely at the quality of children's play, their interactions, and their developing skills and strategies. Sometimes she stopped to write something in the notebook she was carrying, focusing on illustrations of behaviors that demonstrated children's growing abilities. More than manager, her role had changed to one of observer—observing not only the children, but her own planning process at work.

Once she had surveyed the classroom activities, her attention focused on that area where adult intervention might be most needed. Children in the science setting were having fun manipulating the new objects placed in the area, but not using the weight and large measure to its full advantage. Even though they might not be able to use some materials in a sophisticated manner, Denise sometimes purposely placed materials that might encourage children to intellectually stretch, hoping to create a curiosity for new ideas. In this activity, she entered into the play scenario and spent a few minutes teaching the children how to use the scale. Her teaching was brief and to the point, as she tried to continue in the actual play activity and not have it appear like a lesson. In this example, her role became that of a "play tutor," as she took over the play to give instruction on a particular skill.

Her role changed once again in the housekeeping corner. Keeping the pretend theme, she asked for information, hoping to extend, and perhaps clarify the dramatic play. However, unlike that of the science setting, Denise's questions were never designed to take control of the play; rather they were designed to give control of the content and actions to the children. Here, her role was that of a co-player; she played side by side with the children, offering suggestions which the children might choose to take up or not if they pleased.

And finally, Denise took on the role of reflective listener as she moved to the "I can do" area. The children were excitingly describing some of their activities. Denise attempted not only to listen, but to hear the children's intended messages. Further, she tried to take note of some of their outside activities. For example, she learned that Jason had a new puppy and that the scratches on his arms and legs happened when the puppy got a little too rambunctious. And that Keisha's mom had taken a second job that keeps her out late at night. She seemed to know that in understanding the children's outside world, she might better be able to make real-life connections between home and school in her future conversations with children.

Though Denise's roles changed throughout these independent and small group activities, her approach to language and literacy remained the same. The activities she encouraged provided multiple opportunities for children to engage in purposeful integrated oral and written language experiences. In each setting, the contexts were supportive of interactions between adults and children, and among the children themselves as they used oral and written language to explore their interests. And in the course of pursuing their topic, these activities invited, encouraged, and supported language and literacy use for young children.

Sharing Time

At about 9:45, Denise makes her last few visits to individual children and small groups around the room. She interacts with a number of them, suggesting that they might want to share their activity with the rest of the class. She announces, "It's time to clean up. In two minutes, we'll have sharing time."

This is the sign for the children to stop playing and to begin to put away the materials used in their activities. Denise watches to see that the materials are put back in the places designed for them, and that all the children are equally contributing to the task. As they finish, she tells them to join her in the circle area, where the whole group focus activity had previously taken place. Once all the children have arrived, Denise says:

"I noticed so many interesting things going on during activity time. Some of you had the opportunity to work at the table making 'I can do' flashcards. Would anyone like to share their drawings and writings?"

Vanessa immediately raises her hand, and goes before the group with her flashcard.

"I learned how to tie my shoe."

Denise responds, "Can you show us how?"

Vanessa unties her shoe and begins to slowly manipulate the laces to make a bow.

Neil asks, "How did you learn to do it?"

Vanessa, "My mom bought me a book at the grocery store and showed me how." After Vanessa finishes her sharing, Danny shows a picture story to the class. Denise asks, "Tell us what you wrote."

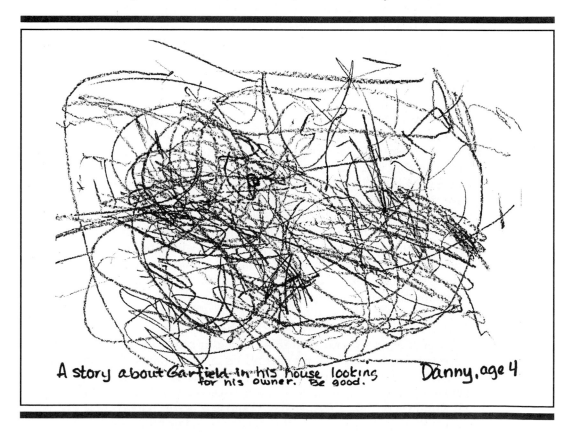

A story about Garfield in his house looking for his owner. Be good.   Danny, age 4

"I wrote a story about Garfield in his house looking for his owner. His owner told him that he better be good," said Danny. Denise replies, "That's really interesting," and then pointing, "What are you trying to do here?" "That's a letter 'A'." Denise then praises Danny for writing his story.

Two other children get an opportunity to share before morning snack time. Sharee shares the pictures that she has cut in the art area, one of which shows her favorite food—pizza. Based on a raising of hands, it is decided that many of the children agree with her. Then Deron shares his new pet—a rat named Henrietta. On his "I can do" flashcard he has made a picture of himself and his rat, and tells everyone that he can take care of her. This creates a great deal of interest from others who would also like to own a pet. Some of the children even take turns patting her, and telling Deron how pretty she is. In each case, Denise listens, then encourages the other children to connect these events with their own personal experiences. As sharing time comes to an end, Denise thanks the participants for sharing, and thanks the group for being a great audience.

Commentary

In the sharing time activity, we observed the importance of the setting and the models for listening and interacting established by Denise. She created a context that was friendly and informal; here, the children could try out their new inventions, interests, and achievements, without fear of failure. Just the "doing" was regarded as a considerable achievement! Even though the decision to volunteer was left to the children, eventually all of them wanted to share some special event with others. And their sharing seemed to draw this young community of learners closer by bringing their outside lives into the classroom.

We also noticed how Denise attempted here to spotlight children's efforts. She became the enabler, encouraging children to interact with others, while she remained carefully in the background. She usually waited until the children had their say before commenting, extending, or demonstrating something related to the sharing with the group. Her efforts made it possible for the participant sharers to feel that their contributions were respected by others. Those who attempted to disrupt the activity were quickly dismissed from the group. Soon all seemed to learn that sharing time was special—a forum for children to display and demonstrate their newly learned skills.

We should also emphasize that the children's efforts to talk about their interests and interact with others was greatly enhanced by the accompanying objects, as in this particular case—papers and a pet. Children at this age are still rather limited in their ability to talk about experiences removed from the activity itself. Thus, the objects allowed for close-up interactions—talk that was based on what the child actually had before him or her. This also gave Denise a better opportunity to respond contingently, since the objects served to help her fill in the gaps when talk was limited.

Reading aloud

And now the day's actions wind down, as children end their morning with storytime. Today Denise has decided to read two books to the children. One is the big book, *In a dark, dark wood* (Melser & Cowley, 1980) with a highly predictable format, and the other book is the narrative, *Ira sleeps over* (Waber, 1972) with a strong storyline. Each relates to the topic of interest, but each has a different purpose. The predictable book is designed to get the children settled down from their busy activities, to join together, to hear the rhythmic patterns of language and to participate as a group. The narrative is designed to enhance children's developing sense of story structure. Denise will use both to entice interest in story reading and concepts about print.

Since the children have heard *In a dark, dark wood* several times before, they are eager and ready to participate in the reading. Denise places the storybook on an easel rather close to the children, and points to the beginning of the sentence as she begins to read. When she comes to a predictable pattern, her voice slows down to cue the children to respond to the repetitive lines. Being familiar with the story, the children giggle and respond altogether, as if they were singing a favorite song.

Next, Denise shows them the book, *Ira sleeps over*—a story that is new to the group. It's about a little boy, Ira, who plans to sleep over at a friend's house for the very first time. He's a bit worried because he wants to bring his teddy bear along for the night, but is scared that his friend might laugh at him. However, once he recognizes that his pal also has a teddy bear, Ira realizes that good friends don't ridicule each other. Denise believes that the story will "hit home" with many of the children who are just beginning to experience being away for a night at a friend's house.

Denise begins by showing the cover to the children, and asking, "What do you think this story might be about?"

"It's a little boy with a teddy bear."

"Do any of you have a favorite stuffed animal?" asks Denise. She encourages the children to tell her a little bit about their toys.

"When is your toy especially important to you?"

"When I'm sick . . . and I feel yucky," says Chris.

"I take Snoopy everywhere I go," says Sara.

"Well," Denise replies, "This story is about a little boy named Ira, who is invited to sleep over at his friend Reggie's house. Let's see what happens in the story."

Denise begins to read, stopping at various points to show children the pictures, and to elicit their reactions, comments or questions. Several times, she reminds the children of what has gone on before in the story, and then says, "I wonder if Ira will really sleep over?" or "What will Ira do?" After a few responses from the group, she says, "I'd bring my teddy bear over to my friend's house if I were scared—would you?" As the story is about to reach its conclusion, Denise stops and asks the children for their predictions on how they feel the story might end.

"I don't think he's gonna sleep over. Its too scary for him."

"Nah, he will, you'll see. He'll take his teddy bear with him."

The children are all surprised to see at the end that Reggie also has a special teddy bear, just like Ira.

Denise then asks, "Was Reggie a really good friend to Ira?" The children all nod their heads. "Why?"

"Cause he didn't laugh at 'im."

"He knew Ira was scared but he didn't say anything."

"I'd like you to think about what you'd do if you were Ira." This question elicits a number of responses from the children about their own experiences. Denise signals the ending of the discussion by saying, "Next time when we read the story, maybe we can pretend what we would do if we were Ira."

Commentary

This storybook reading session worked well at a number of levels. First, at its broadest level, the session focused on a number of important concepts about print. In the shared book experience, for example, Denise pointed to the beginning of each sentence, demonstrating that words are the medium through which the story is conveyed rather than through the illustrations alone. In her reading, she also demonstrated that print is read from left to right, and from top to bottom as she pointed to the words in each sentence. Further, she encouraged children to actively participate in the reading, using a story with rhythmic and highly predictable language. By hearing these rhythmic patterns, teachers can enhance phonemic awareness, which according to many studies (Juel, Griffith & Gough, 1986; Stanovich, 1986) is crucial for later success in reading. Specifically, then, Denise focused on the following concepts of print, as defined by Marie Clay (1979):

- ❏ Print is read from left to right, and from up to down.
- ❏ Oral language can be written down and then read.
- ❏ Words are different from pictures.
- ❏ Words carry meaning and can be read.
- ❏ Illustrations carry meaning but cannot be read.

At the next level, Denise began to focus on a story's structure. She selected a well-structured story, with a clearly delineated setting, theme, characters and plot to enhance children's comprehension. This story involved a highly salient event for children at this age level; consequently, it invited a good deal of discussion and interest among them. Throughout the reading, Denise attempted to encourage the children to relate these story episodes to their own life events. In this way, she tried to make the story personally meaningful to each child in her room.

We noticed that her reading related to the framework of a "grand conversation" (Clay, 1991). Basically, it encourages teachers to:

- ☐ Prepare children for listening by building their anticipation to the events in a story. Some might call this a teaser, or a preview. Before reading, a teacher might show children some of the pictures in the story and ask them to guess what the story is about. Or, a teacher might pose a question, like, "Have you ever slept over at a friend's house?" to initiate the reading. In any case, the focus here is to encourage children to actively listen and to relate the story happenings to real-life events.

- ☐ Guide children's listening throughout the reading. Comments, reactions, and brief questions can engage those little wandering minds at times by reiterating story sequences, and building connections. It is important, however, that these mini-discussions do not become so extended as to distract themfrom enjoying the language of the story, or its overall meaning. Young children are easily sidetracked. Guided comments, therefore, should remain focused and directed toward the resolution of the story.

- ☐ Extend children's understanding of the story. A quick retelling by the teacher, or a guided retelling from the children help to recap the main points of the story, and begin to highlight the key elements of story structure: its setting, plot, theme and resolution. From here, a story discussion can focus on evaluating and comparing stories with others like it (as well as characters and plot), and relating story events to personal or classroom activities.

Finally, at the last level, we noticed that Denise made an effort to connect story readings with the theme of friendship. Too often in classrooms, storyreading is seen as a **decontextualized** event, separate from other activities or happenings in the classroom. Unfortunately, this may give children the impression that reading is not a particularly functional activity, but one merely for enjoyment. While its uses for pure pleasure are laudable, we believe that storybook reading can serve to stimulate new ideas, reflections and extensions in children's knowledge. Denise's comments in *Ira sleeps over* are a good example. In her questions, she encouraged children to examine the characteristics of a good friend using the book to enhance their understanding on the topic of friendship. Through these kinds of linking experiences, storybook reading can become a more integral part of the curriculum, serving to bind all classroom activities together.

Today's activities are over, and the children are now on their way home. Once alone, Denise will reflect and make comments in a journal, which she will share with her aide. At the same time, she will plan the culminating activity for the topic study of friendship. Based on children's interest in the book *Stone Soup* (Brown, 1975), they have decided to have a gathering with parents, friends, and siblings. Each family has been sent a special invitation, asking them to bring a vegetable that will be shared with others in making a wonderful vegetable soup. This activity will symbolize the comforts and joys of friendship: giving, sharing, and connecting with others.

Making Weekly Plans

Let's step back now and see how Denise actually brought this construction to life in the day-to-day. Look at the planning sheet displayed in Table 6.4.

TABLE 6.4 ♦ A WEEKLY PLAN FOR THE TOPIC STUDY, "ME AND MY FRIENDS"

KEY ACTIVITIES	OBSERVATIONS TO BE MADE
Whole Group Focus Time	
(Day 1) Draw body images of the children. The children lie on a sheet of butcher paper while the teacher draws around the body shape. Children are invited to paint their features, clothes, and so on, on cut-outs. After being decorated, the images are displayed around the room.	Feelings of self Body image Language use
(Day 2) Play the "Each of us is different" game. Blindfold one child (or have him/her close eyes) and try to guess who one of the children in the group is by feeling their faces and/or their body. Point out that while each of us has eyes, nose and other similar features, we're all different, but all special.	Features noted Language use Likenesses and differences Connections to each other as a group
(Day 3) Create a friendship tree. Suggest to the children how all can be friends to one another. Talk about the various aspects of friendship, including sharing, having fun together, getting angry with each other. Paint the outline of a tree on a large sheet of butcher paper and invite the children to paint pictures of themselves on the friendship tree.	Self-image Attitudes toward others in class Cooperation Language use Fine motor coordination
(Day 4) Play the trust game. Set up a mini-obstacle course in room. Discuss with the children, "What is a friend?" Focus on the issue of trust. Pair up the children. Then have one child	Ability to work "cooperatively" Language use Contribution to discussion Attitudes toward others

close his/her eyes, and the other lead the first
through the obstacle course. Notice the trust
that occurs between friends.

(Day 5) Create an "I like you because . . ." book. (This will take several days). Have the children sit in a circle. Ask each child to say, "I like you because . . ." about the child sitting to the left of him/her. Record their comments on large paper. Then have each child draw a picture of the friend. Staple together all the drawings and comments and create a classroom Big Book for all friends in the community to see.	Concepts about print Language use Oral language Fine motor coordination

Play & Small Group Activity Time:

(1) Stock the book corner with books about friendship. Read them to small groups of children. Post a chart poem or two and read these as well. Encourage children to "pretend read."	Book handling Storybook reading behaviors Speech-to-print matching Favorites
(2) Make up "Guess who" riddles by asking individual children to tell you their favorite activity, their favorite food, what they like to do most at home. Suggest clues that reflect the child's positive characteristics. During sharing time, read riddles to the group and have them guess who the child is.	Self-image Oral expression Favorite activities Understanding of others
(3) Start a "Me Museum" (ongoing). Select two children per week. Ask them to bring in photos, hobbies, crafts and other articles that show others a little bit about them. Display these on a bulletin board and shelves. At the end of the week, have featured children "show and tell" about each item in their collection.	Building a sense of community Sharing with others Sense of self Oral expression Favorite interests
(4) Create a writing center for pen pals. Collect old valentines. Help children share a message of love to a pen pal in the classroom. Let children write their own way. Then help them transcribe their message. Place these in a classroom post office to be distributed at a later time.	Developing a community of friendships Emergent writing status Fine motor coordination Concepts about print
(5) Construct homemade telephones in the science area. Get a length of tubing (like an old hose), and push a funnel into each end. Let children talk into one end while a second child listens at the other end.	Oral expression Ability to hold a conversation Cooperation

You'll find that language and literacy activities are subtly woven throughout the activities. Children are encouraged to actively engage in experiences which encourage them to develop skills in using language in conversation, to attend to and follow oral directions, and to record their ideas through pictures and/or words, as they attempt to convey the meaning of their ideas to others. But these language and literacy goals are never taken out of context; rather, they are viewed as integrally bound together with the more comprehensive curricular aims and intentions. In a very real sense then, it is the topic that drives children's curiosity and interest to *use* language and literacy.

Notice how the first whole group activities launch the children into the topic study by building on what they already know and encouraging exploration. This plan reflects the belief that before children can be good friends to others, they must first understand themselves. By day 3, these activities have stimulated children's curiosity, setting the stage for their contributions in the form of ideas and questions about others. They are asked to reflect on the question: "Who are these individuals in the classroom and what are their interests?" Denise encourages children to forge linkages with others in the classroom by framing these explorations in a positive direction. She wants all the children to see themselves as having a unique and special role in the classroom community.

Denise has also created a number of play activities which are designed to support and extend the whole group focus endeavors. Notice, here, how the physical environment is consciously used to support the overall learning goals, as we described in Chapter 4. The conversion of the Science Area into a communications corner, for example, stimulates children to spend time together just talking among themselves. In other words, the setting presses children toward certain actions and not others. In working with the physical environment and props, Denise is attempting to create activity settings that foster the very knowledge, skills and dispositions that she has selected to teach. These activities will be used throughout the entire topic study.

With the help of her local librarian, she has also identified a number of interesting stories and predictable texts that will be used throughout the topic study. By gathering all the books prior to the beginning of the unit, Denise will be able to read them at her leisure, and decide which are the most appropriate texts for her young learners.

Making plans like these has several benefits:

- ❑ Plans provide an agenda which can be shared with colleagues, children and their parents. A condensed version of the plans can even be posted for all to see.

- ❑ Making weekly plans encourages forward thinking on the part of teachers and their focusing on large chunks of time, rather than on each day and how to plan for it. Using the week as the unit for planning rather than the day is a form of long-range planning which promotes the interlinking of activities with one another. As a result, the entire topic study moves forward in a cumulative, connected and consistent manner.

❑ Weekly plans tie the day-to-day to overall curricular goals which generally cover a much longer span of time. Too often, we lose sight of our overarching curricular goals in the incredible detail of the day-to-day. When planning week-to-week, it is much easier to keep these goals in mind, selecting daily activities that are linked more explicitly to them.

❑ Weekly plans make daily planning an easier task—a boon to busy teachers. Having a clear sense of what will be done each day before the week begins reduces anxiety and enhances the opportunity to enjoy daily work with young children.

Making Daily Plans

We find it easier to work from weekly to daily planning. From our overview, we can now create a daily plan, which is displayed in Table 6.5.

TABLE 6.5   SAMPLE OF A DAILY PLAN, WEEK 1, DAY 1

GROUP PATTERN	WHAT	WHERE	PROPS	HOW PROCEDURES	WHY
Whole Group	Draw body images of the children & cut them out	Circle area	Butcher paper Markers Scissors Paints	Encourage children to lie down straight	Body image Knowledge of facial features Orality
	Conversation with child	Circle area	Same		Invite discussion
	Encourage child to paint facial features and clothes on paper	Circle area	Same	Have aide available to help with paint and placement of features	
Small Group Activities	Homemade telephones	Science corner	Hose Tape Funnels	Carry on a conversation with peer	body image orality
	Dress-up and make-up	Housekeeping corner	Safe cosmetics Dress-up clothes		pretend reading
	Reading	Book corner	Books about friendship, self image		
	Pen pals	Writing table			Emergent writing
Reading aloud	Brown bear	Circle area			Participatory reading
	Leo the late bloomer	Circle area	old valentines		Self image Predictable text Story structure

Here, Denise's aim is to briefly indicate what she plans to do, what props she will need to have available, and what procedures are important to initiate these activities. She is comfortable with this format, and keeps her daily lesson plans on a clipboard located at her desk.

From our point of view, the function of daily plans is to remind teachers of the lesson's learning goals and to guide in the implementation of activities. These plans may also be posted for children and serve as an organizer for their day.

In any case, they should be kept as simple and as easy to write up as possible. How teachers choose to display this information on paper, therefore, is obviously subject to personal preference.

· ·

Let's Review . . .

In Chapters 5 and 6, we have examined child-centered activity planning from whole to part, focusing on the overall aims of our curriculum program to the more specific day-to-day details. In these chapters we share our belief that the activities we prepare for our young learners should be congruous with our knowledge of children's interests, needs and motivations, and not merely subordinated to our external logic and values.

Effecting these goals in real-life educational settings, however, is not an easy task. It requires thoughtful planning and a clear understanding of our goals of teaching: the knowledge, processes and strategies, as well as dispositions for learning. Nevertheless, the complexity of planning should not prevent us from accepting the challenge of preparing and using curricular activities that place children at the forefront. Given our expanded understanding of childhood and language and literacy processes, this is a challenge we can hardly ignore.

Our goal is to encourage cumulative, consistent and continuous development in language and literacy learning for early childhood. Toward that end, the child-centered activity planning presented in these chapters attempted to accomplish the following key objectives:

❑   to extend teacher's thinking about curricular activities, and ultimately their role in curriculum development

❑   to encourage thoughtful planning by articulating basic goals for selection and organization of content, language and literacy experiences, attitudes, and teaching strategies

❑   to view language and literacy processes as tools to enhance children's thinking

❑   to provide a model which supports teachers' intentions to offer language and literacy activities that respect children, their ways of knowing and their use of spoken and written language.

....

Let's Explore . . .

1. Observe an early childhood classroom. List all the language and literacy activities carried out in one morning. Evaluate their effectiveness in terms of your understanding of developmentally appropriate goals and objectives for this age level.

2. Visit a preschool for a morning. Observe how circle time activities are conducted. Based on guidelines in Chapters 5 and 6, evaluate the circle time activity for child involvement. Does it encourage child-initiated inquiry and active participation? How might you restructure this time for greater involvement?

3. Design a play setting of your own choice. Write up a brief lesson plan stating your goals, and include the specific props required and any recommended procedures.

4. Create a weekly lesson plan on a particular topic. Write up, in broad outline form, specific whole group focus activities, small group activities, and literature selections for child involvement.

5. Observe a teacher's role during small group activity time. Does he or she interact, or primarily monitor during free-choice time? Could this time be utilized more effectively by teachers for language and literacy purposes? How?

6. Create a card file of predictable books and interesting storybooks for young children.

....

Literature Selections

Brown, Marcia. (1975). *Stone soup*. New York: Scribner.
Brown, Myra. (1967). *Best Friends*. Chicago: Children's Press.
Browne, Anthony. (1989). *Things I like*. New York: Knopf.
Carle, Eric. (1971). *Do you want to be my friend?* New York: Crowell.
Cohen, Miriam. (1967). *Will I have a friend?* New York: Collier Books.
Hill, Elizabeth. (1967). *Evan's Corner*. New York: Holt, Rinehart, and Winston.

HOBAN, RUSSELL. (1969). *Best friends for Francis*. New York: Harper and Row.

KRAUS, ROBERT. (1971). *Leo the late bloomer*. New York: Windmill Books.*

LANGSTAFF, JOHN. (1974). *Oh, a-hunting we will go*. Boston: Houghton-Mifflin.

LOBEL, ARNOLD. (1971). *Frog and toad together*. New York: Harper and Row.

MARSHALL, JAMES. (1972). *George and Martha*. Boston: Houghton-Mifflin.

MARTIN, BILL. (1967). *Brown bear, brown bear, what do you see?*. New York: Holt, Rinehart, and Winston.

SILVERSTEIN, SHEL. (1964). *The giving tree*. New York: Harper and Row.

STEIG, WILLIAM. (1971). *Amos and Boris*. New York: Farrar, Straus & Giroux.*

UDRY, JANICE. (1961). *Let's be enemies*. New York: Harper and Row.

VIORST, JUDITH. (1972). *Alexander and the terrible horrible no-good very bad day*. New York: Antheneum.

WABER, BERNARD. (1972). *Ira sleeps over*. Boston: Houghton-Mifflin.*

WELLS, ROSEMARY. (1973). *Noisy Nora*. New York: Dial.

WILDSMITH, BRIAN. (1974). *The lazy bear*. New York: Franklin Watts.

* Books read in week 1. The other books listed could be read throughout the topic study, and then placed in the book corner for all children to enjoy.

Instructional Mainstays

DLTA participation stories outdoor verses

**Integrated
Activities with
Stories**

**Integrated
Activities
Outdoors**

LEA storytelling obstacle course games

invented spellings environmental print puppetry prop boxes

**Integrated
Activities with
Spoken Words
& Print**

**Integrated
Activities with
Objects, Playtime &
Special Events**

caption pictures finger plays literacy-related celebrations
writing center play

emergent storybook wordless
reading picture books

bookmaking **Integrated
Activities with
Books** predictable books

action books shared reading

CHAPTER 7

Engaging Children in Integrated Language and Literacy Learning Activities

Rapidly turning pages of a book, young Leslie reads while Jessie looks on:

Leslie: *"Once uponna time . . .Once uponna time. . . . Once uponna a time. . . . Once uponna time." (She closes the book). "There I readed it."*

*L*anguage experiences for young children are active, interactive events. Children's innate interests and need to communicate provide the real impetus for language and literacy learning. Creating opportunities for child-centered learning, then, should capitalize on children's natural curiosity by providing a wealth of experiences from which they may gain insight into these communication processes.

In this chapter, we describe a number of the experiences, routines, and activities that have been used successfully by early childhood educators as they move toward child-centered integrated language and literacy learning. We've organized these activities in categories to encourage variations with similar types of materials. First, we'll give a general description of the instructional activity, and then give some basic procedures for ways to initiate the activity in classrooms. Finally, we'll describe a number of variations and additional resources for teachers. These activities, to a great extent, represent **mainstays:** instructional procedures that provide the framework for language and literacy throughout the early childhood years.

Integrated Activities with Storyreading

Directed Listening and Thinking Activity

General Description

We want to delight our young audiences during storyreading sessions as well as make them aware of story composition, and common conventions of print. Created by Russell Stauffer (1970), the directed listening and thinking activity (DLTA) is designed to involve children in constructing meaning from stories and developing an understanding of story structure. With frequent use by teachers, it is thought that children will begin to internalize how a typical story or expository text is constructed so that informed inferences and judgements can be made.

The DLTA may be used with a story or an informational book. In fact, it is good to use both types of books so that children may begin to develop the ability to comprehend multiple text structures. The basic structure of the DLTA, regardless of the type of book, involves three components:

❑   Planning and preparing children for listening
❑   Reading the story
❑   Discussing the story after reading

Basic Procedures

In the following example of DLTA, we will use one of our favorite books, *Abiyoyo* (1986) by Pete Seeger:

A. Plan and prepare children for listening with open-ended questions and discussion.

In choosing stories to read to children, it is important to carefully plan what you read to them. Make sure the book is on the appropriate conceptual level and, for young children, is one that might hold their interest. Especially for young children, too much text on a page sometimes causes attentions to wander. Share your favorites—your appreciation is contagious and will encourage the children to share their own favorites with you. For example, we selected *Abiyoyo* because we loved the story's rhythm and its emphasis on ethnic diversity.

Build interest in the story by having a pre-reading discussion. Hold the book so that children can see the cover. In *Abiyoyo*, a man is telling his young son a story. Tell them: "This is a father telling his son a story. Does any one in your family like to tell stories? Are some of them scary? This story is about a monster named Abiyoyo. While I read, try to think about what you would do if you were the little boy. How would you deal with this very scary monster?" Try to think of creative solutions.

B. Read the text. As you read the story, hold the book so that all children can see the illustrations. Stop at several episodes and ask the children what they think of the selection so far and what they think might happen next. A simple: "Oh, I wonder what may happen next, " or "I'd be scared, what about you?" will elicit children's predictions of the coming events in the story.

C. Discuss the reading. Once the story is complete, you might encourage children's responses by asking: "What did you think about the story? What did you like best about it? Were there things in the story you did not expect? In the case of *Abiyoyo*, what were some of the phrases that made us really laugh?" Simple questions like these will encourage children to retell the story in a more natural way than through formal questioning. At the same time, you will have achieved your goal in encouraging children to sequence story events, and to make judgements about the story.

Language Experience Approach

General Description

The language experience approach (LEA) is a child-centered strategy for stimulating reading and writing development. It is based on the following philosophy developed through work by Russell Stauffer (1970) and Roach Van Allen (1968) among others, all from the child's point of view:

What I think is important.

What I think, I can say.

What I can say, I can write.

What I can write, I can read.

The language experience approach represents a very natural way for integrating language: listening (to others), speaking, reading and writing by using children's oral language for reading material. It offers a powerful approach for helping children make the connections that:

❑   oral language is associated with written language

❑   reading progresses from left-to-right and from top to bottom

❑ letters have certain shapes and sounds

❑ combinations of letters make words

Building language experiences are easily incorporated in the early childhood classroom. A cooking project, a classroom trip, a holiday event, or a visitor, creates excitement and enthusiasm for writing group stories together.

Basic Procedures

The language experience approach, a whole group focus activity, follows a common procedure:

1. Begin with oral language. Generally, an LEA lesson begins with an exciting class experience: a classroom trip to see Santa Claus, a walk in the woods, a holiday, or a goldfish who just passed away. Remember, many simple events are fascinating to young children. Initiate a discussion by asking open-ended questions. For example, "What did we see on our walk today? What colors did we see? How does it remind you of the season?"

2. Write down children's comments. Do not try to rephrase what they say. Rather, the power of language experience is that it reflects the *children's* language, not yours. The children's sentence structure and dialect should be preserved; just as children's spelling will be conventionalized eventually, so will their ways of expressing ideas from reading others' writing.

We recommend that you write these ideas on a large sheet of chart paper, so that all children can see you write. Use a dark magic marker and write down children's words quickly, but legibly. As you write, read the word aloud. Be sure to use good spacing between words and accurate punctuation. Sometimes it is particularly fun to attribute certain comments to a child. For example, you can write, "Jennifer said, 'Today our goldfish died and I feel sad.' 'I really miss him,' replied Darrell." Later on, when the experience story is completed, Jennifer and Darrell will have the opportunity to read their particular lines. It is a wonderful way to encourage children's participation in these discussions.

Keep these stories rather short to fit on one experience chart paper. They can be hung up (at the child's eye level) for further reference in the writing center. Some of the children will want to re-write the stories for themselves.

3. Read the story back to the children. Point to each word (reinforcing the concept of *word*) and move your hand, emphasizing left-to-right progression. Then encourage the children to join you for a second reading. Let the individual children read their own sentences.

4. Read the story on successive days. Encourage children to independently read the story without your leadership.

Variations

1. Language experience stories can also be effectively used with individual children. Encourage a child to dictate a story. These stories may be placed on a bulletin board or bound and put in the library setting.

2. Any simple experiment or cooking recipe performed by the children can be translated into an experience story. For example, one of our favorites is to ask children to make a peanut butter sandwich, and then have them "dictate" the recipe. They soon realize that direction-giving can be a complicated activity indeed.

Participation Stories

General Description

Young children love participation stories because they all get a chance to become actively involved in storytelling. There are several different types:

a. Action and sound stories: in this type of participation, the audience repeats a refrain, adds bodily actions, or represents a small character part.

b. Choral speaking: in this type, all children participate in reciting a selection, with special solo parts and voices. It generally requires practice.

Both types add variety to a storyreading session. But the success of participation stories depends on the active participation of every child in the group. As a result, participation stories are an excellent strategy for bringing your classroom together as a community of learners.

Table 7.1 shows versions of each type.

Basic Procedures

1. Participation stories can be adapted from familiar folktales or any story that allows for repetition and active involvement.

2. Before reading it to the group, know the selection well. Read it through to the class with a sense of anticipation, and intonation.

3. Look for possibilities of contrasting your voice (such as high/low, or fast/slow).

4. Invite the class to participate together. Encourage the children to create motions or sounds that the verse might suggest. Emphasize the fact that the child must stop at the end of each verse.

TABLE 7.1   PARTICIPATION STORIES

AN ACTION POEM: LET'S PRETEND
Bernice Wells Carlson, 1965

Oh, let's pretend! Yes, let's pretend
That we are something new.
Let's pretend we're lots of things
And see what we can do.
David is a cowboy
Riding up a hill,
(*Ride pony.*)
Until his pony stumbles
And David takes a spill.
(*Fall down.*)
Jeannie is an autumn leaf,
She twirls and twirls around.
(*Dance with many turns.*)
She twists and turns and twirls again,
And tumbles to the ground.
(*Bend way over.*)
Kevin is an airplane
Flying high and grand,
(*Extend arms and glide around room.*)
Until he sees an airport
Where he has to land.
(*Bend knees until extended arms touch floor.*)
Sally is a firefly,
Flitting in the night,
(*Dance with jerky motions.*)
Until the morning comes
And she puts out her light,
(*Kneel down and curl up.*)
Kenny is a snowman
Who smiles and looks around.
(*Stand still and smile.*)
Until the Sun smiles back at him
And he melts to the ground.
(*Gradually kneel as if melting.*)

What else can you pretend?
What do other people do?
If you will act it out,
I'll try to do it, too.

A SOUND STORY: LITTLE DUCK
Linda Leonard Lamme, 1981

This is a group participation story. The teacher reads the story aloud. Then each group of players take the part of an animal. The players give their sound effects whenever their name is mentioned.

cow — moo, moo	cat — meow, meow
horse — neigh, neigh	duck — quack, quack
pig — oink, oink	mouse — squeak, squeak
dog — bow-wow	rooster — cock-a-doodle-doo

The animals on Oak Hill Farm were noisy one morning. The rooster (cock-a-doodle-doo) was crowing. The cow (moo,moo) was mooing. The dog (bow-wow) was barking, and the cat (meow, meow) was meowing. Everybody was looking for little duck (quack, quack). Little duck (quack, quack) was gone. The cow (moo, moo) looked all through the sweet clover in the pasture. But no little duck (quack, quack). The horse (neigh, neigh) galloped into the next field. But no little duck (quack, quack). The fat, fat pig (oink, oink) pushed all the mud out of his puddle. But he could not find little duck (quack, quack).

Then the animals hurried down to the pond once more to look for little duck (quack, quack). They all called him. (Everybody shouts.) But no little duck (quack, quack). The animals were quiet as they walked back to the barn. They had looked everywhere, but could not find little duck (quack, quack).

Suddenly, a little mouse (squeak, squeak) came scurrying out of the barn. How he squeaked! He led the animals back into the barn and over to his nest in a quiet corner. And there was little duck (quack, quack) asleep on the mouse's (squeak, squeak) nest. What a shout the animals gave! (Everybody shouts.) They had found little duck (quack, quack). They woke him up with their shouting. (Everbody shouts.) Little duck (quack, quack) was rushed back to the duck pond, where, after all, little ducks (quack, quack) belong.

CHORAL READING: LITTLE BROWN RABBIT
Linda Leonard Lamme, 1981

Teacher: Little brown rabbit went hoppity-hop
Class: Hoppity-hop, hoppity-hop!
Teacher: Into a garden without any stop,
Class: Hoppity-hop, hoppity-hop!
Teacher: He ate for his supper a fresh carrot top,
Class: Hoppity-hop, hoppity-hop!
Teacher: Then home went the rabbit without any stop,
Class: Hoppity-hop, hoppity-hop!

5. Read the verse together several times, and allow for different children to participate in various parts.

Resources

CARLSON, BERNICE WELLS. (1965). *Listen & help tell the story*. New York: Abingdon.

DORIAN, MARGERY. (1974). *Telling stories through movement*. Belmont, Calif: Pittman Learning.

Storytelling

General Description

Nothing is more magical than a story well told. Modeled by an animated teacher, the children soon learn the joys of listening to a story and watching a storyteller. After hearing a favorite, children are sure to say, "Do it again. Tell us the part about . . ." What is unique about storytelling is that the teacher's expression and eyes are all concentrated on the audience, and not just glancing at them as the story is read.

But there are special skills in telling good stories. It comes through thoughtful story selection and careful preparation that is well-suited to the young audience. As you read a selection, think about the following considerations:

❑ Is this story best conveyed through telling or through reading?

❑ Is the story appropriate for my group?

❑ Is the story appropriate for my particular setting?

❑ Is the mood and style suitable for my personality?

❑ Does the story have enduring interest for children?

Basic Procedures

There are five basic steps, according to guidelines by Sorenson (1981), in preparing a story for storytelling:

1. Know the story. Read it aloud repeatedly. Get to know the setting, characters, and their actions, and the mood and style of the story will be felt throughout the preparation.

2. Analyze the story. For example, you might ask: Should this story be adapted in any way? Should it be cut or elaborated in certain sections?

What effects could be used, such as narration, songs, realia, gestures, or voice inflections?

3. Read and reread. Read the story repeatedly until you know it well. Then leave it for a day or two. At the end of that time, check yourself to see how well you remember it. Consider which of the author's phrases or words you'd like to retain. For example, this phrase from the *Gingerbread Boy* is really necessary to make the story come alive:

> "Run, run as fast as you can
>
> You can't catch me,
>
> I'm the gingerbread man!"

4. Create a cue card for yourself. Make an abstract of the story structure, or use any form that is useful to remind yourself of the key events in the story. An example of an outline is shown below:

Title: The Little Engine that Could

Author: Watty Piper

Telling time: About 10 minutes

Little train carrying wonderful things to good little boys and girls on the other side of the mountain could go no longer.

One: Shiny new engine
        Passenger train: pull the likes of you?
        Off he steamed to the roundhouse
Two: Big engine
        Freight engine: pull the likes of you?
        Off he steamed to the roundhouse
Three: Kind train
        Rusty old engine: I can not, I can not, I can not.
        Off he went to the roundhouse
Four: Little blue engine
        Never been over the mountain: I think I can, I think I can,

Resolution: The little blue train helps them over the mountain so the good little boys and girls can have toys to play with.

Comments: Could be used to encourage selective choral reading

---

5. Rehearse the story. Practice telling it into a recorder or in front of the mirror. Time yourself. If the story is too lengthy, think of episodes that might be cut without losing the overall texture of the story. For example, the freight train episode in "The Little Engine that Could" could be excluded without significantly affecting the structure of the story.

Variations

Roller stories and flannel boards are particularly useful to have in your classroom as storytelling props. Roller boxes can be made from a box, and two wood dowels (see Figure 7.1). Using cut butcher paper or shelf paper, let children draw the pictures in the story. Paste or staple these pictures together to make a long roller movie. You may provide narration to accompany the pictures in the form of captions, spoken narrative, or even children's retellings of the story.

Flannel boards are easily constructed by stapling a large piece of flannel to plywood. Characters and scenery can be made from flannel, felt or oaktag. Covering oaktag by laminating pieces will make the parts last longer. Glue heavy grade sandpaper or velcro on the backs of the pieces to make them stick to the flannel. You may try to brush the flannel if the pieces do not stick well.

For the first telling, introduce the story and move the flannel pieces onto the flannel board as you tell the story. During the second telling, let the children take turns moving the pieces. These pieces can be stored in labelled shoe boxes in the library setting for children's independent or emergent story readings.

Figure 7.1

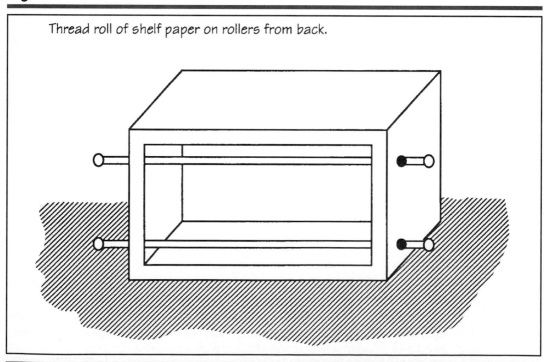

Thread roll of shelf paper on rollers from back.

Resources

The following stories are particularly well-suited for storytelling:

FLACK, MARGERY. (1932). *Ask Mr. Bear*. New York: Macmillan.
GAG, WANDA. (1938). *Millions of cats*. New York: Coward-McCann.
GALDONE, PAUL. (1972). *The three bears*. New York: Scholastic.
PIPER, W. (1954). *The little engine that could*. New York: Platt & Munk.
MELSER, JUNE & COWLEY, JOY. (1980). *In a dark, dark, wood*. New
     Zealand: The Wright Group.
SEUSS, DR. (1940). *Horton hatches an egg*. New York: Random House.
SLOBODKINA, ESPHYR. (1947). *Caps for sale*. Glenview, IL: Addison-Wes-
     ley Publishing Co.
ZUROMSKIS, DIANE. (1978). *The farmer in the dell*. Boston: Little, Brown
     & Co.

Integrated Activities with Creative Movement Inside and Outdoors

Games

General Description

Inside or outdoor activities encourage children to follow directions, and practice language, such as color names, shapes, and numbers all at the same time. These games are also designed to enhance their gross motor coordination. However, since they involve the convergence of a number of skills, you might choose to play the game at varying levels. For example, at a beginning level in the "Cross the River" game, the emphasis might be solely on color names. Then once children are capable of a more complex task, you might combine the activity with colors and shapes. In any case, we suggest starting at a comfortable pace to allow children to feel able to master the skills before moving on to a more difficult level.

Basic Procedures for Several Games

• •

Cross the River

1. Use 8 1/2" by 11" construction paper in a number of basic colors. Paste different geometric shapes on them, such as a triangle, square, rectangle, or circle. The number of colors and shapes will depend on children's skill level.

2. Arrange these papers on the ground and put masking tape on them to assure no slippage.

3. Tell the children that they are going to try to cross a river by stepping on stones. Each child must follow your directions. Then say, "Step on the green square, now to the red circle, and onto the blue rectangle," and so on.

4. To make this activity even more challenging, encourage the children to hop on two feet, to skip, or to leap to the next color.

Red Rover

1. Using two pieces of rope, mark off two end boundary lines.

2. Select a leader. Have the other children stand in back of one line, with the leader facing them between the two lines. When ready, the leader calls out, "Red rover, red rover, let (select a child's name) come over."

3. The child must try to cross the space and the opposite rope before he or she is caught by the leader. Any child caught must now stay in the center to help the leader catch his or her new prey.

Red light, green light

This so-called old-fashioned game remains ever-popular with young children.

1. Children line up alongside each other.

2. Select a leader. The leader stands with his or her back to the rest of the children, approximately 25 feet away.

3. The leader calls, "1-2-3 green light." This means that the players can run as fast as they can toward the leader. Then the leader calls, "1-2-3 red light." This signals that all children must stop running.

4. Quickly, the leader turns to see if anyone is still moving. Those who are caught must return to the starting point. The first player who joins the leader is the winner of the game.

Obstacle Course

General Description

Creating an obstacle course is an effortless way to enhance children's ability to listen and follow directions, and to use their physical skills at the same time. It provides an excellent opportunity for children to play a game with rules with no winners or losers. This game can be played inside if space is available; however, we prefer to plan an obstacle course outside using some of the structures on the playground. It is important, however, always to have an adult supervise the activity as the children engage in the play.

Basic Procedure

1. Use movable playground equipment, cardboard boxes, barrels, ropes, or tires to create your obstacle course.

2. Once ready, encourage the children, one at a time, to follow your directions to get through the course without upsetting or moving the objects.

3. Try encouraging the children to:
- ❑ broad jump over a rope that is on the ground.
- ❑ run around a series of tires.
- ❑ crawl through a tube or a large cardboard box.
- ❑ tip-toe around a tree.
- ❑ skip between two chairs.

Variation

After the children have practiced several times, let them attempt to go through the course as quickly as possible. Encourage them to try to beat the clock, working against their own time rather than in competition with others. This strategy avoids excessive competition which often discourages their trying new activities for fear of failure.

Outdoor verses

General Description

Outdoor verses encourage children to use language as they explore moving creatively and playing outdoors. Children particularly enjoy them after being indoors or following a long spell of rain. It lets them blow off steam while at the same time learn to develop strength and control of their bodies through activity. Table 7.2 describes some verses we use often with young children.

TABLE 7.2   OUTDOOR VERSES

RUNNING ACTIVITIES
(from Maxim, 1990)

Organize the children so there is a good deal of space between them. Then ask them to run in the following ways:

- Run in a large circle.
- Run quickly or slowly.
- Run with very long strides.
- Run toward me.

Then, for variety, try to:

- March like a toy soldier.
- Bounce like a rubber ball.
- Jiggle like jelly.
- Flitter like a snowflake.
- Flop like a rag doll.

JACK BE NIMBLE

Cut a slit in the plastic top of a container. Pull an orange or yellow kerchief through it. Now you have created a candlestick!

Recite the rhyme, "Jack be nimble." Let each child take a turn by jumping with both feet over the candlestick as the last line is recited. A fun way to encourage children to learn each other's name, substitute their name for *Jack*.

> Jack, be nimble
> Jack, be quick
> Jack, jump over the candlestick!

ACTION VERSES

While playing outdoors, use the following rhymes to encourage various body movements:

> Little frogs, little frogs,
> Hop to the wall;
> Little frogs, little frogs,
> Please come back, I call.
>
> Little lions, little lions,
> Run to the door;
> Little lions, little lions,
> Give a great big roar.
>
> Little ducks, little ducks,
> Waddle to the gate;
> Little ducks, little ducks,
> Hurry—don't be late.
>
> Little birds, little birds,
> Fly to the swings;
> Little birds, little birds,
> Flap and flap your wings.

Integrated Activities with Spoken Words and Print

Caption Pictures

General Description

Most children attempt to communicate ideas first through pictures, then through writing at some later time. Caption pictures allow children to see their ideas in written form (see Figure 7.2). As they draw, color or cut and paste, teachers can offer to write a sentence or two about their project. This might involve simply labelling objects in their pictures, or writing out their descriptions for them. In this way, children can begin to associate spoken with written language, and can see how their language can be written down and spelled.

Figure 7.2

My story looks like a dog, but it isnt. Its called the bear's hunt.

Alexandra age 3

Basic Procedures

1. You might want to give a small group a specific topic at times. For example, following a special event like apple-picking, children might be asked to draw pictures about their special experiences. Generally, a short discussion about recent events at home or at school is all it takes to get children started in a conversation.

2. Offer to write out a sentence or two about the child's experience. Be sure to print the letters clearly and say the words as you write. Read the sentence once again after it is completed.

3. Ask the child if he/she would like to read the sentence.

4. This activity has the potential for producing a book illustrated and written by one or more children.

Variation

Child-dictated stories can also occur after reading a favorite story-book. Have a child retell the story and write down this retelling. This produces wonderful stories from a child's point of view, in the child's own language. It offers another opportunity for a child to illustrate his or her own book.

Environmental Print

General Description

Environmental print—signs, labels, and charts—can provide an essential way to organize your classroom environment and also provide children with important written language experiences. Labels and signs can be used to indicate children's cubbies, where different items in the classroom belong, and important procedures and routines for the class to follow. Particularly for young children, rebus or picture writing along with the printed word is especially useful to help them make sense of the message. After all, in their real-world environment, young children use multiple cues to develop print–meaning associations.

We recommend two key features to keep in mind when infusing your environment with print:

❑   Make sure the print is at eye level for the children. Hang labels and signs at heights easy for them to see.

❑   Point out the labels to the children and refer to them as part of your normal routine. Encourage them to read these labels, to copy them if they are interested and to use them in their play. Strategies such as pointing to a sign, and saying "Look, the sign says 'sorry, we're closed,'" will make signs and labels more salient to children in their everyday activities.

Basic Procedures

1. Display signs and labels in functional settings, simulating a context that might encourage children to read print as if it were in their real-life environment. For example, placing a sign such as "come in, we're open" in front of a play setting when it is available for play gives children an authentic reason to read.

2. Encourage volunteers and aides to emphasize specific words or letters, and to extend children's understanding of these labels by pursuing their questions about meaning.

Variations

1. Interactive charts listing classroom jobs, the daily schedule, weather, and attendance will demonstrate the important functions of print in the classroom. At first, you will have to interpret these charts and model their uses. But soon the children will be able to use them quite independently as part of the daily classroom routine.

2. The "Morning Message" has become a popular technique for giving children opportunities to see meaningful written language being constructed. A morning or afternoon message, written as the children watch, briefly tells about a significant event for the classroom on that day. For example:

"Today is the longest day of the year."
"We are going to plant a tree today."

Over time, children begin to look at the chalkboard for each day's special message. Once the message is written, you can encourage the children to reread it, and discuss the day's upcoming events.

Finger Plays

General Description

Finger plays are child-oriented verses, rhymes, or short stories with accompanying hand motions. They promote language development by encouraging children to engage in a pleasurable repetition of words and free use of voices. Children enjoy these rhythmic jingles and are easily captivated by their words and motions. They can be used for many purposes, including:

❑   relaxing children and directing excess energy
❑   developing memory skills
❑   providing small and large motor activity
❑   developing listening skills and following directions.

In Table 7.3, we list several of our favorites.

Basic Procedures

1. Gather the children together in a circle. Say the rhyme and show them the accompanying actions. Be sure to use motivating facial and verbal expressions.

2. Repeat the rhyme, then say to the children, "Please help me say it while I do the motions."

3. Repeat the rhyme once again with the children and invite them to join you in the finger action. Watch as they participate in the play. Some children will clearly have difficulty in mastering the accompanying movements; others will be more facile in their small motor coordination. These observations will be useful in creating developmentally appropriate activities to enhance young children's physical coordination.

Resources

CARLSON, B. (1965). *Listen and help tell the story*. New York: Abingdon.
CHAMBERS, D. (1977). *Literature for children: The oral tradition; story-telling and creative drama*. Dubuque, IA: William C. Brown.
DORIAN, M. & GULLAND, F. (1974). *Telling stories through movement*. Belmont, Calif: Pittman Learning.
MAXIM, G.W. (1990). *The sourcebook*. Columbus, OH: Merrill.
MOORE, V. (1972). *Pre-school story house*. Metuchen, NJ: Scarecrow Press.

Invented Spelling

General Description

Children learn to write by writing. Even before receiving any type of formal instruction, young children have been shown to have considerable and reliable knowledge about their language's phonology. As we have noted, children first begin by experimenting with writing: scribbling, drawing letter-like forms, incorporating writing in pictures and using letters in nonsystematic ways. But shortly after this experimental period, children begin to use invented spelling. They begin to use letters in a systematic, though nonconventional way to represent speech sounds.

TABLE 7.3   FINGER PLAYS

THE BEEHIVE

Maxim, 1990

Here is a beehive
(Close fingers together, thumbs inside.)
But where are the bees?
Hidden someplace where nobody sees.
Soon they'll come out of their hive.
One, two, three, four, and five.
(Open one finger as you say each number.)

MY HANDS

(Follow actions as rhyme indicates.)
My hands upon my head I place,
Upon my shoulders, upon my face.
At my waist and by my side,
And then behind me they will hide.
Then I raise them way up high,
And let my fingers swiftly fly.
Then clap one, two, three,
And see how quiet they can be.

TEN FINGERS

I have ten little fingers.
    (Hold up hands.)
They all belong to me.
    (Point to self.)
I can make them do things.
Would you like to see?
    (Point to eyes.)
I can open them up wide,
    (Spread fingers.)
Shut them up tight,
    (Make tight fist.)
Put them together,
    (Fold fingers together.)
Jump them up high,
    (Reach above heads.)
Jump them down low,
    (Touch floor.)
Fold them quietly,
    (Fold fingers together.)
And sit (or stand) just so.

Rhea Paul (1976) recognized the following developmental patterns among her young children's invented spellings. They used:

- ❏ beginning representation of initial phonemes
- ❏ initial and final phonemes written
- ❏ separated short vowel sounds from surrounding consonants and attempted to include them in the spellings
- ❏ spelling more conventionally

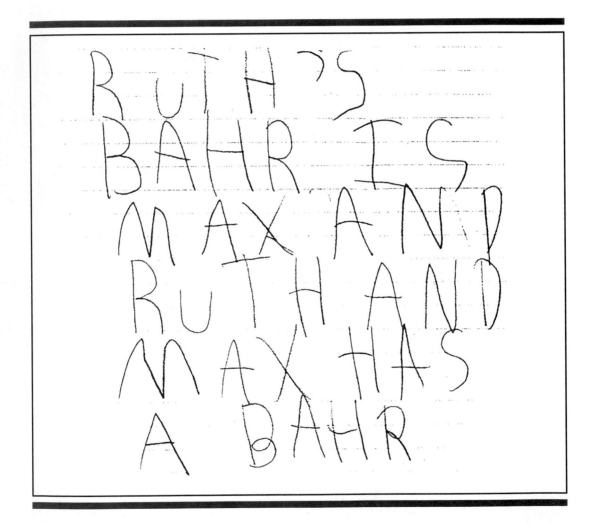

Rather than merely an artifact of preconventional writing, invented spelling offers teachers a window into young children's emerging conceptions of written language.

Basic Procedures

1. Look for opportunities to talk about writing. For example, when you write a caption on a child's picture, you might ask "What letter should I write for this picture of an animal?" Or you might talk with a child about a picture he or she is drawing and say, "You can write about your picture—what letter(s) do you need?"

2. Provide writing opportunities for children. This will encourage them to use their invented spellings. At the drawing table, for instance, you might suggest that they include words in their pictures.

3. You will find that letters representing parts of words or several words will be run together (because children's notions of *word* is still evolving). In fact, sometimes letters will be scattered all over the pictures that they make. As you might imagine, this makes it a bit hard to decipher a child's meaning. We suggest that you be ready by asking, "Will you read this to me?"

4. It is important to encourage all forms of invented spelling. Teachers cannot hurry children beyond a particular stage to more readable invented spellings. Rather, children's invented spellings will become increasingly more conventionalized when they are encouraged to write often and to write for a wide variety of purposes and audiences.

Writing Center

General Description

A writing center holds an uncanny fascination for young children. Here is a place in the classroom where they can experiment with writing, collaborate with their peers, and get responses from one another. As this center contains a variety of writing implements and materials like paper, pencils, crayons, chalk and chalkboard, children can frequent it for a wide variety of purposes during their busy day. Naturally, they will use their preconventional forms, such as scribbling, drawing, random letters, and invented spelling in their writing. Still, these writings will serve important purposes: to write stories, invitations to a party, make lists and create signs. A far cry from rigid coloring books or worksheets, these constructions serve the creative needs and emergent skills of young writers.

The writing center can be a cozy, relatively small area, where about three to four children can comfortably play. It should be in a place, however, that can be monitored, to avoid any inappropriate use of the materials. A table and several chairs, low level shelves to store materials, and a bulletin board to display written products will provide the basic set up for the writing center.

Adapted from Schickedanz (1986), the writing supplies listed in Table 7.4 might be included in your center.

Basic Procedures

1. Invite the children to visit the writing center during free choice time, or any time during the day when they need to write things down.

2. Keep this area well stocked with materials. Children go through paper rather quickly, and pencil tips are easily broken. By keeping this area continually attractive, you will be offering encouragement to visit the center regularly.

3. During free play, visit the center frequently. You might want to write with the children to model these behaviors, or offer encouragement and help, when needed.

4. On occasion, you can make suggestions for specific writing tasks. For example, during the Valentine season, you might encourage the children to write special notes to each other. Or, following a special visit from a community worker, you can suggest that children write a thank-you note, expressing their appreciation. However, it is important to keep these ideas at the suggestion level and not make them into assignments. Remember, writing is a wonderful form of play for young children.

TABLE 7.4   WRITING MATERIALS FOR THE WRITING CENTER
Pencils (large sized for little hands)
Pens
Markers
Crayons
Paper (different sizes to encourage different types of writing)
Clipboard
Chalk
Small chalkboards
Eraser
Paste and glue
Scissors
Pretend stamps
Stationery/envelopes
Mail box (can be made easily from a shoe box)
Yarn (for creating books)
Hole punch
Library-size envelopes
Alphabet letter stamps and ink pads
Old magazines

Variations

1. Theme-based centers seem to create natural writing opportunities. For example, by establishing a dramatic play area, like a fire or police station, or a doctor's office, children may incorporate written language in their activities as an integral part of these settings.

2. For a fun home-based activity, try creating a "writing suitcase" (Rich, 1985) for young children to take home on the weekends. You can include some of the materials from the writing center and place them all in a suitcase (or even better, a briefcase). Keep it relatively simple, however, and let the individual child's imagination take over.

3. Collect your old food circulars, brochures, catalogues, and junk mail for the writing center. Children get a good deal of practice in reading and writing by filling out forms and looking for sale items. In addition, their small motor coordination can be enhanced by opening envelopes and manipulating paper.

Integrated Activities with Objects, Playtime, and Special Events

Celebrations

General Description

A formal tribute to a job well done, celebrations are designed to allow us to share our discoveries and activities with others in our theme-based explorations. Celebrations are public displays, highlighting children's efforts and achievements and bringing the outside world in.

We always try to end our topic or theme-based units with a celebration. They serve a number of important functions:

- ❏ They honor child-centered explorations and creative endeavors.
- ❏ They encourage connections between school and home, inviting parents to share in children's learning activities and achievements.
- ❏ They serve to formally end the unit by presenting our young learners' final interpretations and discoveries.

Basic Procedures

1. Let celebrations become a regular part of your child-centered curriculum planning. They represent culminating activities, bringing children's learning to the public's eye.

2. Try to think of different forms of celebrations. For example, creating a videotape of children's learning activities is sure to bring parents together. Or, inviting other classes to see and learn more about indoor gardening is a special way to call attention to children's learning. Celebrate what you've learned from stories by dressing in character costumes for a day and having a parade. Your children's enthusiasm will encourage many more potential ideas.

3. Considering parents' busy work schedules, be sure to organize these celebrations thoughtfully in advance. Also, think of the following options:

- ❏ Invite parents to a bagel breakfast or a morning tea to celebrate children-published works. It is often easier for parents to participate when they can schedule events before work.
- ❏ Involve adults other than parents. Senior citizens from the local center are always appreciative audiences.
- ❏ Invite members from the community to join in celebrating our young children's efforts—the local fire chief, a police officer, and other local workers are important figures to young children and are likely to be a very responsive audience.

Variation

Celebrations offer a wonderful opportunity to involve children in writing. Whenever possible, a written invitation from them should be created to announce each special event. Even if a parent is unable to attend, invitations still provide important information regarding the classroom's activities.

Literacy-related Play

General Description

Play themes are prompted by settings and props. Children generate ideas for dramatic play from their environment. Set up a post office area, for example, with a mail box, delivery pouch, stationery and envelopes, and just watch as children engage in post office-like play. By including literacy objects in housekeeping, book corner and art areas, children begin to incorporate print in very natural ways in their dramatic play themes.

Think about the following criteria when selecting literacy props in dramatic play settings:

- ❑ Appropriateness: Can the prop be used quite naturally and safely for young children? For example, we have included note pads, and large pencils in play settings, but have avoided metal clips or staplers, which might require close supervision by an adult.

- ❑ Authenticity: Is the prop a real item that children might naturally find in their environment? We recommend real props such as phone message pads, and old, nonworking telephones (easily provided by the local telephone company), instead of toy objects.

- ❑ Utility: Does the prop serve a particular function that children may be familiar with in their everyday life? We strategically place props in certain areas. For example, props associated with a kitchen, like coupons, or recipe cards, and message pads are placed in close proximity to one another so the children can easily incorporate the literacy props in play.

It is best to begin with a relatively small number of print props, then gradually add more to keep the areas interesting. Children's spontaneous actions will give you ideas for including new props, arising from their specific interests.

Guided by these criteria, ideas for print props that might be included in typical dramatic play themes for young children are listed in Table 7.5.

Basic Procedures

1. Children's dramatic play must remain a child-initiated activity; it is not a time for teachers to attempt to teach particular literacy-related skills.

2. Most of these props will be used by the children in the context of play quite naturally. As teachers, we can enhance children's play by responding contingently to their play initiatives. For example, when a child wishes to order a pizza we can respond by asking, "How much does it cost?" "Can I order extra cheese?" to encourage more complicated exchanges; but still, children should continue to take the lead in directing the play.

3. At times, it may be most useful to serve a monitoring role, encouraging children by visiting only briefly, influencing the play less directly.

Variation

Observing children at play offers an excellent opportunity for evaluating language and developing literacy capabilities. Play is a highly con-

TABLE 7.5   PRINT OBJECTS TO ENHANCE CHILDREN'S DRAMATIC PLAY

Neuman & Roskos, 1991a

HOUSEKEEPING/KITCHEN AREA

Cookbooks	Small message board
Blank recipe cards	Calendars of various types
Labelled recipe boxes	Notepads of assorted sizes
Small plaques/decorative magnets	Pens, pencils, markers
Personal stationery	Large plastic clips
Food coupons	Books to read to dolls/animals
Grocery store ads/fliers	Telephone book
Play money	A telephone (a real one)
Empty grocery containers	Emergency number decals

POST OFFICE

Envelopes of various sizes	A tote bag for mail
Assorted forms	Computer/address labels
Stationery	Large plastic clips
Pens, pencils, markers	Calendars of various sizes
Stickers, stars, stamps, stamp pads	Small drawer trays
Post Office mailbox	Posters/signs about mailing

LIBRARY

Library book return cards	Stickers
Stamps for marking books	ABC index cards
A wide variety of children's books	Telephone
Bookmarks	Telephone book
Pens, pencils, markers	Calendars of various types
Paper of assorted sizes	Posters of children's books
A sign-in/sign-out sheet	File folders

textualized event for children; their language skills will likely be far more sophisticated in the play context than in any formal testing situation.

Prop Boxes

General Description

Prop boxes are dramatic play activities, all bundled together in a decorative box, for children to play with at home, on weekends, or vacations. They provide a marvelous opportunity to encourage parents to play with their children, and to make them aware of children's emerging literacy understandings. They also have the potential of enhancing children's learning of literacy outside the school context.

Prop boxes are based on popular themes for young children. For example, we constructed a box to look like a school house; we included props like an alphabet book, chalk and a chalkboard, a pointer, as well as writing implements and paper. (This provides an excellent opportunity for those children who will be entering kindergarten to play "school"). Another favorite of ours is a grocery store. Inside the decorated grocery box we included a grocery apron and hat, a book on buying groceries, as well as a stamper, cereal boxes, play money, coupons and similar items.

These prop boxes are designed to encourage children to incorporate literacy behaviors through their dramatic play activities. They are inexpensive to make, yet provide for hours of creative play for children on their own, with peers, and with parents as well.

Basic Procedures

1. Use a box that is large enough to hold a number of props. Decorate it according to a particular theme. We tend to focus on themes that include literacy related play such as: a post office, detective's precinct, doctor's office, or a hospital.

2. Try to solicit some real-life props from local merchants or offices. For example, the local dentist office often provides free toothbrushes, brochures, and buttons for children, as well as clipboards, and chart paper. Keep these boxes replenished with materials on a regular basis.

3. Let children sign out prop boxes for specific periods of time. Be sure to get a parent's agreement before it goes home.

4. Encourage children to talk about their play when they return the boxes. This will stimulate others to want to take them home.

Puppetry

General Description

Feltboard figures and puppets are natural stimulants for encouraging children to tell stories. Props such as stuffed animals, hand puppets, life-size puppets, and puppet-like figures used on a flannel board provide points of departure for young children to create, tell, and retell stories. Sometimes children show more spontaneity and vocal expression when sharing ideas through puppets. Those who might appear shy in dramatizing stories actually become quite animated when acting with puppets. After all, it's the puppet who is speaking, and not them!

Performing with puppets provides meaningful opportunities for the creative and dramatic use of language. It also encourages sharing and coordinating ideas, since part of the success and fun of the drama is dependent on negotiating a story with others.

Basic Procedures

1. A language- and literacy-enriched classroom environment should include puppets that are virtually indestructible (for example, sock puppets), as well as more temporary puppets (for example, paper bag puppets).

2. Try to include puppets that are specifically related to favorite stories and are easily used for retelling (for example, *The three bears*; *The three billy goats gruff*), as well as puppets that are not specifically related to any story. Remember children are active storytellers; they will naturally make up stories as they play with these puppet characters.

3. Place these materials in an area accessible to the children. We recommend the library setting as a way to encourage spontaneous dramatic play based on stories.

4. Allow children to create their own unscripted stories. Giving children particular lines to memorize at this age seems to take away from the sheer magic of puppet play.

5. Making puppets can be fun (see Figure 7.4). We recommend that you keep it relatively simple. Three types are particularly suited to young children (Sorenson, 1981).

❏ Puppets covering the hand or fingers. These can easily be made from paper bags. Glove and finger puppets can include different characters attached to each finger.

❏ Puppets attached to sticks. These are heads and bodies attached to, or drawn on tongue depressors, dowels, clothespins, or large spoons.

❏ Puppets from odds and ends. Any materials can be used to make puppets. Collect egg cartons, buttons, popsicle sticks and have a scrap box for fabric, yarn, fringe and other interesting materials, and let the children create their own puppets.

Variation

Try creating paper bag prop stories, an idea developed by Susan Mandel Glazer (1989). Get three to five large brown paper bags. Put a book familiar to the children in each of these bags. Fasten the book jacket or a photocopy of a picture from the book on the front of each bag to identify its contents. Then put props associated with each story in the appropriate bag. These props might include simple puppets for each main

Figure 7.4

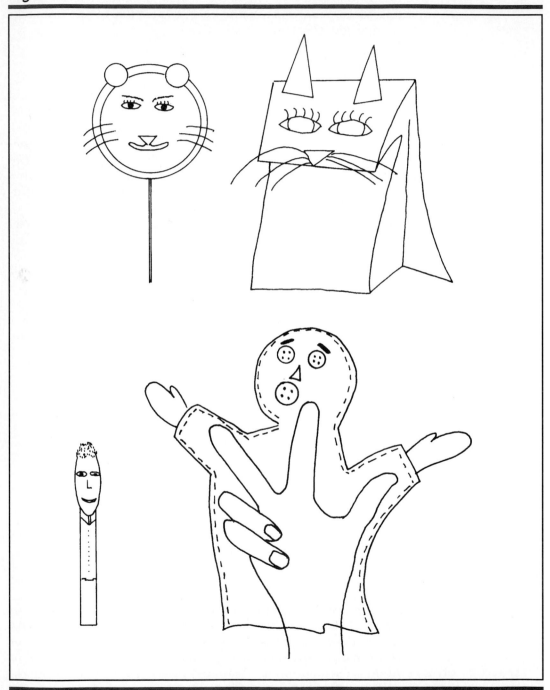

character, as well as props to identify important elements of the setting. For example, "The Three Pigs" can be made into a paper bag prop story by providing sock puppets of the three pigs, and the wolf, as well as different types of material to represent each house. Make these materials easily available in the library setting and let the children have a go at acting out a story during free choice time.

Resources

The following books easily stimulate children to play with puppets:

BARRET, J. (1970). *Animals should definitely not wear clothing.* New York: Antheneum.

CARLE, ERIC. (1972). *The very hungry caterpillar.* New York: Collins-World.

DE REGNIERS, BEATRICE. (1972). *Red riding hood.* New York: Atheneum.

EASTMAN, P. (1960). *Are you my mother?* New York: Random House.

JOHNSON, C. (1959). *Harold and the purple crayon.* New York: Harper & Row.

PERRAULT, C. (1978). *Cinderella.* New York: Thomas Y. Crowell.

SLOBODKINA, ESPHYR. (1947). *Caps for sale.* Glenview, IL: Addison-Wesley.

STEIG, WILLIAM. (1973). *Sylvester and the magic pebble.* New York: E.P. Dutton.

Integrated Activities with Books

Action Books

General Description

Action books are picture books with pop-ups, pull-tabs, lift-flaps, or other movable parts. As reported by Bohning and Radencich (1989), these books do not have impressive characters or story structure. Rather, they are designed to link the marvel of movement with text and illustrations. Because of their moveable parts, they provide young children with opportunities to participate in and enjoy the interactive nature of reading.

Action books are a natural medium to use with young children by helping them: 1) connect reading with real life experiences; 2) encourage active involvement while reading; and 3) begin to use books for enjoyment. By providing some kind of hands-on involvement in reading, these books serve as a natural transition between the concrete world and the abstract dimensions of book reading.

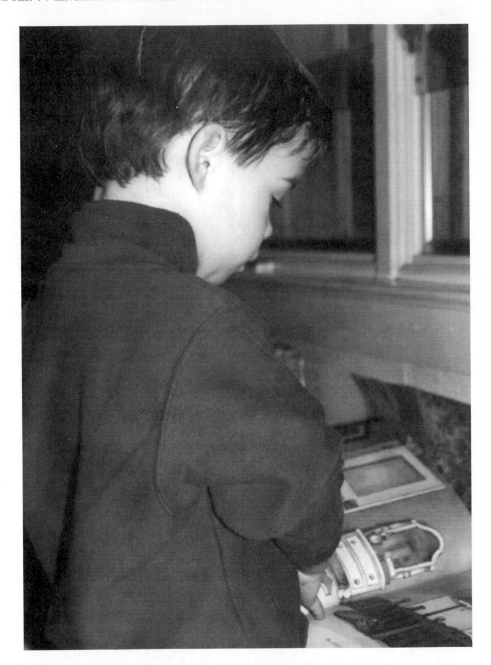

Basic Procedures

1. It is best to read these books with children in a small group setting. In the first reading, teachers should model how to use various pieces in the book.

2. Let children take turns participating in the reading. Since many of the objects in the book are rather delicate, it is important to stress proper care in using the pieces, like lift-ups, or string.

3. Once the children have gotten the knack of the three-dimensional features in action books, place them in the library setting for independent reading. Together, children and their friends will spend a good deal of time literally playing with print.

Resources

CARTER, D.A. (1988). *How many bugs in a box?* New York: Simon & Schuster.

HAWKINS, C., & HAWKINS, J. (1985). *Old Mother Hubbard*. New York: Putnam.

HELLARD, S. (1986). *Billy goats gruff*. New York: Putnam.

HILL, E. (1985). *Spot goes to the beach*. New York: Putnam.

KUNHARDT, D. (1984). *Pat the bunny*. Racine, WI: Western Publishing Co.

LUSTIG, L. (1979). *The pop-up book of the circus*. New York: Random-House.

WHITE, E. & P. (1984). *The touch me book*. New York: Western Publishing Co.

ZELINSKY, P. (1990). *The wheels on the bus*. New York: Dutton.

Book-making

General Description

Children know they are readers and writers when they write their own books. These child-generated products may be placed in your library setting along with other published books! We have used these books for a variety of purposes: for recording favorite picture books, collecting artifacts from seasons, creating autobiographies of each child, as well as noting "my favorite things." Really, once you get started, the possibilities are endless.

Basic Procedures

Below are listed the basic instructions for three types of books. The first two, the flip book and the accordion book, are easily constructed within class time. The third book-making project involves more work, yet yields a more permanent product—one that will probably remain in a family's collection of "famous" published works forever. For this project, we recommend that you recruit parents to help in making these books.

Flip books (Routman, 1991)

Young children are captivated with flip books. These are easy to make and can be used for scenes from a book, language experience stories, and are perfect for children's retellings of cumulative tales.

1. Take five sheets of 8 1/2" × 11" paper. Fold them in gradually increasing sizes as shown in Figure 7.5.

2. Assemble all pages and staple from inside at the top.

Figure 7.5

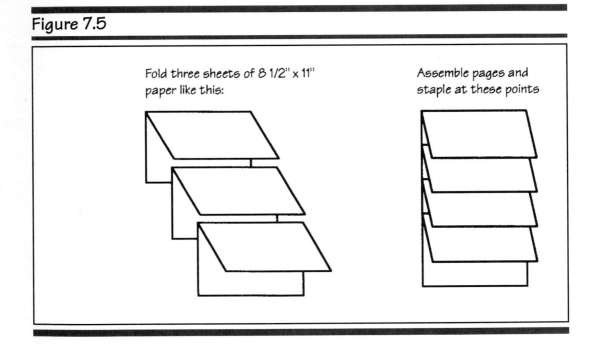

Fold three sheets of 8 1/2" x 11" paper like this:

Assemble pages and staple at these points

Accordion books

Accordion books are an excellent resource for encouraging children to develop a story's sequence. Like flip books, however, they may be used for many purposes. Using two sheets of paper, approximately 5" × 8", they fold out just like an accordion.

1. Paste two sheets of paper together. Fold them back and forth like an accordion.

2. Cut two pieces of cardboard for covers. Paste sheets of paper on each side of cardboard (see Figure 7.6).

Figure 7.6

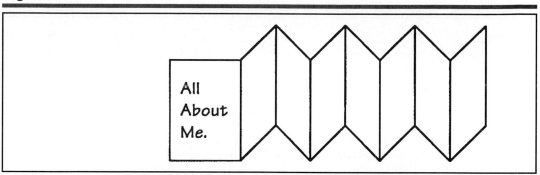

All
About
Me.

Book binding

Created in six steps, these books are bound for permanency. Children may dictate or write an exciting text with accompanying illustrations. When the books are completed, be sure to set up opportunities for the children to act like "authors" and share them with others. See Figure 7.7.

Making big books

The following procedures have been recommended by Heald-Taylor (1987) for creating big books (see Figure 7.8):

1. Selections. Make big books from selections that are relatively short, with repetitive language.

2. Format for the book. There are several formats you can choose:
   - Replica book: This is an exact copy of the original
   - New illustrations: You write the text and let the children be your illustrators
   - Child-composed book: Here you may use the format of the story to create a new version (for example, adapting the familiar *Brown Bear Brown Bear*, by Bill Martin to "Red dragon, red dragon, what do you see?")

3. Prepare the text. Write one or two sentences of the story on enlarged manuscript paper (12" × 18"). For easy viewing, place these sentences at the top of the page so that the children can see it easily. Be sure to include a cover page.

4. Leave at least three quarters of the page available for illustrations.

5. Protect the book by laminating the covers. Place an envelope in the back so that children can sign the big book out to share with friends and family.

6. Bind the book. Attach the pages with a heavy duty stapler, or punch three holes and use metal rings.

Figure 7.7

STEP I

Fold sheets of paper in half.
Stack into a packet.
Staple or sew pages together to form base of book.

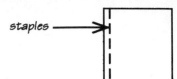

staples

STEP II

Cut cardboard about one inch larger than packet of pages to form cover of book.
Match left edge evenly and adjust so that the packet is 1/2 inch from top, bottom and right hand sides.

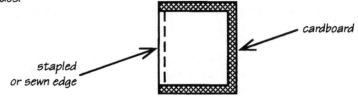

cardboard

stapled
or sewn edge

STEP III

Tape packet to inside edge of cardboard and along the outside to form cover and book pages.

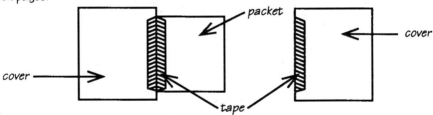

packet

cover

cover

tape

STEP IV

Cover outside with a sheet of material that is 2 inches larger than desired book size.
Miter corners.
Suggested materials:

construction paper (cover with clear contact to preserve and strengthen)

contact paper	cloth	fabric	burlap
shelf paper	old shades	felt	canvas
wall paper			

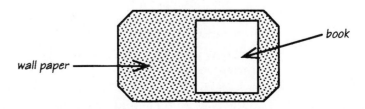

wall paper

book

Figure 7.7 (*continued*)

STEP VI

Put inside colored facing paper to inside cover (front and back) to form lining and finish of book.

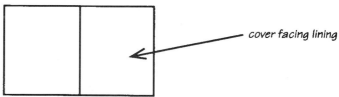

cover facing lining

SUGGESTIONS

If a child has written a book already, have child write it complete with illustrations before binding. Then follow Steps I through VI to make the book.

Remember, you will need extra pages in the book as follows:
  2 blank pages (one front and other back)
  A page for dedication, introduction, preface or Table of Contents.

Use Table of Contents when child is binding a collection of poems of stories.

Unless you are using high grade paper, write only on one side—especially if you are using magic markers or colered ink or paint to make illustrations. Many of these elements soak through the paper and make reading the other side impossible.

Figure 7.8

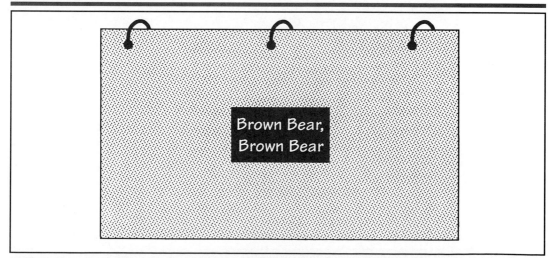

Brown Bear,
Brown Bear

Emergent Storybook Reading

General Description

Getting children to interact with books is a critical feature of the early childhood classroom. In addition to reading aloud to children, an important dimension of the storybook reading program in preschools and kindergartens is to provide opportunities for children to independently *read* books by themselves (and to one another). Known as "emergent storybook readings" (Sulzby, 1985), these reading opportunities seem to facilitate growth in reading by giving children occasions to practice what they have learned in interactive storybook readings. They also allow children to explore new dimensions of books and reading on their own.

Reading aloud to the children on a regular basis seems to be especially important in promoting these independent readings. After children have heard a book read several times, they often gravitate to these same books in the library setting, and pretend to read them. These emergent efforts represent meaningful attempts by children to act as if they were already readers; in a sense, they are beginning to grapple with the symbolic features of print, long before they are able to read conventionally.

Basic Procedures

1. Place books that have been repeatedly read aloud to children in the classroom library.

2. Set up a library setting, with the following key features (Morrow & Weinstein, 1986):

    - Partition a library setting in the classroom. Make it large enough to accommodate four or five children at a time, and provide some kind of comfortable setting, including large pillows, small chairs, a rocking chair.

    - Use open-faced book shelves

    - Provide a wide variety of books and print. Include wordless picture books, favorite fairy tales, informational books, and magazines.

    - Include props, such as library-sized pockets, in/out trays, and stamps to encourage library play.

    - Create literature-related displays.

3. Change books and displays on a regular basis (for example, according to holidays), and encourage children to use the library during free choice time.

Predictable Books

General Description

Predictable books are ideal for promoting young children's active participation in story reading. These books can take a number of forms. In some, predictability involves the use of repetitive language patterns. *Brown bear, brown bear, what do you see?* (Martin, 1970), for example, is a favorite of many as children are introduced to a succession of characters who ask, "What do you see?"

Predictability can also take the form of rhyming phrases. One of our personal favorites is *Chicken soup with rice* (Sendak, 1962), which includes the irresistible refrain, "eating once, eating twice, eating chicken soup with rice." In addition, there are some predictable books that have a cumulative sequence of events. In *The little red hen* (Galdone, 1973), no animal friends can be found to help the little red hen bake her bread, each answering "Not I" to her requests. New events are added with each new story episode. These books make reading a truly interactive event.

Basic Procedures

1. Read selections you love. Your positive attitude is infectious and will encourage children to actively participate in the readings.

2. Start with books that have easily learned patterns (for example, *Brown bear*), and then move on to books with more complex structures (for example, *Green eggs and ham*).

3. Read the title and show the picture on the cover of the book to the children and ask, "What do you think this book might be about?" Encourage children to use both picture and word cues as they make their predictions.

4. Read the book aloud to the children. When coming to a predictable line, use your voice and hand motions to encourage the children to read along with you.

5. Let the story's lines and rhymes carry much of the meaning. Stopping at various points in predictable text often interrupts the beautiful flow of language and repetitive patterns.

Resources

(Many more are included in Appendix C and in the References section, both located at the back of the book.)

Carle, E. (1969). *The very hungry caterpillar*. Cleveland, Ohio: Collins-World.

de Paola, Tomie. (1978). *Pancakes for breakfast*. New York: Harcourt Brace Jovanovich.

Galdone, Paul. (1975). *Henny penny*. New York: Houghton Mifflin.

Galdone, Paul. (1975). *The gingerbread boy*. New York: Houghton Mifflin.

Hutchins, Pat. (1972). *Goodnight, owl!* New York: Macmillan.

Keats, Ezra Jack. (1972). *Over in the meadow*. New York: Four Winds.

Westcott, Nadine. (1980). *I know an old lady who swallowed a fly*. Boston: Little, Brown.

Shared Reading

General Description

The shared reading process brings predictable books and "big books" together to create one of the most powerful techniques for engaging children in literature. Developed by Don Holdaway (1979), the strategy is patterned after the bedtime story routine. It involves increasing the size of predictable books, called "big books," so that large groups of children can have an intimate experience in a manner similar to that of a parent and child. With a big book, all the children can see the pictures and the words of the story clearly while it is being read.

One of the objectives of the shared reading process is to induce a desire among children to return to the book on subsequent days. Repeated readings enhance:

❏   children's understanding of books and response

❑   opportunities for oral practice of the language through group participation

❑   awareness of the special structures of a story, which may be used in reconstructing and decoding in later independent readings

Basic Procedures

1. Introduce a book for shared reading to the whole class. An art easel, or an old wooden podium is useful to rest the big book on while reading the book to the children.

2. Take primary responsibility for reading the selection the first time, but at the same time, encourage children's active participation.

3. During the course of the week, read the selection many times in unison, pointing to the text as you read. At each session, consider one of the following strategies (Heald-Taylor, 1987):

❑   Read the story and encourage the children to read the refrain.

❑   Read one line of text at a time, and the children repeat in unison first along with you, then alone as a group.

❑   Read most of each sentence and pause for the children to fill in the missing word.

❑   Let the children read the text in unison, first with your support, then without.

❑   Let individual children rehearse a section from the text and *read* it independently.

4. Discuss the story by asking, "What did you like most about the story?," or "Can you retell the story in your own words?"

5. Engage children in a variety of activities which may allow them to further interpret the selections through puppetry, movement, role play, dramatization or art activities.

6. Following repeated readings, place the big books into the classroom library or reading corner so the children can enjoy the selection on their own or with others.

Wordless Picture Books

General Description

Wordless picture books tell a story but use no words at all. These books encourage children to use their emerging language abilities in creating their own interpretations of stories. The use of wordless books tends to enhance highly creative story tellings that change with each rereading. Carrying a very definite storyline, the pictures enable children to use their beginning awareness of story structure in developing a story all their own.

Basic Procedures

1. Gather the children in a circle and introduce the book. Since these books are quite unique to most children, describe how it contains no words at all. Consequently, this type of book requires the children to become active, creative storytellers.

2. Guide the children through the book, encouraging them to interpret each picture and to predict what may happen next. Be open to many story interpretations. It is important, however, to remind children of the basic thread of the story in order to have them successfully generate a reasonable story line together.

3. Go through the wordless book several times, inviting the children to tell the story as they go along.

Variations

1. Encourage the children to tape-record their own interpretations of the story. Place the wordless picture books and these tapes in the listening center. These interpretations will be delightful for others to listen to during free choice time.

2. As a group activity, create a language experience story together which represents the classroom's unique interpretation of the story.

3. Make the wordless picture book come alive by using the opaque projector. Each picture can be magnified to encourage greater group participation throughout retellings.

Resources

ALEXANDER, MARTHA. (1970). *Bobo's dream*. New York: Dial.
DE GROAT, DIANE. (1977). *Alligator's toothache*. New York: Crown Books.
GOODALL, J. (1970). *Jacko*. New York: Harcourt Brace Jovanovich.
MAYER, MERCER. (1967). *A boy, a dog, and a frog*. New York: Dial.
MAYER, MERCER. (1974). *Frog goes to dinner*. New York: Dial.
TURKLE, BRINTON. (1976). *Deep in the forest*. New York: Dutton.
WARD, LYND. (1973). *The silver pony*. Boston: Houghton-Mifflin.

Let's Review . . .

In this chapter, we tried to include our favorite **mainstays:** language and literacy procedures that can be used successfully throughout the year. These classroom strategies can help in fine-tuning developmentally appropriate teaching in language and literacy for young children. As is true of any activity, of course, do not hesitate to experiment and modify these strategies to meet the special needs of your children. However, take particular note that these activities emphasize a wholistic approach to literacy learning: they encourage an integration of language processes, and social interaction among children, and offer many opportunities for children to demonstrate their developing abilities in a safe and satisfying language environment.

Let's Explore . . .

1. Select a particular topic for study in your early childhood class (for example, seeds, or "me and my friends"). Adapt two or more of the strategies in this chapter to the selected topic. Try these ideas out on your group of children. Evaluate the instructional strategies according to the topic and the needs of your students.

2. Write out an objective in language and literacy that you would like to accomplish with your young children. Adapt an activity used in this chapter to meet this need. Be sure to include props and procedures in developing your ideas.

3. Prepare a small booklet for parents. Adapt a number of activities that can be used easily (and inexpensively at home) to encourage parent–child interactions in language and literacy activities. Have the children create a decorative cover. This will surely grab parents' attention!

Assessment

Basic Concepts

systematic
observation

patterns of
language &
literacy behaviors

language and
literacy in-use

How To

Observe

- decide on
  skills &
  processes
  to observe

- establish
  predictable
  time(s)
  to observe

- select multiple
  data sources

Record

- teacher
  observations

- children's
  constructions

- interviews
  with parents
  & children

Organize

- into language
  and literacy
  folders

- into language
  and literacy
  portfolios

Interpret

- influences
  - beliefs
  - development
  - curricular
    goals

- activities
  - normative
  - summative

- reporting

CHAPTER 8

Assessing Language and Literacy Learning

"Tell me about when I was little . . ."

Two certainties necessitate the assessment of children's language and literacy development in educational settings. One is that children's ability to use language and literacy is certain to change and the other is that change is certain to demand response from adults. Both of these certainties impact the educational work we do.

Noting change in systematic ways, talking about it intelligently, and acknowledging it in teaching constitute the process of assessment. We refer to these actions as the process of assessment because they are behaviors which can recur. And it is their recurrence which makes assessment ongoing and useful in educational work.

Volumes have been written on the purposes, procedures, and processes of assessment. Central to much of this discussion is the very human behavior of observation. What is observed? By whom and when? How is it done and what for?

For educational purposes, sometimes we observe by using a formal or **standardized** test as our lens for looking at behavior and performance. What is seen through it may be used to select children for specific educational programs, to ascertain achievement, and to inform instruction in a broad and general way.

At other times our observational lens may be informal, consisting of narratives, rating scales or checklists completed at certain times during a program year. Because these devices for looking are closer to the day-to-day teaching we actually do, they tend to inform our instruction in more specific ways.

Whether assessment is formal or informal, however, all educators agree that its overall goal is to provide descriptive records of children's learning while enlarging adult's understanding and informing their teaching. In this chapter it is not our intent to enter the longstanding and ongoing discussions of assessment nor to grapple with the many issues that surround it, such as the appropriateness of "paper–pencil measures," and the validity of standardized testing. Instead we are interested, here, in how early childhood teachers can observe children's language and literacy behaviors under natural conditions, interpret what they see, and use their interpretations to inform their own teaching as well as the parents of the children in their charge. From this perspective, assessment involves practical matters: (a) what to observe, when, and how to record it; then (b) how to organize our observations and interpret them so as to assist and stimulate children's language and literacy growth. Before plunging into these practicalities, though, we need to discuss three key ideas fundamental to the evaluation process.

- ❑ Plan observations systematically.
- ❑ Search for language and literacy behavioral patterns.
- ❑ Focus on behavioral patterns that reveal genuine development and growth.

We need to recognize, first, that observation is critical to the assessment process. But there is more to observation than merely watching what children do and listening to what they say. If observation is to serve assessment, then it must be **systematic**. And if it is to be systematic, then it must be **planned.**

Planning systematic observations of children's language and literacy learning and growth includes at least two considerations. First, thought needs to be given to what will be observed with respect to language and literacy. In the main, our thinking here focuses on children's functional use of spoken and written language, for example, the social and creative ends to which children use it. For instance, to what extent do they use spoken language to express their wants and/or use printed language to claim ownership of their possessions? And we also want to note their understanding of the technical aspects of language or its form. For example, we are interested in their pronunciation of words and their storybook reading behaviors. In Table 5.2 in Chapter 5, we suggested a number of language and literacy behaviors which could become the targets of planned, systematic observation.

Second, having decided on the behaviors to be observed, the means for recording them need to be determined. This is especially challenging for teachers of young children because they must find ways to carefully gather information on the run. Furthermore, since young children have difficulty explaining themselves, teachers must record with sufficient detail so as to reveal *how* children may be thinking and feeling as well as to describe *what* they are doing (Cohen, Stern & Balaban, 1983).

Third, we need to understand that evaluation is a search for **patterns of behavior**, not simply details or traces of behavior. What this implies is that taking just one look, obtaining one measure or collecting one name-writing sample will not do. For instance, we may note on a particular day that 4-year-old Dervon seems unable to settle conflicts using language, resorting to jabs and punches. But, most likely we would not judge Dervon's ability to use language in conflict situations from this one event. We would give him another chance, observing what he does in different situations and at other times. To detect patterns of language and literacy behavior, then, the assessing we do must include multiple sources of information which are gathered over some period of time. And it is our close examination of these diverse indicators of behavior that enhances the credibility of the interpretations we make about children's language and literacy growth.

And finally, because it is impossible to look at everything associated with language and literacy development at once, much less jot it down, teachers need to have a frame of reference for their looking, a template that outlines what will be viewed. For observation purposes, it makes sense to utilize the organizer (theme/topic) selected as a framework within which to conduct ongoing observations of children's language and literacy development. For one reason, the organizer, with its related learning goals, embraces important language and literacy behaviors we need to watch. And for another, it provides a practical way to consistently and clearly integrate instruction and assessment.

As a result, observation of language and literacy growth can become embedded in daily activities which reflect intended knowledge, skill, and disposition learning outcomes. In other words, language and literacy behaviors are observed as children use them to pursue other ends. Hence the focus of observation is on **language and literacy in use,** not as behaviors separate from the broader curriculum nor as discrete entities.

This last point is an extremely important one, especially with respect to early literacy development. Recall the ecological perspective we discussed in earlier chapters. It reminds us that spoken language and literacy development are closely tied to the specific social and cultural contexts within which they occur. These complex behaviors and processes develop both as individual intellectual achievements and social ones. Consequently, the course of development of spoken and written language is not neatly linear. Different children evidence growth at different ages and in different ways. Observation, then, must focus on the clear descriptions of children's uses of language and literacy in their attempts to construct meaning from their experiences. It is these evolving **behaviors-in-use** which indicate genuine language and literacy growth.

In this chapter, then, we outline how to plan for the systematic observation of patterns of language and literacy behavior embedded in the day-to-day classroom activities designed to achieve broad and content-rich curricular goals. Our emphases are twofold: (1) knowing what to observe with respect to language and literacy and the means for gathering evidence, and (2) organizing and interpreting the observational data we obtain so that the time spent observing and recording has been worthwhile.

Observing and Recording Language and Literacy Behaviors

When planning for the systematic observation of language and literacy behaviors-in-use, follow these guidelines:

• •

First . . .

Consider the three broad domains of language and literacy and their respective performance indicators that we presented in Chapter 5, Table 5.2 (p. 143). Although certainly not an exhaustive listing, these may be used as observable indicators of children's developing use of spoken and written language processes. When used in integrated instructional planning, they become the targets of observation for the purposes of assessing children's language and literacy development and growth.

For example, in the seed study Beth focused on observing the children's abilities to use language for getting and giving information about seeds, to follow oral and written directions when conducting experiments, and to record their ideas with accuracy through pictures and words. In her topic study of friendship, on the other hand, Denise directed her observations primarily toward oral language skills and strategies, noting the children's abilities to speak confidently, listen attentively to others, and to "turn-take" in conversation.

While the listing of language and literacy performance indicators in Table 5.2 provided a useful observational tool for Beth and Denise, it is only one among many useful lists which may be used to guide the observation of language and literacy behaviors. Others are included within this chapter and additional sources of language and literacy observation guides are provided in Appendix C.

• •

Next . . .

Plan for a continuous cycle of observations of individuals and the whole group.

Begin by determining *a predictable time or times each day* for observation purposes. Recall Denise's sample of a weekly plan (Table 6.5). As you may have noticed, she indicated performance indicators in specific language and literacy domains that she would observe during both whole group focus and small group activity time. In a similar fashion, you may decide to observe certain language and literacy behaviors during whole group time, small group activity time and/or sharing time.

Observe for 5–7 minutes each day at the times pre-selected, focusing on behavioral indicators of language and literacy development. Initially gather impressions about the group as a whole. Then focus on individual children. Continue until all the children in your class have been observed.

But, don't stop when you reach the end of the class list. Start all over again, thereby creating a *continuous cycle of observations*. What you may have missed the first time around, you may note the next time and so on. Plan for whole group observations as well as those of individual children. And conduct your observations in the natural flow of activities which address larger curricular goals.

Now . . .

Select ways to record and date observations from multiple sources.

Because teachers are above all responsible for the safety and well-being of young children, it is impossible for them to make near-perfect records of what children do and say. But they can jot, chart, check off, and mechanically record children's behaviors on a regular basis. They can gather samples of children's drawings, stories, constructions and language. And they can converse with children and their primary caregivers in various ways. When pulled together, the accumulated bits of information from these different sources reveal patterns of development and growth in children's language and literacy.

Quite simply, teachers need to select ways to collect and date information from three sources: (1) what they themselves observe; (2) what children produce; and (3) what children and their parents tell them in interviews and surveys.

As Figure 8.1 illustrates, gathering information from these multiple sources is more likely to portray what children know with greater accuracy. Greater accuracy, in turn, facilitates the teacher's ability to pinpoint appropriate language and literacy learning goals for individual children.

Ways to Gather Teacher Observations

One way to document what is happening in children's language and literacy learning is to *record exactly what you see and hear*. Use simple

Figure 8.1   Gathering Data from Multiple Sources

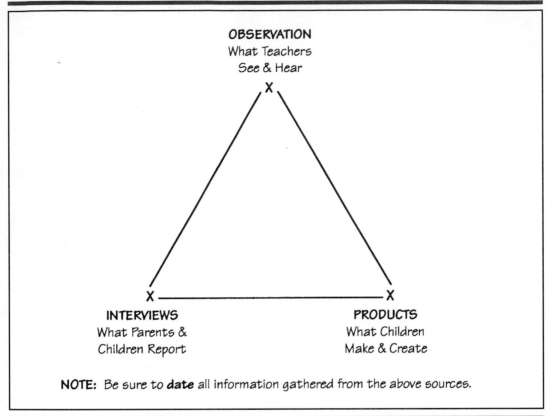

NOTE: Be sure to **date** all information gathered from the above sources.

words and phrases. What you note about the group and/or an individual child can be jotted down on mailing labels or post-its, as in Figure 8.2.

And kept in a class notebook with a page or two per child, as in Figure 8.3 on page 251.

Over time, a substantial record can be built up which profiles a child's language and literacy tendencies, preferences, and skills.

Another way to record observations of children's language and literacy behaviors is to *keep a log or notebook*. For example, Joan, a day care teacher, maintained a notebook of children's activity in the book corner. She kept the notebook in the book corner area and on a regular basis she recorded who was doing what in this area. (See Figure 8.4 on page 252.)

In this case, a notebook provided a means for documenting the literacy growth of a whole group. But it can just as easily be used to record the language and literacy behaviors of individual children. Designate one or two pages for each child. Then regularly log in the behaviors (actions and language) of individual children on a rotating basis.

Figure 8.2   Using Mailing Labels to Record Observations

9/18 Sean (age 4) <u>Book Corner</u>
- Looked at pictures in 2 books
- turned pages l → r
- pointed at words under pictures

10/18 Sean   <u>Office Play Area</u>
- scribbled and mailed 3 letters
- signed name ZĒ∧
- intermixed alphabet letters and scribble.
- knew mailing routine

11/19 Sean   <u>Office Play Area</u>
- talk-reads book in office
- points at
- scribbles down phone message (3x)
- signs name ZEA∧

Figure 8.3   Maintaining Observations

Sara (age 3)

- 10/12 - Listened attentively to our story today

- 10/19 - Pointed to and named pictures in storybook

- 10/26 - Invited her friend Larisha to play "babies"

- 11/2 - Attempted to make her name on a drawing

Figure 8.4   Keeping a log of observations

> **BOOK CORNER LOG**
> **The Four Year Olds**
>
> 9/18 James talk-read *Are You My Mother?* to Darren
>
> Linda looked at pictures in Richard Scarry's *Best Word Book Ever*
>
> Mark and David still doing puppet shows
>
> 9/20 Sergio asked Miss Jane to read *Bread and Jam For Frances* to him
>
> Brandon and Paul recited the ABC's while looking at *Wildsmith's ABC*
>
> Mark and David tried to stage a puppet show but had trouble keeping an audience

Yet another way to record what children do and say is to use ready-made *checklists*. Resources for locating a variety of these are provided in Appendix C. Checklists are simple and efficient to use, presenting an intact listing of possible behaviors. Be mindful, however, that such lists represent only a sampling of behaviors. To obtain a comprehensive view of children's language and literacy, checklists should be augmented with more detailed descriptions of what children actually do and say.

Finally, *mechanical devices* can be used to obtain samples of language and literacy behaviors. When done systematically, the periodic audiotaping or videotaping of children's activities provides a valuable means for examining children's language and literacy development in depth.

For example, audiotaped samples of a child's language and literacy may be obtained by recording storybook reading at different times throughout the year. Below, Jan, a prekindergarten teacher explains:

I include a blank audiotape among the supplies parents are requested to provide for their children. If parents are unable to provide one or forget, I have a supply available.

At three different times during the year, I invite the child to read a favorite storybook to me. I take notes during the storybook reading, using the following guide (adapted from Sulzby, 1985):

Table 8.1   Informal Observation Guide During Storybook Reading

Child's Name _____ Age _____ Date _____
Storybook _____
_____

Directions: Circle one in each category.

(1) Holds book:
   (a) properly (right side up)
   (b) improperly (upside down)

(2) Handles book:
   (a) properly (front to back, turns pages left to right)
   (b) improperly (back to front, flips through pages in book, skips pages)

(3) Reads book by:
   (a) attending to each picture, labeling objects, not forming a story;
   (b) attending to pictures and "making up" a story from the pictures;
   (c) attending to pictures and "telling" a version of the story;
   (d) attending to pictures and forming the written story (sounds like reading);
   (e) attending to print, reading some words correctly and inventing the rest;
   (f) attending to print, but preoccupied with word recognition;
   (g) attending to print and reading fluently.

(4) Retells story:
   (a) relying on pictures & needing help to recall details;
   (b) without book & demonstrating knowledge of details;
   (c) without book with reading-like intonation;
   (d) without book & including key story elements: setting, characters, plot, theme

Other observations:

I also record each session on the child's personal audiotape so I reflect more carefully on the child's use of language and story sense and make comparisons over time.

I use the form in Table 8.2 to document the child's growth in language use and storybook reading (adapted from Morrow, 1989 & Sulzby, 1985; 1990). When conferring with parents, I use this information to demon-

---

TABLE 8.2   Observation of Storybook Reading Attempts

Child's Name_____ Age _____

Storybook #1: _____

Storybook #2: _____

Storybook #3: _____

	I	II	III

Literature Awareness   Date
1. Expresses story preference
2. Recalls gist of story
3. Attends to illustrations

Book & Print Awareness
1. Orients to book properly
2. Knows where to begin
3. Knows pictures related to print
4. Reads by attending to pictures
5. Reads by attending to print

Story Sense
1. Observes story sequence
   (beginning, middle, end)
2. Retells using key story
   elements
3. Comments on story

Special Notes:

strate how their child is developing as an emergent reader. It is also a wonderful way to convey to parents the steps involved in emergent literacy by having them listen to the audiotape, noting how their child attempts to read.

Audiotaping can be used in similar ways to gather oral language samples and other literacy behaviors, such as children's ability to make predictions about a story using pictures as cues.

Videotaping provides another mechanical means for documenting what children do and say. When video equipment is available, the activity in specific areas of the environment can be videotaped regularly. Because the video camera sees all, the tapes can be viewed repeatedly to analyze how an area is used as well as the behaviors of individual children in the area.

To get started, use the step-by-step procedure for observing videotapes of children's behavior given in Table 8.3.

Anecdotal records, logs, checklists and mechanical devices are valuable ways for teachers to document what they see and hear. Teachers need to select at least one of these ways and to use it frequently and consistently. It is a means of providing evidence of children's development and growth *from the teacher's point of view.*

As important and powerful as it is, however, the teacher's point of view is but one point of view. It must be balanced by other sources of information if the teacher is to target her teaching to the language and literacy needs of groups as well as individual children.

Ways to Collect Children's Constructions

The drawings, writings, play-stories, block constructions and art projects children invent and construct are concrete expressions of their thinking and feeling. These, more than any other, indicate the child's point of view and should be included in the assessing we do. Consequently, teachers need to plan ways to preserve what children create on their own terms.

For the most part, children's constructions can be sorted into two groups: those that involve expendable materials, such as paper and clay, and those that use nonexpendable materials, like blocks and play props (Kuschner, 1989). Constructions in both groups can be rendered permanent for evaluation purposes in a few simple ways.

(1) Use photography to capture massive block structures, clay figures, play scenes, and creations made with small manipulatives. Keep photos in personalized albums with an accompanying brief description of the object or activity. Or make individual picture books, that reflect a child's constructions with materials.

TABLE 8.3   OBSERVING USING VIDEOTAPES

Step 1. Videotape a 10–15 minute segment of a specific activity (e.g., shared reading time) in a specific location (e.g., housekeeping).

Step 2. Watch the entire videotaped segment to obtain a general sense of children's activity. Record the location of the activity and the participants.

Step 3. Select who you want to observe. Target an individual or a small group.

Step 4. View the videotape at five minute intervals. Stop the tape after each five minute interval and jot down what your target child or children are saying and doing. Use key nouns and verbs only. Excerpts of an individual observation and a small group observation are provided.

Step 5. Summarize observations, stating the gist of the activity and key features of children's language and literacy use.

SAMPLE FIVE MINUTE OBSERVATION OF AN INDIVIDUAL CHILD
Location: Book Corner

Who	Action	Language
Jonathan	Picks up book	
	Walks to rocker	
	Sits.	
	Turns pages left to right	
	Talks softly. Looks at pictures	
	Rocks back and forth	
	Closes book.	
	Watches others at play.	
	Calls to James	C'mere.

SAMPLE FIVE MINUTE OBSERVATION OF A SMALL GROUP
Location: Housekeeping

Who	Action	Language
Lakisha	Cooks at stove	Dinner! Dinner! You guys.
	Handles pots & pans	
	Sets table	
Monica	Approaches table	I'm here, Mom.
	Sits down	
L.	Puts food on table	Delicious time. Delicious time
M.	Pretends to eat	M-M-M. Delicious time.

(2) Photocopy children's writing attempts periodically. Keep them in the child's folder or in a writing sampler as evidence of writing development.

(3) Collect signed paintings and drawings at regular intervals. Date each and maintain in a folder or an art scrap book. Or design an art gallery area where art work is framed and hung for an extended length of time.

(4) Periodically have children write and sketch what they do, or act as a scribe for them. These descriptions can be preserved in albums or big books, something like Figure 8.5.

Figure 8.5

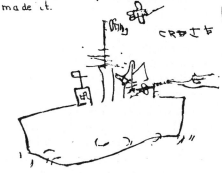

Our Big Book of What We Play Every Now and Then...

The Black Center

This is an aircraft carrier. We took 4 of these big things and a helicopter and one of these little things and a motorized van and we put them all together. The helicopter and the motor cycle battled. Chucky, Jason, and of course me, Jeremy Michael Walton made it.

Unlike teacher observation which can follow a planned schedule, collecting samples of children's constructions is much less predictable. Consequently, ready access to a camera, a copy machine, chart paper and markers is of utmost importance. These tools should be kept in locations that are easy to access at a moment's notice. Under these conditions, they will be used more frequently and regularly—two essentials if children's constructions are to become permanent artifacts in the assessment process.

Ways to Conduct Interviews

Interviews are an excellent way for teachers to enrich their understanding of language and literacy growth in individuals and in child development more generally. The primary purpose of an interview is to find out what a person is thinking and to learn about his or her opinions, beliefs and preferences.

For the most part, interviews of parents and children seem to work best when they resemble friendly conversations. Like most conversations, they should include a greeting of some kind, an expression of interest, taking turns at speaking, some pausing, and a leave-taking, or a way of saying "the end" to the conversation.

Somewhat different from day-to-day conversations, though, interview conversations have an explicit purpose—a clear expectation that the talk is about some specific thing. They also contain a lot of questions and repetition, requesting the interviewee to explain something so the interviewer understands. In short, the overriding aim of the interview is to gather information, but to do so in a friendly way (Spradley, 1979).

Interviews may be conducted in a variety of ways—some more conversation-like than others. With young children in particular, one effective way to interview them is to invite them to do something, like play, draw or hold an object. As they do, they can be encouraged to talk and thereby reveal their interests, preferences and understandings. Take drawing, for example. We ask young children to draw their favorite play area in the classroom. As they do, they explain why they like to play there, somewhat like Julia (age 4) in Figure 8.6.

Often we audiotape such interviews, later analyzing each child's oral language along with the drawing that he or she produced. Usually we ask them to sign their piece, thereby collecting a name-writing sample as well. As an alternative to drawing, children can hold and talk about their favorite toy, stuffed animal or book, providing another concrete means around which to conduct an interview.

As children approach kindergarten age, interviews in the form of surveys may be used more frequently, for example, attitude and interest surveys. These consist of a series of questions or statements about a specific

Figure 8.6

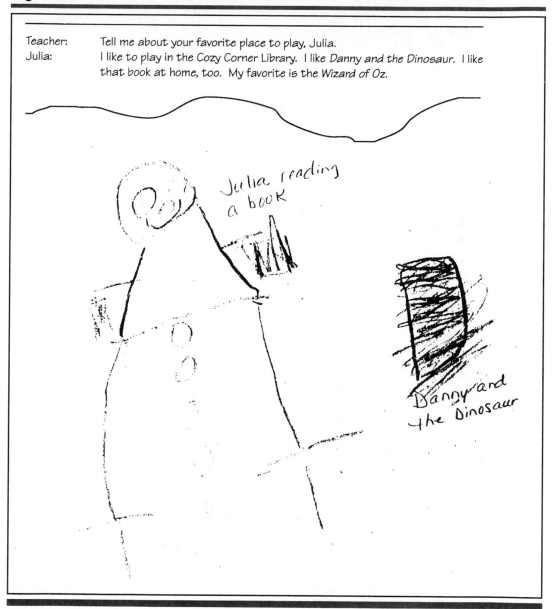

Teacher: Tell me about your favorite place to play, Julia.

Julia: I like to play in the Cozy Corner Library. I like *Danny and the Dinosaur*. I like that book at home, too. My favorite is the *Wizard of Oz*.

topic or activity, for example, reading. The child responds to each by marking **Yes** or **No** or an **X** on a picture or word which best represents his or her opinion. The "How I Feel" Survey in Table 8.4 is one example. Using a format similar to this survey, other more informal and shorter

---

TABLE 8.4   HOW I FEEL

Child's Name_____Age_____Date_____

What to do:

- Draw a face to show how you feel.
  - Draw a (☺) face if you feel this way a lot.
  - Draw a (😐) face if you feel this way sometimes.
  - Draw a (☹) face if you never feel this way.
- Put the face you want in the box.

1. I like to find out things for myself.	
2. I like to look at and read books.	
3. I like other people to read to me.	
4. I like to share my ideas by: talking—	
         drawing—	
         writing—	
5. I keep trying even when things are hard to do.	

---

surveys can easily be constructed by the teacher to ascertain children's feelings and opinions about other aspects of their lives, such as play activities, storytime activities and outdoor games.

Interviewing parents can consist of very informal chats as they come and go from the early childhood program. These provide an excellent opportunity to learn about children's eating habits, sleeping habits and literacy habits; for example, bedtime favorites and writing activities.

TABLE 8.5	JUST TO CHECK YOUR SHARED BOOK ACTIVITIES

Child's Name _____ Date _____

	(IF YES, PLEASE MARK X)					
	M	T	W	TH	F	S/S
1. Did you read a story to your child?	—	—	—	—	—	—
2. Did you hold your child while you were reading?	—	—	—	—	—	—
3. Did you and your child have a conversation about the book before, during, and after you read it?	—	—	—	—	—	—
4. Did you relate the stories in the book to real life events?	—	—	—	—	—	—
5. Did your child see you reading?	—	—	—	—	—	—
6. Did your child have related reading activities?	—	—	—	—	—	—
7. Did you point out other examples of words or letters inside and/or outside your home, for example, signs	—	—	—	—	—	—
8. Did your child work with his/her book alone?	—	—	—	—	—	—
9. Did you monitor your child's TV viewing and talk about the program(s)?	—	—	—	—	—	—
10. Did you explain unfamiliar words or experiences to your child?	—	—	—	—	—	—

(From *Shared Book: A Parent Guidebook*, ABE Program, Ashtabula County, OH.) (under auspices of Ohio Dept. of Education, Dept. of Adult & Continuing Education)

Keep post-its handy in your pocket to jot down information learned about these habits when on the run.

Interviews can also take the form of **life histories** about children. This can begin as early as infancy. Parents can be invited to dictate, tape record or write down their children's biographies, relating observations of their children's development, such as eating and sleeping habits, first steps and words, and humorous and tender moments.

Periodically, too, it is helpful to have brief sit-down conversations with parents in the classroom while children play. This is an appropriate time to initiate general surveys which ascertain such things as family reading habits, literacy activities, and routines. The shared reading checklist in Table 8.5 is one example. After explaining the purpose of the survey and completing the first few items, encourage parents to complete the survey at home and return it within the next few days. Interview information gathered in this way enlarges the teacher's understanding of children's literacy experiences outside the school doors, revealing how variable these may be.

Interviews can also be conducted within the parent conference format. In this situation, interviews are necessarily more structured and less likely to resemble casual conversation. Interviews within this context, nevertheless, do open up opportunities for parents to provide background information and insights related to specific issues, concerns, and needs relative to their children's language and literacy growth. For instance, this time can be used to explore parents' perceptions of their children's language and literacy development in depth, how and when they read to their children and how they engage their children in conversation.

Teacher observations, children's constructions, interviews: these multiple sources of information lay the foundation for accurate and thoughtful assessment. By looking at all of them, it is easier to see the patterns of behavior that profile a child's language and literacy development. And it is the recognition of these patterns which guides the interpretations we make about children's growth and progress as language users.

Organizing Observations From Multiple Sources

Having gathered data from different sources, teachers are next faced with the task of keeping it together in an efficient and convenient manner. Like so many things we do, this is often easier said than done. Pulling together and maintaining notes, drawings, audiotapes, interview data, and checklists for 15 to 20 different children demands well-developed organizational skills.

To keep it simple, we will discuss two means for organizing observational data: folders and portfolios. These have many features in common, but with one main difference. Portfolios call for greater child and parent involvement than folders, which complicates matters somewhat. We will begin with folders, since their contents and organization may serve as the forerunners of portfolios.

Using Language and Literacy Folders

It is a fairly common practice to maintain folders on children. At the very least, these may contain identifying information and medical data. Their usefulness in language teaching, however, can be maximized when they are used to collect, organize and display a set of observations in an ongoing manner.

Begin by deciding what types of observational data with respect to spoken and written language you will maintain in the folder. Be alert to the inclusion of data from multiple sources. For example, you may decide to include a narrative summary from daily anecdotal notes, a checklist of language and literacy behaviors, audiotaped language samples, and drawing/writing samples. Below are a number of examples from a language and literacy folder. These were collected by Theresa, a day-care teacher in charge of a group of 3- and 4-year-olds. The samples featured in Figure 8.7 are those of 4½-year-old Julia.

Next establish a routine for entering observations into each child's folder. You may choose to do this weekly, monthly or only several times a year. Whatever the schedule, be sure to date entries and samples. We recommend using a folder with multiple pockets so observations from one point in time can be kept together. Or color code the observations from a specific time period, using colored dots on the data sources to indicate the time frame, for example, orange dots on samples collected in the Fall. In this way, ongoing observations from different points of time may be assured.

Periodically, study the folders, summarizing patterns of language and literacy development you detect. Jot down what you notice in the form of summary statements, which may read something like this:

(1) Susan (age 5) demonstrates an increasing ability to understand and use words in meaningful contexts. For example, she effectively uses spoken language to collaborate in activities with others, that is, in play negotiations and in carrying out small group projects.

(2) Tony (age 4) expresses story preferences (for example, *Curious George* by H.A. Rey) and accurately recalls familiar stories without the aid of pictures (such as in *The Tiny Seed* by Eric Carle).

Summary statements become the basis for making judgments about children's language development and growth. They are helpful during parent conferences, serving as main ideas around which to gather the details of behavior. They can also be applied to final evaluations, facilitating the decision-making associated with them.

As individual folders begin to bulge with observational data, storing them may present problems. Consider hanging files in file cabinets, crates which are stackable or in sturdy cardboard boxes. If pocket folders are used, they are easily stored like books on a book shelf.

Folders are a popular and efficient means of housing and organizing the ongoing observing we do as teachers of young children. We may do

Figure 8.7   Ongoing observations

10/22 Negotiated play roles with friends
in Housekeeping.

10/29 Recognized own name on list of
helpers.

11/5 Listened attentively during sharing time.

11/12 Wrote letters to friends at Writers' Table.

11/19 Made Tissue Turkey, referring to
written directions.

Writing Sample
10/23

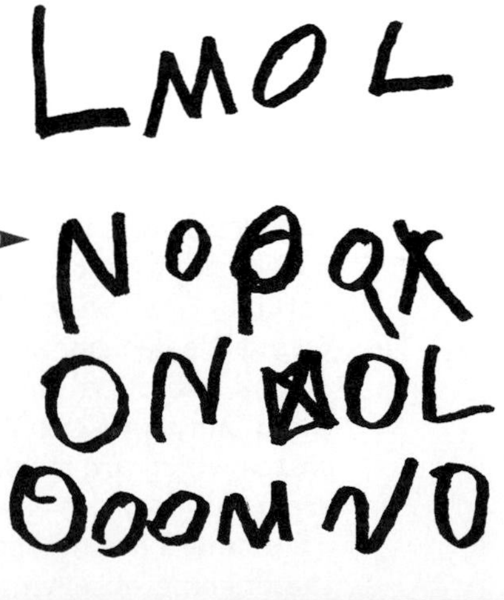

LMOL

NOₚQₓ
ONꞰOL
ƟooMVO

Figure 8.7   (continued)

Informal Observation Guide During Storybook Reading

Child's Name _Julia_   Age _4 ½_ Date _10/15_

Storybook _Come over to My House by T. LeSieg_

Directions: Circle one in each category.

(1)   Holds book:

    (a)   properly (right side up)

    (b)   improperly (upside down)

(2)   Handles book:

    (a)   properly (front to back, turns pages left to right)

    (b)   improperly (back to front, flips through pages in book, skips pages)

(3)   Reads book by:

    (a)   attending to each picture, labelling objects, not forming a story;

    (b)   attending to pictures and "making up" a story from the pictures;

    (c)   attending to pictures and "telling" a version of the story;

    (d)   attending to pictures and forming the written story (sounds like reading);

    (e)   attending to print, reading some words correctly and inventing the rest;

    (f)   attending to print, but preoccupied with word recognition;

    (g)   attending to print and reading fluently.

(4)   Retells story:

    (a)   relying on pictures & needing help to recall details;

    (b)   without book & demonstrating knowledge of details;

    (c)   without book with reading-like intonation;

    (d)   without book & including key story elements: setting, characters, plot, theme

Other observations:

- Shared details about her own home
- Mentioned relative who had lived in England.
- Pointed to the words "Come over to my house. Come over and play" at several points throughout her "reading."

Figure 8.7   (continued)

Child's Name _Julia_   Age _4½_ Date ___11/3___

What to do:

- Draw a face to show how you feel.

    - Draw a ☺ face if you feel this way a lot.

    - Draw a 😐 face if you feel this way sometimes.

    - Draw a ☹ face if you never feel this way

- Put the face you want in the box.

1.	I like to find out things for myself.	
2.	I like to look at and read books.	
3.	I like other people to read to me.	
4.	I like to share my ideas by: talking -	
	drawing -	
	writing -	
5.	I keep trying even when	

well to consider them as places where we accumulate slices of language and literacy behavior over time. Taken together, they provide evidence of language development and growth in the whole child.

Using Language and Literacy Portfolios

Unlike folders which are developed and maintained exclusively by the teacher, portfolios contain examples of work which the learner sees fit to display. In them are demonstrations of accomplishments as a speaker, a listener, a writer and a reader. Since making decisions about accomplishments of this sort is just emerging in very young children, parents and/or others close to the young child can become participants in the creation of a portfolio.

In many ways, this collaboration is a continuation of those baby books many parents maintained on their children and which recounted the first few years of life. While in the earliest months the parent took full responsibility for documenting his or her child's history, this responsibility can be increasingly shared with a child until he or she can assume full responsibility for documenting his or her own history.

Language and literacy portfolios should be outgrowths of children's language and literacy folders. From the collection of direct observations, documents, and child interviews systematically gathered and maintained in the folder, children may periodically select (with parental assistance) those items they wish to keep as "special." On a post-it or an index card, an adult should record why the child selected that particular item. In addition, parents and others may comment about the piece. These comments should also be recorded and clipped onto the item. Finally, an adult should review the portfolio contents with the child, conversing about what has been done and where it might lead—somewhat in the style of looking at a scrap book or family photo album.

To get started with language and literacy portfolios, the following procedures have proved helpful (adapted from Tierney, Carter & Desai, 1991).

(1) Establish ownership for the language and literacy portfolios.

Make sure that children understand that their portfolios belong to them—that they make them with the assistance of their parents and other adults. Like baby books, scrap books, and personal photo albums, portfolios are a personal record of one's life experiences and achievements. So, no two portfolios will be exactly alike. Mine is mine and yours is yours.

One way to get this point across is to discuss it with each parent and child together at registration time. Another is to have a meeting or two for parents: (a) to provide examples (you may have someone present his or her portfolio) and (b) to discuss the concept of portfolios as a form of assessment and how parents can talk to their children about them. A third way is to consistently view the portfolio as the child's possession, treating it with the same care you would other objects the child holds dear.

(2) Make and post a list of items a language and literacy portfolio may contain.

Using the array of items gathered from documenting what children do, list possibilities for inclusion in the portfolio. For example, Ruth, a prekindergarten teacher, provided the listing in Table 8.6 for the children in her classroom and their parents (Table 8.6).

(3) Personalize portfolios.

From our point of view, this is a family matter. Parents and their children should decide together how they want to personalize their portfolios. Some may want to construct their own portfolio cases and others may simply want to design the cover of a pocket folder. One preschool teacher handles it this way.

At the beginning of each program year I invite the parents and their children to get together. When they arrive I explain the concept of portfolios and why I encourage their use in my classroom. I emphasize the importance of our working together to keep memories of the important learning that their children do.

Next I invite each parent and child to personalize a holder for these memories together. In my classroom, all portfolio cases are pocket folders with a strip for punched inserts. Such inserts may be papers or plastic holders for securing bulkier items. Although all of the cases are the same shape and size, none of their covers is alike. Each portfolio cover bears the personal signature of its owner.

I show the parents and children some examples of how others have personalized their folders. I have many materials available for them to get started: scissors, glue, yarn, tagboard, construction paper, gummed stars and stickers, colored chalk and pencils, markers and so on. I tell them that this may be just a beginning and that they can alter their holder at any time with only one stipulation. The child needs to be involved in any alterations. I make the point that what counts is not so much how the portfolio looks (some scrap books look very plain), but what it contains.

As parents and their children work together at tables, they get to know one another. These introductory conversations create a sense of community for the class and stimulate an acceptance and respect for differences as well. Most finish on the spot and the children place their portfolios on the shelf I have provided in the classroom.

(4) Establish a selection and review process.

Portfolios reflect what children can do and simultaneously point them in new learning directions. Hence, they can become the centerpiece of periodic parent conferences. It is helpful, then, to organize the portfolio selection and review process around this existing event which is well known and accepted.

TABLE 8.6   Some Suggestions for Portfolios

—drawings

—scribble messages

—pictures of block constructions

—a list of favorite books, poems, or songs

—an inventory of personal books

—an audiotape of pretend reading

—a list of favorite games

—parent's report of "firsts," for example, first tooth, first word, first joke and so on

Once a number of items have been accumulated in individual folders, the process of selecting and reviewing items for the portfolio can be treated as a routine activity, much like shared reading or block play. Viewed as an opportunity for private time between teacher and child, individual appointments can be scheduled during free choice or free play. At this time, collected samples may be shared and children encouraged to select those seen as special for inclusion in their portfolios.

During the selection process, the teacher should probe to determine what makes the piece special and record this information on a post-it or index card, attaching it to the piece. The teacher can also ascertain what individual children would like to do next, using this as an opportunity to challenge and stretch their thinking. This, too, should be jotted down and attached to the piece. Periodically, the teacher should list out these ideas as potential learning goals and confer with parents about them.

As parent conference time approaches, invite parents to stop by and to review their children's portfolios *with them* in a casual way, much like they would look at a family photo album. In the course of this portfolio sharing, parents become witnesses to their children's language and literacy learning activities and processes in a very concrete way. As a result, they become better informed about what their children are capable of doing, allowing them to become more effective teachers and decision-makers in their children's education.

At parent conferences, the parent has an opportunity to add items to the portfolio (from school and home), to comment on what the child has selected, and to confer with the teacher about future learning goals. The parent's comments about the child's work should be noted and attached to appropriate pieces in the portfolio. In addition, the parent and teacher should summarize what the child has accomplished and potential directions for new learning. One copy of this summary may go in the child's language and literacy folder (not the portfolio) for the teacher's use and another retained by the parent.

When a program year draws to a close or when children leave a program, they should take their portfolios with them, since these are their property. Parents should be encouraged to preserve their children's portfolios and share them with their future teachers.

Although at first glance it may appear that portfolios add more work to an already time-consuming assessment process, they may in the long run actually save time. First, activities associated with portfolios can easily become a regular part of day-to-day learning activities, not something done in addition to learning. Second, the nature of data gathering for portfolio purposes spreads around the job of gathering and selecting items for assessment by including parents. Third, the process deeply involves parents *and* children, making them full participants in, not merely recipients of assessment activity. Put simply, they now shoulder some of the responsibility for appraising how well we are all doing, whereas before the teacher carried this responsibility alone. And finally, portfolios provide an extremely rich way to document what children can do, lending credibility, validity and accuracy to curriculum development and instructional programming.

Interpreting Observations From Multiple Sources

As professionals, early childhood teachers must assess children's behaviors and performance. By definition, assessment involves appraisal of the qualities of what is observed. And all appraisals are interpretations—intelligent attempts to make sense out of bits and pieces of information. Interpretation, then, is at the heart of assessment.

Two factors are essential if interpretation is to serve assessment meaningfully. One is how much the teacher already knows about what is being assessed. With respect to language and literacy in the early years, this includes knowledge about children and how they learn as well as language and literacy development. Obviously, the more the teacher knows about these areas, the more insightful his or her interpretation of children's language and literacy behaviors.

Another factor is the nature of the information made available for interpretation. Of importance is its quality and range. The more representative the information, the greater the likelihood of accuracy in constructing meaning about a child's behavior and performance. This is why evidence from multiple sources (observations, children's products, parent information) is so valuable; as a collection, it provides a clearer picture of a child's growth.

When both of these factors are present—teacher knowledge and multidimensional sources of information—patterns of behavior indicative of children's language and literacy growth are more easily detected. Such patterns reflect how well children are developing as speakers, listeners, writers and readers. Furthermore, they inform the instructional decisions teachers must ultimately make.

But, how is this done? How do teachers *interpret* children's language and literacy behaviors for the purposes of assessment?

The Act of Interpretation

In its broadest sense, interpretation is an act of meaning making. Something is observed and the observer interprets or constructs meaning about it, using his/her beliefs, knowledge and intentions. But in educational work, simply making interpretations will not suffice. Because teachers are responsible for informing and guiding the learning of others, they must also understand what influences the interpreting that they do.

Interpretation for educational purposes, then, involves awareness in at least three areas: an awareness of one's beliefs about language and literacy development, an awareness of universal sequences in language and literacy development, and an awareness of overarching language and literacy curricular goals. In combination, these sources of knowing influence the interpretations teachers make and the conclusions they eventually draw.

Becoming Aware of Personal Beliefs.

All teachers have beliefs about language and literacy development. And, of course, having beliefs is quite natural.

What is crucial, however, is that we become aware of our beliefs. We can make our beliefs more explicit by simply stating them out loud or writing them down every now and then, like so.

I believe:

(1) Language and literacy development are interrelated;

(2) There is no one way to learn language or literacy;

(3) Language and literacy are best learned in contexts of use;

and so on . . .

Examining one's own beliefs creates an opportunity to assess them and to readjust them, when necessary, in light of new evidence.

Becoming Aware of Universal Sequences of Development.

Although our understanding of how language and literacy develop is itself still developing and is not fixed, there are expected or normative levels of functioning which have emerged. This is more so the case with oral language development than with literacy development. Because literacy development is so closely tied to the specifics of the young child's social and cultural contexts, its course of development is more variable. Nevertheless, there are distinct patterns of behavior in early reading and writing which can influence interpretations of development in the literacy domain.

Based on existing theory and research, some fairly stable patterns of development in language and literacy are described in Table 8.7. They provide a frame of reference for interpreting how children are progressing as speakers, listeners, readers and writers. We stress, though, that these lists are not prescriptions of what children should be doing at certain ages. Rather they should be viewed as guideposts we can be aware of in our efforts to interpret children's language and literacy growth.

TABLE 8.7   GUIDE TO CHILDREN'S LANGUAGE AND LITERARY GROWTH

LISTENING
Developmental Patterns

Characteristics

Age 2 Understands most simple words and sentences. Likes to hear commercial "jingles" and catchy tunes. Listens to simple stories. Likes nursery rhymes.

Age 3 Likes to hear familiar sounds (animals, transportations, household). Likes one-on-one reading experiences. Has rather short but attentive listening span.

Age 4 Listens longer to stories. Still likes one-on-one experiences. May bring favorite stories to be read. Follows simple directions.

Age 5 Seems content to listen for a period of time. Enjoys stories, songs, finger plays, and rhymes. Can follow more directions. Carries on conversations.

SPEAKING
Developmental Patterns

Characteristics

Age 2 Has favorite word: "No!" Tries to say simple words; may use short sentences and carry on simple conversations. Names simple objects (body parts, pictures). Likes short responses.

Age 3 Can carry on a conversation. Uses simple words and short sentences (3 to 4 words). May carry on a monologue. Asks "why" to gain adult attention.

Age 4   Is quick to pick up new words. Learns words for ideas, actions, and feelings. Combines more words. Is integrating rules of grammar; may have difficulty with irregular past tense or plurals. Is boastful and quarrelsome. May carry on a monologue. Talks about imaginary companion. Experiments with language. Asks "why" for knowledge.

Age 5   Has highly socialized speech. Is a continual talker. Uses "because" sentences. Has wide vocabulary, uses 6- to 8-word sentences. Can verbally compare two or more objects.

READING
Developmental Patterns

Characteristics

Age 2   May recognize objects, turn pages in books, point to or name objects.

Ages 3, May learn to read simple words (some memorize or remember).
4, and 5 May identify words that look alike or different. Recognize a few words (own name, logos, signs, television words, food containers).

WRITING
Developmental Patterns

Characteristics

Age 2   Scribbles; repeats radial or circular pattern. Uses whole-hand grasp, whole-arm movement. Fills whole page. Is fascinated by markings.

Age 3   Prints large, single, capital letters anywhere on page. Likes to draw and paint (images are large, simple, and incomplete).

Age 4   May recognize a few letters, including own name. May write name or a few capital letters (large and irregular). Likes to draw and paint. Human figures are "stick," drawings crude. Draws circles and squares.

Age 5   Prints first name (large, irregular letters increasing in size). Frequently reverses letters and numbers or writes from right to left. Prints numbers (uneven and medium-sized). Can write some capital and lowercase letters. Has better grasp on writing utensils. Likes to draw and paint. Pictures are more complex and complete. Combines squares and circles. Likes to copy a model. May ask about spelling.

(Adapted from Barbara Taylor, *A child goes forth: A curriculum guide for preschool children* 7th Ed., pp. 99-114. Macmillan Publishing Co. NY, 1991).

Becoming Aware of Curricular Goals.

The language and literacy curricula that child care programs follow—no matter how simple or complex—contain what the adults of those programs view as essential goals in children's language and literacy development and growth. How well children are developing as users of oral and written language is inevitably judged against these goals, either explicitly or implicitly. Hence, teachers must have a working knowledge of the curricula they are using and be aware of their overarching language and literacy goals. In many ways (some subtle and some not so subtle) these become the standard for assessing children's levels of language functioning.

In Table 5.2 (Chapter 5) we shared some broad language and literacy curricular goals. Your awareness of these may prompt you to become aware of those which overarch the specific child care program where you teach or plan to teach. As long-range goals, these can provide another point of reference for the assessment and interpretation of children's language and literacy behaviors.

Although awareness of the influences on interpretation is informative, it must inevitably give way to action if assessment is to be served. It is one of those instances where knowing why must activate knowing how. And it is to the know-how or the act of interpretation we next turn.

In general, the actual task of interpretation involves the systematic examination of information about children's language and literacy behaviors. It is embedded in two types of activities: forming impressions and drawing conclusions. Both include sorting through information, summarizing and synthesizing it.

Forming Interpretive Impressions.

Formative activities occur as we go along. At regular intervals in the program year (perhaps every four weeks or so), information may be entered into children's language and literacy folders or their portfolios and a general review of the contents conducted. Such information needs to be varied coming from the multiple sources mentioned in the previous section, such as anecdotal notes, checklists, play and work samples, parent reports, self-evaluations and comments.

In reviewing the contents, it is important that teachers document their first impressions in some way. An easy way to start is to scan the materials and to jot down things noticed, somewhat like a preschool teacher did for a preschooler in Table 8.8.

From observations like these, summary statements about a child's language and literacy behavior can be developed. Summary statements combine and condense information into a few key points which profile an individual's current behavior and performance. Continuing with the example provided above, the statements in Table 8.9 illustrate this

TABLE 8.8   EXAMPLE OF DOCUMENTING A TEACHER'S FIRST IMPRESSIONS ON A PRESCHOOLER

What I notice about Julia (age 4 1/2). . .

(1) . . . demonstrates skills in using language to engage others in conversation; she speaks in complete sentences.

(2) . . . handles a book properly, that is she turns pages left to right.

(3) . . . distinguishes between picture and print when storybook reading, that is she runs her finger along the print as she "reads" the story.

(4) . . . retells stories, including essential elements: main characters and the action.

(5) . . . names most alphabet letters correctly.

(6) . . . uses learned letters in random fashion for writing.

TABLE 8.9   EXAMPLE OF DOCUMENTING SUMMARY STATEMENTS ON A PRESCHOOLER'S LANGUAGE AND LITERACY BEHAVIOR

(1) J. attends to and follows directions.

(2) J. speaks confidently, showing an awareness of grammatical rules.

(3) J. uses language to achieve her goals and to express her intentions, interests and preferences.

(4) J. demonstrates an awareness of story sequence—beginning, middle, end.

(5) J. produces letter strings in a variety of written formats, for example, lists, letters and stories.

(6) J. knows that spoken language can be written down, then read.

(7) J. handles books appropriately, demonstrating left-to-right, top-to-bottom orientation.

teacher's attempt to summarize young Julia's language and literacy behaviors at one point in the program year.

Using the summary statements as indicators of patterns in Julia's language and literacy development, the teacher now interprets this information, deciding on the quality and appropriateness of this child's language and literacy performance. In other words, the teacher brings meaning to the statements, using what she knows and what she believes.

Based on her analysis and interpretation of the evidence, this teacher decides that Julia is progressing nicely as a speaker, listener, reader and writer at this point in time. The child demonstrates excellent storybook reading behaviors, even stating reading preferences (dinosaur books). She plays cooperatively with others, assisting in the development of sometimes quite elaborate play themes. She consistently uses language over physical action to make her wants and desires known.

But in particular, note how the teacher's interpretation and resulting assessment are buttressed by concrete evidence which has been collected into a folder. Put simply, the teacher has a rationale for her assessment of Julia. And by repeating this process periodically during a program year, the teacher can rather easily construct a well-informed and clear assessment of Julia's language and literacy growth.

Formative activities, then, provide an opportunity for teachers to systematically document their general impressions about a child's language and literacy development in a substantial and credible way. Moreover, they make the overall assessment process more manageable and efficient, serving as periodic reviews which may form the basis for drawing conclusions about development over time.

Drawing Sound Conclusions.

Summary activities occur at **termination points** in programs, for example, at the end of the year or in transitions from one program level to another—prekindergarten to kindergarten, for instance. Their purpose is to determine the appropriateness of development at a key point in time, assessing progress thus far as above average, average, or below average.

At these times the entire contents of a folder or portfolio may be reexamined and/or the periodic summaries reviewed. Based on this evidence, the teacher can draw conclusions about the typicality, quality and appropriateness of an individual child's growth.

How the teacher records his or her conclusions may take a variety of forms. Some may prefer a narrative, others a checklist and still others may use continua of performance indicators, like those illustrated in Table 8.10. Note in particular how the continua reflect the language and literacy processes targeted for development and observation as listed in Table 5.2 from Chapter 5. In short, what is assessed is integrally connected to what children are learning and what teachers are teaching about language and literacy.

Reporting Interpretations To Others

The process of interpretation, however, does not end with the synthesis of information by teachers. Interpretation only becomes truly meaningful and useful when successfully reported to those who care about assessment the most—the children and their parents. How to discuss interpretations requires not only communicative skill but also a fine

TABLE 8.10   EXAMPLE OF CHILDREN'S PERFORMANCE INDICATORS

Child's Name_____Age _____Date_____

	Usually	Somewhat	Seldom
SPOKEN LANGUAGE			
1. Uses language as a tool			
2. Turn-takes in conversation			
3. Applies social conventions			
4. Applies grammatical rules			
5. Speaks clearly and confidently			
6. Understands/uses words in context			
7. Attends to and follows directions			
8. Listens to stories, songs, rhymes			
9. Plays with rhyming words/sounds			
10. Uses increasing number of words			
11. Develops and tells stories			
12. Retells familiar stories accurately			
LITERACY			
1. Grasps/manipulates writing tools			
2. Records ideas . . .			
using drawing for writing			
using pictures + scribble for writing			
using scribble for writing			
using letterlike forms for writing			
using letter forms randomly			
using invented spellings			
using conventional spellings			
3. Writes/recognizes own name in print			
4. Aware of print permanency			
5. Aware of print orientation			
6 Aware of print-meaning associations			
7. Uses pictures to "read" a storybook			
8. Uses pictures & print to "read" book			
9. Expresses story preferences			
10. Recalls details from familiar stories			
11. Aware of story sequence			
12. Handles books properly			

TABLE 8.11   EXAMPLE OF CHILDREN'S PERFORMANCE REPORTING

REPORTING IN CONFERENCES

Before . . .
- Make a list of points to cover. (Hint: Think of 3 to 4 adjectives that really characterize the child's language and literacy behaviors.)
- Inform parent(s) of the purpose of the conference.
- Prepare a comfortable meeting area. (Hint: Arrange to sit side-by-side.)

During . . .
- Stand, greet and thank parent(s) for coming.
- Provide data (information) in a clear way.
- Seek information from the parent(s).
- Synthesize information & arrange for ongoing actions.
- Record key ideas & any proposed activities. (Hint: Provide a copy for parent(s)).

Closing . . .
- Summarize the main points.
- Reiterate plans for continued action & communication.
- Express thanks.

(Adapted from Ellen Kronowitz, *Beyond student teaching.* 1992, NY: Longman Publishing Co.)

sense of audience on the teacher's part. Although each teacher develops a unique style of communication, there are some tried and true reporting behaviors that perhaps should become habits for us all.

As we close this chapter, we need to reiterate that assessment is a meaning-making process. And this being so, people, not things, are at its center. Teachers, parents, and children bring meaning to assessment activities, procedures and products. Together they can invent and control the tools and procedures of assessment so that teaching and learning may be served, and so that all may participate fully in developing a language for life within children.

Let's Review . . .

We began this chapter by discussing three key ideas that undergird the assessment process: that observations should be systematic and therefore planned; that the process is essentially a search for patterns of language and literacy behavior; and that language and literacy behaviors-in-use should be the focus of observation, revealing genuine development and growth.

With these ideas in mind, we described how to implement an assessment process, beginning with considerations of those language and literacy skills and processes which may become the targets of observation. Next, several ways to record observations were discussed and illustrated. These were divided into three types: teacher's observations, children's constructions, and interviews. How to organize information from these diverse sources was presented in two formats: folders and portfolios. Finally, how to interpret and judge the observations we gather was examined, stressing the importance of one's own personal beliefs about language and literacy development, an awareness of universal sequences of development and familiarity with curricular goals. Summary statements were offered as one means of consolidating and interpreting information for use in formative and summary assessment activities.

In closing, we cautioned and reminded ourselves that language and literacy assessment is a means, not an end unto itself. It is undertaken and conducted by responsible and informed adults for the betterment of children, assisting them in their development of a language for life.

· ·

Let's Explore . . .

1. Brainstorm and list items you would suggest be collected and placed in young children's language and literacy portfolios to showcase themselves as emerging readers and writers. Star those you think are *musts* and provide an explanation for each of your choices.

2. Pretend you are the teacher of a wonderful group of 4- and 5-year-olds in a day care program and that you are planning to use language and literacy portfolios as your assessment mechanism. Outline a presentation you will make to the parents of the children, orienting them to the concept and describing their role in the process.

3. Using the topic study you prepared in Activity 4 in Chapter 5, develop an assessment component for it. List the specific language and literacy skills you will observe. Establish a predictable time to observe. Decide what you will collect and how. Then indicate the format you will use to organize the data that you will gather.

A Literature Sampler

Action books

CARTER, D.A. (1988). *How many bugs in a box?* NY: Simon & Schuster.
HAWKINS, C., & HAWKINS, J. (1985). *Old Mother Hubbard.* NY: Putnam.
HELLARD, S. (1986). *Billy goats gruff.* NY: Putnam.
HILL, E. (1985). *Spot goes to the beach.* NY: Putnam.
KUNHARDT, D. (1984). *Pat the bunny.* Racine, WI: Western Publishing Co.
LUSTIG, L. (1979). *The pop-up book of the circus.* NY: Random House.
WHITE, E. (1984). *The touch me book.* NY: Western Publishing Co.
ZELINSKY, P. (1990). *The wheels on the bus.* NY: Dutton.

Informational Books For Young Children

ASCH, F. (1985). *Bear shadow.* Englewood Cliffs, NJ: Prentice Hall.
BARTON, B. (1979). *Wheels.* NY: Crowell.
BESSAR, M. (1967). *The cat book.* NY: Holiday House.
BONNERS, S. (1978). *Panda.* NY: Delacorte.
CARRICK, D. (1985). *Milk.* NY: Greenwillow.
COLE, J. (1987). *The magic school bus inside the earth.* NY: Scholastic.
GACKENBACH, D. (1984). *Poppy the panda.* NY: Clarion.
GIBBONS, G. (1984). *Tunnels.* NY: Holiday House.
HUTCHINS, R. (1960). *The amazing seeds.* NY: Dodd, Mead & Co.
KRAUS, R. (1945). *The carrot seed.* NY: Harper & Row.
KETTLEKAMP, L. (1959). *Kites.* NY: William Morrow & Co.
LANE, M. (1981). *The squirrel.* NY: Dial.
LESIEG, T. (1961). *Ten apples up on top.* NY: Beginner Books.
LOWREY, J. (1971). *Six silver spoons.* NY: Harper & Row, Publishers Inc.
MAESTRO, B. & DELVECCHIO. E. (1983). *Big city port.* NY: E.P. Dutton.
MAY, J. (1971). *Why people are different colors.* NY: Holiday House.
MILES, M. (1969). *Apricot ABC.* Boston, MA: Little, Brown & Co Inc..
MONJO, F.N. (1969). *The drinking gourd.* NY: Harper & Row, Publishers Inc.
NORRIS, L. & SMITH, H. (1979). *An oak tree dies and a journey begins.* NY: Crown Publishers.

O'BRIAN, W. (1968). *Ear book.* NY: Random House.

ROCKWELL, A. (1972). *Machines.* NY: Macmillan.

SCARY, R. (1989). *All about cars.* NY: Golden Book.

SELSAM, M. (1966). *When an animal grows.* NY: Harper & Row, Publishers Inc.

SPIER, P. (1980). *People.* NY: Doubleday & Co.

SWALLOW, S. (1973). *Cars, trucks and trains.* NY: Grosset & Dunlap.

WHITE, F. (1969). *Your friend the tree.* NY: Alfred A. Knopf.

WILDSMITH, B. (1971). *The owl and the woodpecker.* Oxford: Oxford University Press.

WILDSMITH, B. (1974). *Squirrels.* Oxford: Oxford University Press.

YOUNG, R. (1990). *A trip to Mars.* NY: Orchard Books.

Old Favorites

BROWN, M.W. (1944). *A child's goodnight book.* NY: W.R. Scott.

BROWN, M.W. (1957). *Goodnight moon.* NY: Harper & Row, Publishers Inc.

BURTON, V.L. (1943). *The little house.* Boston, MA: Houghton Mifflin.

DE REGNIERS, B. (1972). *Red riding hood.* NY: Atheneum.

HOLLING, H.C. (1942). *Paddle-to-the-sea.* Boston, MA: Houghton Mifflin.

KEPES, J. (1953). *Five little monkeys.* Boston, MA: Houghton Mifflin.

KRAUS, R. (1954). *A very special house.* NY: Harper & Brothers.

KUSKIN, K. (1959). *Just like everyone else.* NY: Harper & Row, Publishers Inc.

LIONNI, L. (1968). *Frederick.* NY: Pantheon.

McCLOSKEY, R. (1942). *Make way for ducklings.* NY: Viking.

MINARIK, E.H. (1962). *Little bear's visit.* NY: Harper & Brothers.

NESS, E. (1967). *Sam, Bangs, & Moonshine.* NY: Holt, Rinehart and Winston Inc.

PERRAULT, C. (1955). *Cinderella.* NY: Thomas Y. Crowell.

SCHEER, J. (1965). *Rain makes applesauce.* NY: Holiday House.

SEUSS, DR. (1950). *Bartholomew and the Oobleck.* NY: Random House.

STEIG, W. (1970). *Sylvester and the magic pebble.* NY: Simon & Schuster.

THURBER, J. (1944). *Many moons.* NY: Harcourt Brace Jovanovich.

UDRY, J.M. (1957). *A tree is nice.* NY: Harper & Brothers.

ZOLOTOW, C. (1972). *William's doll.* NY: Harper & Row.

Picture Books For Young Children

AARDEMA, V. (1991). *Borreguita and the coyote, a tale from Ayutla, Mexico.* NY: Knopf.

AHLBERG, A. & J. (1978). *Each peach, pear, plum: An I-spy story.* NY: Viking Press.

AHLBERG, A. & J. (1986). *The jolly postman or other people's letters.* Boston, MA: Little, Brown & Co.

ANNO, M. (1978). *Anno's journey.* NY: Philomel Books.

BARRET, J. (1970). *Animals should definitely not wear clothing.* NY: Atheneum

BROWN, M. (1972). *The runaway bunny.* NY: Harper & Row, Publishers Inc.

BUSH, J. (1991). *The fish who could wish.* Brooklyn, NY: Kane/Miller Book Publishers.

CARLE, E. (1971). *The grouchy ladybug.* NY: Crowell.

CREWS, D. (1978). *Freight train.* NY: Greenwillow.

DAHL, R. (1991). *The minpins.* NY: Viking.

FLACK, MARGERY. (1932). *Ask Mr. Bear.* New York: Macmillan.

FLEMING, D. (1991). *In the tall, tall grass.* NY: Holt, Rinehart & Winston Inc.

FREEMAN, D. (1962). *Bear.* NY: Viking.

GAG, WANDA. (1938). *Millions of cats.* NY: Coward-McCann.

GAMMELL, S. (1988). *Song and dance man.* NY: Knopf.

GREELEY, V. (1991). *White is the moon.* NY: Maxwell Macmillan International.

HILL, ELIZABETH. (1967). *Evan's Corner.* NY: Holt, Rinehart & Winston Inc.

HOBAN, RUSSELL. (1969). *Best friends for Francis.* NY: Harper & Row.

HOBAN, T. (1971). *Look again.* NY: Macmillan Publishing Co.

KRAUS, ROBERT. (1971). *Leo the late bloomer.* NY: Windmill Books.

LANGSTAFF, JOHN. (1974). *Oh, a-hunting we will go.* Boston: Houghton-Mifflin

KELLOGG, S. (1974). *The mystery of the missing red mitten.* NY: Dial Press.

McCLOSKEY, R. (1957). *Time of wonder.* NY: Viking Press, Inc.

McCLOSKEY, R. *One morning in Maine.* NY: Viking Press, Inc.

PROVENSEN, A. & M. (1967). *The Mother Goose book.* NY: Random House.

WABER, BERNARD. (1972). *Ira sleeps over.* Boston: Houghton Mifflin.

WELLS, ROSEMARY. (1973). *Noisy Nora.* NY: Dial.

WILDSMITH, B. (1962). *Brian Wildsmith's ABC.* NY: Watts, a subsidiary of Grolier.

YABUUCHI, M. (1985). *Whose footprints?* NY: Philomel.

YOLEN, J. (1987). *Owl moon.* NY: Philomel Books.

YOUNG, E. (1989). *Lon Po Po: A red riding hood story from China.* NY: Philomel Books.

ZUROMSKIS, DIANE. (1978). *The farmer in the dell.* Boston: Little, Brown & Co.

Predictable Books For Young Children

ARUEGO, J. & DEWEY, A. (1989). *Five little ducks.* NY: Crown Publishers.

BROWN, M. (1957). *The three Billy Goats Gruff.* NY: Harcourt Brace Jovanovich.

CARLE, E. (1969). *The very hungry caterpillar*. Cleveland, OH: Collins–World.

CAMERON, P. (1961). *"I can't," said the ant*. NY: Coward-McCann.

DE PAOLA, TOMIE. (1978). *Pancakes for breakfast*. NY: Harcourt Brace Jovanovich.

EASTMAN, P.D. (1960). *Are you my mother?* NY: Random House.

EMBERLY, B. (1967). *Drummer Hoff*. Englewood Cliffs, NJ: Prentice Hall.

GALDONE, P. (1972). *The three bears*. NY: Scholastic.

GALDONE, P. (1975). *Henny penny*. NY: Houghton Mifflin.

GALDONE, P. (1975). *The gingerbread boy*. NY: Houghton Mifflin.

GALDONE, P. (1975). *The little red hen*. NY: Scholastic.

HOBERMAN, M.A. (1978). *A house is a house for me*. NY: Viking.

KEATS, EJ. (1972). *Over in the meadow*. NY: Four Winds.

HUTCHINS, P. (1972). *Goodnight, owl!* NY: Macmillan.

JOHNSON, C. (1959). *Harold and the purple crayon*. NY: Harper & Row, Publishers Inc.

LOBEL, A. (1979). *A treeful of pigs*. NY: Greenwillow.

MARTIN, B. (1967). *Brown bear, brown bear, what do you see?* NY: Holt, Rinehart and Winston Inc.

MELSER, J. & COWLEY, J. (1980). *In a dark, dark, wood*. New Zealand: The Wright Group.

PIPER, W. (1954). *The little engine that could*. NY: Platt & Munk.

SENDAK, M. (1962). *Chicken soup with rice*. NY: Harper & Row, Publishers Inc.

SEUSS, DR. (1960). *Green eggs and ham*. NY: Random House.

SEUSS, DR. (1940). *Horton hatches an egg*. NY: Random House.

SLOBODKINA, ESPHYR. (1947). *Caps for sale*. Glenview, IL: Addison-Wesley Publishing Co.

SPIER, P. (1971). *Gobble, growl, grunt*. Garden City, NJ: Doubleday & Co.

STOTT, D. (1990). *Too much*. NY: Dutton.

WESTCOTT, NADINE. (1980). *I know an old lady who swallowed a fly*. Boston: Little, Brown & Co.

Storybooks For Young Children

ADOFF, A. (1973). *Black is brown is tan*. NY: Harper & Row, Publishers Inc.

BABBITT, N. (1989). *Nellie: A cat on her own*. NY: Farrar, Strauss & Giroux.

BAKER, K. (1990). *Who is the beast?* NY: Harcourt Brace Jovanovich.

BERENSTAIN, S. & J. (1978). *The Berenstain bears and the spooky old tree*. NY: Random House.

Brown, M. (1967). *Best friends*. Chicago: Children's Press.

BROWN, M. (1075). *Stone soup*. NY: Scribner.

BROWNE, A. (1989). *Things I like.* NY: Knopf.

BRYLANT, C. (1982). *When I was young in the mountains.* NY: E.P. Dutton.

BURTON, V. (1939). *Mike Mulligan and his steam shovel.* NY: Houghton Mifflin.

CARLE, E. (1971). *Do you want to be my friend?* NY: Crowell.

COHEN, MIRIAM. (1967). *Will I have a friend?* NY: Collier Books.

DePAOLA, T. (1975). *Strega Nona: An old tale.* Englewood Cliffs, NJ: Prentice Hall.

FEDER, J. (1979). *Beany.* NY: Pantheon Books.

HAZEN, B. (1988). *The gorilla did it.* NY: Aladdin Books.

KEATS, E.J. (1962). *The snowy day.* NY: Viking.

KRAUS, R. (1971). *Leo the late bloomer.* NY: Windmill.

LEEMIS, R. (1991). *Mister Momboo's hat.* NY: Cobblehill Books/Dutton.

LIONNI, L. (1966). *Frederick.* NY: Pantheon.

LOBEL, A. (1972). *Frog and toad together.* NY: Harper & Row, Publishers Inc.

MAESTRO, B. (1978). *Busy day: A book of action words.* NY: Crown Publishers.

MARSHALL, JAMES. (1972). *George and Martha.* Boston: Houghton Mifflin.

McPHAIL, D. (1990). *Lost!* Boston: Little, Brown & Co.

NESS, E. (1965). *Tom tit tot.* NY: Charles Scribner & Sons.

OTEY, M. (1990). *Daddy has a pair of striped shorts.* NY: Farrar, Strauss & Giroux.

PRESTON, E. (1974). *Squawk to the moon little goose.* NY: Viking Press.

RASKIN, E. (1966). *Nothing ever happens on my block.* NY: Atheneum Publishers.

ROCKWELL, H. (1973). *My doctor.* NY: Macmillan Publishing Co.

SCHEER, J. (1964). *Rain makes applesauce.* NY: Holiday House.

SENDAK, M. (1973). *Where the wild things are.* NY: Harper & Row, Publishers Inc.

SEUSS, DR. (1957). *The cat in the hat.* NY: Random House.

SHEARER, J. (1977). *Billy Jo Jive: Super private eye: The case of the sneaker snatcher.* NY: Dell Publishing Co.

SILVERSTEIN, SHEL. (1964). *The giving tree.* NY: Harper and Row, Publishers Inc.

SPIER, P. (1977). *Noah's ark.* Garden City, NJ: Doubleday & Co.

STEIG, W. (1969). *Sylvester and the magic pebble.* NY: Simon & Schuster.

STEIG, WILLIAM. (1971). *Amos and Boris.* NY: Farrar, Strauss & Giroux

SURANY, A. (NY). *Ride the cold wind.* NY: G.P. Putnam & Sons.

UDRY, JANICE. (1961). *Let's be enemies.* NY: Harper and Row, Publishers Inc.

VIORST, JUDITH. (1972). *Alexander and the terrible, horrible, no-good, very bad day.* NY: Atheneum.

WABER, B. (1967). *An anteater named Arthur.* Boston, MA: Houghton Mifflin.

WABER, BERNARD. (1972). *Ira sleeps over.* Boston: Houghton Mifflin.

WELLS, ROSEMARY. (1973). *Noisy Nora*. NY: Dial.
WILDSMITH, BRIAN. (1974). *The lazy bear*. NY: Franklin Watts

Wordless Picture Books

ALEXANDER, M. (1970). *Bobo's dream*. NY: Dial.
DAY, A. (1985). *Good dog, Carl*. La Jolla, CA: Green Tiger Press.
DE GROAT, D. (1977). *Alligator's toothache*. NY: Crown Books.
GOODALL, J. (1970). *Jacko*. NY: Harcourt Brace Jovanovich.
MAYER, M (1967). *A boy, a dog, and a frog*. NY: Dial.
MAYER, M. (1974). *Frog goes to dinner*. NY: Dial.
TURKLE, B. (1976). *Deep in the forest*. NY: Dutton.
UTCHINS, P. (1968). *Rosie's walk*. NY: Macmillan.
WARD, L. (1973). *The silver pony*. Boston: Houghton Mifflin.

Beginning Chapter Books That Can Be Read to Young Children

BLUME, J. (1970). *Freckle juice*. Scarsdale, NY: Bradbury.
BLUME, J. (1980) *Superfudge*. NY: Dutton.
CAMERON, A. (1988). *Julian secret agent*. NY: Random House.
CLEARY, B. (1968). *Ramona the pest*. West Caldwell, NJ: William Morrow
    & Co.
DAHL, R. (1964). *Charlie and the chocolate factory*. NY: Knopf.
HOWE, J. & HOWE, D. (1979) *Bunnicula*. NY: Atheneum.
McCLOSKEY, R. (1950) *Henry Huggins*. NJ: William Morrow & Co.
PARISH, P. (1963). *Amelia Bedelia*. NY: Harper & Row, Publishers Inc.
WHITE, E.B. (1952) *Charlotte's web*. NY: Harper & Row, Publishers Inc..
WILLIAMS, M. (1958). *Velveteen rabbit*. NY: Doubleday.

Books That Extend Language Play For Young Children . . ..

AYLESWORTH, J. (1990). *The complete hickory dickory dock*. NY:
    Atheneum.
BROWN, M. (1988). *Party rhymes*. NY: Dutton.
HABER, J. (DESIGNER), WESTCOTT, N. (ILLUSTRATOR), & CULBERTSON, R.
    (PAPER ENGINEERING). (1991). *The pop-up, pull-tab, playtime house
    that Jack built*. Boston, MA: Little, Brown & Co.
HENNESSY, B.G. (1990). *Eaney, meeney, miney, mo*. NY: Viking.

IVIMEY, J. (1990). *The complete story of the three blind mice.* Boston: MA: Little, Brown & Co.

LEAR, E. (1991). *The owl and the pussycat.* NY: G.P. Putnam's Sons.

SILVERSTEIN, S. (1974). *Where the sidewalk ends.* NY: Harper & Row.

SILVERSTEIN, S. (1981). *A light in the attic.* NY: Harper & Row.

Multicultural Literature

AARDEMA, V. (1981). *Bringing the rain to Kapiti plain: Anansi Tale.* NY: Dial.

CLIFTON, L. (1977). *Amifika.* NY: Dutton.

FREEMAN, D. (168). *Cordoroy.* NY: Viking.

GREENFIELD, E. (1977). *Africa dream.* NY: Harper & Row.

HASKINS, J. (1989). *Count your way through Africa.* NY: Carol Rhoda

JOHNSON, A. (1988). *Tell me a story Mama.* NY: Watts

MENDEZ, P. (1989). *The black snowman.* NY: Scholastic.

SEEGER, P. (1986). *Abiyoyo.* NY: Collier-Macmillian.

STEPTOE, J. (1988). *Baby says.* NY: Lothrop.

TAYLOR, M. (1987). *The gold cadillac.* NY: Dial.

A Media & Technology Sampler

Video: Doing things: *Eating, washing in motion*. (1989). Eureka, MT: BoPeep Productions.

These captivating 25 minutes of essentially silent video entice children 19 months to 5 years of age with footage of children and farm animals as they move through daily activities. With a racially diverse cast, the film is accompanied by a teacher's guide with extension ideas.

Film: *Growing, growing* (rev. ed.) (1991). Los Angeles, CA: Churchill Films.

This is a very enjoyable film for kindergarten and primary students, who could watch children planting and taking care of seeds. As the plants grow, the children's activities extend on the concepts into the areas of art and writing stories and songs.

Record: Edge, N. & Hunter, T. (1989). *Music is magic: Linking music and literacy*. Salem, OR: Nellie Edge Resources for Creative Teaching.

From age 1 to 5, children will enjoy this uplifting collection of songs. Traditional favorite tunes are reintroduced with original lyrics which are multiculturally appropriate. The songs easily extend specific literature selections or other literacy activities.

Record: Faires, D. (1989). *Sing, yes! Developmental affirmation songs*. Hazelwood, MO: Shalom Publications.

Based on Jean Illsley Clarke's developmental affirmation, these songs are for all children, beginning in infancy. Focused on the building of self-esteem, these songs are accompanied by guitar and other instruments.

Computer program: *Kindercomp golden edition*. Cambridge, MA: Spinnaker Software Corp.

A computer software program, including matching, counting and adding, it familiarizes a preschooler with letters on the keyboard and the alphabet. The program prompts for a letter match between the lowercase letter on the screen and the capital one on the keyboard. Another game asks for the next successive letter in the alphabet. Correct responses are acknowledged with music, and errors elicit no response.

Cassette: Jack, D. (1990). *Dance in your pants.* Leuccadia, CA: Ta-Dum Productions.

This cassette comes with a book of lyrics so children can sing along as well as move with the lively music. Appropriate for children as young as infants and toddlers.

Tape, and video: King, C. (1981). *Really Rosie.* NY: Caedmon.

Selections from Maurice Sendak's nutshell library of stories, including *Really Rosie*. The songs, sung by Carole King, are delightful renditions of many of Sendak's favorites, among them "Chicken soup with rice," and "Pierre."

Video: Leach, S. & Parker, K. (1988). *A day at the beach: Barney and the backyard gang.*: Allen, TX: The Lyons Group.

This 30-minute video uses lively music and drama to educate and entertain children aged 2 to 8 using the wild imagination of children. The simple plot depicts a multicultural group of children who learn to problem solve through fun and pretend play.

Record: Mahal, T. (1988). *Shake sugaree.* Redway, CA: Music For Little People.

Shake Sugaree is a refreshing collection of children's music, appropriate from infancy through age 6. Folk music from many cultures encourages children to join in with instruments and dancing.

Video: *Moving machines* (1990). Eureka, MT: BoPeep Productions.

These sounds and images of moving construction machinery rivet the attention of children ages 2 through 6 for the full 27 minutes, encouraging conversation as well as active responses.

Computer program: *The new talking stickybear alphabet.* Norfolk, CT: Optimum Resource, Inc.

This computer program is excellent for young children. Advancing on the program Stickybear ABC, this edition affords exposure and practice with letter recognition through both visual and auditory displays. Letters and words beginning with the target letter are synthesized in a natural-sounding language pattern. Only correct responses activate animated pictures. Three different games assess more and less advanced skill levels of recognition.

Tape: Seeger, P. (1984). *Stories and songs for little children.* Fairview, NC: High Windy Audio.

Classic children's songs are featured by this well-known folk singer. Children aged 3 to 8 will be delighted by Seeger's telling the story of the giant Abiyoyo and the little boy with the ukulele.

Tape: *The elephant's child* (1987). Stanford, CA: Windham Hill Records.

Jack Nicholson and Bobby McFerrin tell one of Rudyard Kipling's *Just So Stories* with entrancing quality. The music of Kipling's language, coupled with Nicholson's unforgettable expression is only more enhanced by McFerrin's musical innovations on voice. Children of all ages will love the pictures painted by these storytellers.

Tape, video, book: Thomas, M. (1988). *Free to be you and me.* Arista Records.

A delightful album, book and video highlighting new perspectives about women's and men's roles. Stories told in song and verse, with major stars as contributors. A memorable media selection.

Tape: Walker, M. (1991). *The frog's party.* Albany, NY: Gentle Wind.

This uplifting collection of music encourages nonviolent problem solving, communication skills and healthy interpersonal skills. Infants, toddlers and preschoolers would benefit from this cassette.

Tape: Wise, J. (1987). *The best of Joe Wise: Music for kids.* Chicago, IL: GIA Publications.

Here are some happy, silly songs for young children. The simple and intriguing lyrics center on the children they were written for.

• •

Journals For Teachers . . .

Childhood Education

Association for Childhood Education International
11501 Georgia Avenue, Suite 315
Wheaton, MD 20902

Day Care and Early Education

Human Sciences Press
233 Spring St.
New York, NY 10013-1578

Language Arts

National Council for Teachers of English
1111 Kenyon Road
Urbana, IL 61801.

The Reading Teacher

International Reading Association
800 Barksdale Rd.
P.O. Box 8139
Newark, DE 19714-8139

Young Children

National Association for the Education of Young Children
1834 Connecticut Ave, NW
Washington, DC 20009-5786

APPENDIX C

A Resource Sampler For Teachers

BUTZOW, C. & J. (1989). *Science through children's literature.* Englewood, CO: Teacher Ideas Press, A Division of Libraries Unlimited, Inc.

CARLSON, BERNICE WELLS. (1965). *Listen & help tell the story.* NY: Abingdon.

CHAMBERS, D. (1977). *Literature for children: The oral tradition; storytelling and creative drama.* Dubuque, IA: William C. Brown.

COODY, B. (1992). *Using literature with young children.* Dubuque, IA: William C. Brown Publishers.

CROFT, DOREEN J. (1990). *An activities handbook for teachers of young children* (5th ed.). Boston, MA: Houghton-Mifflin Co.

DAVIES, G. (1983). *Practical primary drama.* Portsmouth, NH: Heinemann Educational Books.

DORIAN, MARGERY. (1974). *Telling stories through movement.* Belmont, CA: Pittman Learning.

GILLIS, J. & FISE, M.E. (1985). *The childwise catalog: A consumer guide to buying the safest and best products for your children.* NY: Pocket Books.

GLAZER, J. (1986). *Literature for young children.* Columbus, OH: Merrill Publishing Co.

Global Literature for Children. Milwaukee, WI: Raintree Publishers.

HAISLET, B. (1976). *The rainbow book: A book of items children can send for free.* Minneapolis, MN: Parkway Press.

HARLAN, JEAN (1988). *Science experiences for the early childhood years.* Columbus, OH: Merrill-Macmillian Publishing Co.

LAMME, L. (1981). *Learning to love literature: Preschool through grade 3.* Urbana, IL: National Council of Teachers of English.

LOUGHLIN, C. & MARTIN, M. (1987). *Supporting literacy: Developing effective learning environments.* NY: Teacher's College Press.

LYNCH, P. (1986). *Using big books and predictable books.* NY: Scholastic Books.

MAXIM, G. (1990). *The sourcebook.* Columbus, OH: Merrill.

MCKEE, J. (ED.) (1986). *Play: Working partner of growth.* Wheaton, MD: Association for Childhood Education International.

Mister Rogers' plan & play book. (1985). Pittsburgh, PA: Family Communications.

MOORE, V. (1972). *Pre-school story house*. Metuchen, NJ: Scarecrow Press.

NEUMAN, S.B. & PANOFF, R. (1983). *Exploring feelings*. Atlanta, GA: Humanics Limited.

NODELMAN, P. (1992). *The pleasures of children's literature*. NY: Longman Publishing Co.

RICHARDS, ROY, COLLIS, MARGARET & KINCAID, DOUG (1987). *An early start in science*. London: Macdonald Educational.

RUSSELL, D. (1991). *Literature for children*. NY: Longman Publishing Co.

STRICKLAND, DOROTHY & MORROW, LESLEY (EDS.). (1989). *Emerging literacy: Young children learn to read and write*. Newark, DE: International Reading Association.

TAYLOR, BARBARA (1991). *A child goes forth: A curriculum guide for preschool children*. (7th ed.). NY: Macmillan Publishing Co.

THOMAS, J. L. (1992). *Play, learn and grow: An annotated guide to the best books and other materials for very young children*. NY: Bowker.

TRELEASE, J. (1982). *The read-aloud handbook*. NY: Penguin.

WILLIAMS, ROBERT, ROCKWELL, ROBERT, & SHERWOOD, ELIZABETH (1987). *Mudpies to magnets*. Mt. Rainier, MD: Gryphon House, Inc.

WINKEL, L. & KIMMEL, S. (1990). *Mother Goose comes first: An annotated guide to the best books and recordings for your preschool child*. NY: Holt.

Sources of Observational Tools for Assessment

COODY, BETTY (1992). *Using literature with young children* (pp. 259-260). Beaumont, TX.

MACHADO, JEANNE (1990). *Early childhood experiences in language arts: Emerging literacy* (4th ed.) (pp. 94–95; p. 164). Albany, NY: Delmar Publishers Inc.

MORROW, LESLEY (1989). *Literacy development in the early years: Helping children read and write* (pp. 184–186). Englewood Cliffs, NJ: Prentice-Hall.

OHIO DEPARTMENT OF EDUCATION (1991). *The Ohio early childhood curriculum guide*. Columbus, OH: Department of Education, Division of Educational Services.

SCHICKEDANZ, JUDITH (1986). *More than the ABCs* (chapter 2). Washington, D.C.: NAEYC.

SULZBY, E. (1990). *Emergent literacy: Kindergarteners write and read* (p. 24). Bloomington, IN: Agency for Instructional Technology.

WATSON, DOROTHY (1987). *Ideas and insights: Language arts in the elementary school* (p.216). Urbana, IL: National Council of Teachers of English.

ALLEN, R.V. & ALLEN, C. (1968). *Language experience in reading.* Chicago, IL: Encyclopedia Britannica.

ALLISON, L. (1975). *The reason for seasons.* Boston, MA: Little, Brown & Co.

APPLEBEE, A. (1978). *The child's concept of story.* Chicago: University of Chicago Press.

BAGHBAN, M. (1984). *Our daughter learns to read and write: A case study from birth to three.* Newark, DE: International Reading Association.

BARTLETT, E. J. (1981). Selecting an early childhood language curriculum. In C. Cazden (Ed.), *Language in early childhood education* (pp. 33–76). Washington, D.C.: National Association for the Development of Young Children.

BARTLETT, F. C. (1932). *Remembering.* Cambridge: Cambridge University Press.

BERNSTEIN, B. (1970). A sociolinguistic approach to socialization. In F. Williams (Ed.), *Language and poverty: Perspectives on a theme.* Chicago: Markham.

BETTLEHEIM, B. (1975). Reflections: The uses of enchantment. *New Yorker,* (pp. 50–114).

BISSEX, G. (1980). *GNYS at work: A child learns to write and read.* Cambridge, MA: Harvard University Press.

BLANK, M. (1982). Moving beyond the difference. In D. F. Farran & L. Feagans (Eds.), *The language of children reared in poverty.* NY: Academic.

BLOOM, L. (1970). *Language development: Form and function in emerging grammars.* Cambridge, MA: The M.I.T. Press.

BOHNING, G. & RADENCICH, M. (1989). Action books: Pages for learning and laughter. *Young Children, 44,* 62–66.

BRUNER, J. (1975). The ontogenesis of speech acts. *Journal of Child Language, 3,* 1–19.

BRUNER, J. (1980). *Under five in Britain.* Ypsilanti, MI: High Scope Press.

CARLSON, B.W. (1965). *Listen and help tell the story.* NY: Abington Press.

CAZDEN, C. B. (1981). *Language in early childhood education.* Washington, D.C.: National Association for the Development of Young Children.

CHOMSKY, N. (1957). *Syntactic structures.* The Hague: Mouton.

CLAY, M. (1975). *What did I write?* London: Heinemann.

CLAY, M. (1979). *The early detection of reading difficulties.* Portsmouth, NH: Heinemann.

CLAY, M. (1991). *Becoming literate.* Portsmouth, NH: Heinemann.

CLAY, M. (1991). Introducing a new storybook to young readers. *The Reading Teacher, 45,* 264–273.

COCHRAN-SMITH, M. (1984). *The making of a reader.* Norwood, NJ: Ablex.

CRAFTON, L. (1991). *Whole Language: Getting started . . . moving forward . . .* Katonan, NY: Richard C. Owens Publishers.

CUMMINS, J. (1979). Linguistic interdependence and the educational development of bilingual children. *Review of Educational Research, 49,* 222–251.

DORIS, E. (1991). *Doing what scientists do.* Portsmouth, NH: Heinemann.

DURKIN, D. (1966). *Children who read early.* NY: Teachers College Press.

DYSON, A. H. (1982). The emergence of visible language: Interrelationships between drawing and early writing. *Visible Language, 16,* 360–381.

ELLEY, W. (1989). Vocabulary acquisition from listening to stories. *Reading Research Quarterly, 24,* 174–187.

ENTWISLE, D. P. (1970). Semantic systems of children: Some assessments of social class and ethnic differences. In F. Williams (Ed.), *Language and poverty: Perspectives on a theme.* Chicago: Markham.

ERVIN, S. (1964). Imitation and structural change in children's language. In E. Lenneberg (Ed.), *New directions in the study of language.* Cambridge: The M.I.T. Press.

FEITELSON, D., KITA, B. & GOLDSTEIN, Z. (1986). Effects of listening to series stories on first graders' comprehension and use of language. *Research in the Teaching of English, 20,* 339–355.

FERREIRO, E. & TEBEROSKY, A. (1982). *Literacy before schooling.* Portsmouth, NH: Heinemann.

GEE, J. (1989). What is literacy? *Journal of Education, 171,* 18–25.

GENISHI, C. (1987). Acquiring oral language and communicative competence. In C. Seefeldt (Ed.), *The early childhood curriculum* (pp. 75–106). NY: Teachers College Press.

GLAZER, S.M. (1989). Oral language and literacy development. In D. Strickland & L. M. Morrow (Eds.), *Emerging literacy: Young children learn to read and write* (pp. 16–26).

GOODMAN, K. (1986). *What's whole in whole language.* Portsmouth, NH: Heinemann.

GOODMAN, K. (1991). Whole language at the chalk-face. In K. Goodman, L. Bridges, & Y. Goodman (Ed.), *The whole language catalog.* Santa Rosa, CA: American School Publishers.

GOODMAN, K. & GOODMAN, Y. (1979). Learning to read is natural. In L. R. & P. Weaver (Eds.), *Theory and Practice in Early Reading* (pp. 137–154). Hillsdale, NJ: Erlbaum.

GOODMAN, Y. & ALTWERGER, B. (1981). *Print awareness in preschool children: A working paper*. Tuscon: University of Arizona.

HALL, N. (1987). *The emergence of literacy*. Portsmouth, NH: Heinemann.

HALLIDAY, M. A. K. (1975). *Learning how to mean: Explorations in the development of language*. London: Edward Arnold.

HARLAN, J. (1988). *Science experiences for the early childhood years*. Columbus, OH: Merrill Publishing Co.

HARSTE, J., BURKE, C. & WOODWARD, V. (1982). Children's language and world: Initial encounters with print. In J. L. & M. T. Smith-Burke (Eds.), *Reader meets author/bridging the gap* (pp. 105–131). Newark, DE: International Reading Association.

HEALD-TAYLOR. (1987). How to use predictable books for K-2 language arts instruction. *The Reading Teacher, 40,* 656–671.

HEATH, S. B. (1983). *Ways with words: Language, life, and work in communities and classrooms*. Cambridge: Cambridge University Press.

HOLDAWAY, D. (1979). *The foundations of literacy*. Portsmouth, NH: Heinemann.

HOUGH, R. A. & NURSS, J. R. (1992). Language and literacy for the limited English proficient child. In L. O. Ollila, & M. L. Mayfield (Eds.), *Emerging literacy* (pp. 42–70). Boston, MA: Allyn and Bacon.

HYMES, J. L. (1991). *Twenty years in review: A look at 1971–1990*. Washington, D.C.: National Association for the Education of Young Children.

JUEL, C., GRIFFITH, P. L. & GOUGH, P. (1986). Acquisition of literacy: A longitudinal study of children in first and second grade. *Journal of Educational Psychology, 78,* 243–255.

JUSCZYK, P. W. (1977). Rhymes and reasons. Some aspects of the child's appreciation of poetic form. *Developmental Psychology, 13,* 599–607.

KATZ, L. (1987). What should young children be doing? *The Wingspread Journal, 9,* 1–3.

KATZ, L. & CHARD, C. (1989). *Engaging children's minds*. Norwood, NJ: Ablex.

KLEIN, A. (1991). All about ants: Discovery learning in the primary grades. *Young Children, 46,* 23–27.

KOUNIN, J. S. & DOYLE, P. H. (1975). Degree of continuity of a lesson's signal system and the task of involvement of children. *Journal of Educational Psychology, 67,* 159–164.

KRITCHEVSKY, S. & PRESCOTT, E. (1977). *Planning environments for young children: Physical space* . Washington, D.C.: National Association for the Education of Young Children.

KUSCHNER, D. (1989). "Put your name on your painting, but . . . the blocks go back on the shelves." *Young Children, 45,* 49–56.

LABOV, W. (1970). The logic of non-standard English. In F. Williams (Ed.), *Language and poverty: Some perspectives on a theme.* (pp. 153–187). Chicago: Markham.

LAMME, L.L. (1981). *Learning to love literature.* Urbana, IL: National Council of Teachers of English.

LEOPOLD, W. F. (1971). Semantic learning in infant language. In A. B.-A. &. W. F. Leopold (Eds.), *Child language: A book of readings.* Englewood Cliffs, NJ: Prentice Hall.

LINDFORS, J. (1987). *Children's language and learning.* Englewood Cliffs, NJ: Prentice-Hall.

LINDHOLM, K. J. (1980). Bilingual children: Some interpretations of cognitive and linguistic development. In K. E. Nelson (Ed.), *Children's language.* NY: Gardner Press.

LOUGHLIN, C. & MARTIN, M. (1987). *Supporting literacy: Developing effective learning environments.* NY: Teachers College Press.

MANDLER, J. M. & JOHNSON, N. (1977). Remembrance of things parsed: Story structure and recall. *Cognitive Psychology, 9,* 111–151.

MASONHEIMER, P., DRUM, P. & EHRI, L. (1984). Does environmental print identification lead children into word reading? *Journal of Reading Behavior, 16,* 257–271.

MAXIM, G. W. (1990). *The sourcebook* (2nd edition). Columbus, OH: Merrill Publishing.

MEEK, M. (1981). *Learning to read.* London: Heinemann.

MENYUK, P. (1991). Linguistics and teaching the language arts. In J. Flood, J. Jensen, D. Lapp, & J. Squire (Eds.), *Handbook of research on teaching the English language arts* (pp. 24–29). NY: Macmillan.

MOORE, G., LANE, C., HILL, A., COHEN, U. & McGINTY, T. (1979). *Recommendations for child care centers.* Milwaukee, WI: Community Design Center Inc.

MORISETT, C. E. (1991, April). *Toddlers' language development: Sex differences in response to social risk.* Seattle, WA:

MORRISON, G. (1988). *Early childhood education today* . Columbus, OH: Merrill.

MORROW, L. M. (1988). Young children's responses to one-to-one readings in school settings. *Reading Research Quarterly, 23,* 89–107.

MORROW, L. & SMITH, J. (1990). The effects of group setting on interactive storybook reading. *Reading Research Quarterly, 25,* 213–231.

MORROW, L.M. & WEINSTEIN, C. (1986). Encouraging voluntary reading: The impact of a literature program on children's use of library centers. *Reading Research Quarterly, 21,* 330–346.

NATIONAL ASSOCIATION FOR THE EDUCATION OF YOUNG CHILDREN (NAEYC), (1991). Guidelines for appropriate curriculum content and assessment in programs serving children ages 3 through 8. *Young Children, 46,* 21–38.

NELSON, K. (1973). Structure and strategy in learning to talk. *Monograph for the Society for Research in Child Development, 38,* Nos. 1 & 2.

NEUMAN, S. B. & ROSKOS, K. (1989). Preschoolers' conceptions of literacy as reflected in their spontaneous play. In S. M. & J. Zutell (Eds.),

Cognitive and social perspectives for literacy research and instruction (pp. 87–94). Chicago, IL: National Reading Conference.

NEUMAN, S.B. & ROSKOS, K. (1990). Play, print and purpose: Enriching play environments for literacy development. *The Reading Teacher, 44,* 214–221.

NEUMAN, S.B. & ROSKOS, K. (in press). Literacy objects as cultural tools: Effects on children's literacy behaviors in play. *Reading Research Quarterly.*

NEUMAN, S.B. & ROSKOS, K. (1991). Peers as literacy informants: A description of young children's literacy conversations in play. *Early Childhood Research Quarterly, 6,* 233–248.

NINIO, A. & BRUNER, J. (1978). The achievement and antecedents of labelling. *Journal of Child Language, 5,* 1–16.

OGLE, D. (1986). K-W-L: A teaching model that develops active reading of expository text. *The Reading Teacher, 39,* 564–570.

OLDS, A. (1988). Places of beauty. In D. Bergen (Ed.), *Play as a medium for learning and development.* Portsmouth, NH: Heinemann.

OLSON, D. R. (1977). From utterance to text: The bias of language in speech and writing. *Harvard Educational Review, 47,* 84–108.

PACE, J. (1990). Making a mini-greenhouse. *Highlights Magazine, 45,* 18.

PALEY, V. (1986). On listening to what children say. *Harvard Educational Review, 56,* 122–131.

PAPPAS, C., KIEFER, B. & LEVSTIK, L. (1990). *An integrated language perspective in the elementary school: Theory into action.* NY: Longman.

PARKER, R. (1983). Language development and learning to write: Theory and research findings. In R. Parker & F. Davis (Eds.), *Developing literacy: Young children's use of language.* Newark, DE: International Reading Association.

PAUL, R. (1976). Invented spelling in kindergarten. *Young Children, 31,* 195–200.

PELLEGRINI, A. (1991). *Applied child study.* Hillsdale, NJ: Lawrence Erlbaum Associates.

PFLAUM, S. W. (1986). *The development of language and literacy in young children* (3rd edition). Columbus, OH: Merrill.

PREISER, W. F. (1972). Work in progress: The behavior of nursery school children under different spatial densities. *Man-Environment System, 2,* 247–250.

QUIN, LISA LOUISE (MAY 1991). "An investigation into how play in the sociodramatic play area of a classroom can encourage and develop reading and writing skills with a group of six, year 2 children." Unpublished paper presented in partial fulfillment for degree of Bachelor of Education Honors, Manchester Polytechnic. England.

READ, C. (1971). Pre-school children's knowledge of English phonology. *Harvard Educational Review, 41,* 1–34.

RESTACK, R. (1988). *The mind.* NY: Bantam.

RICH, S.J. (1985). The writing suitcase. *Young Children*, *40*, 42–44.

RICHARDS, R., COLLIS, M. & KINCAID, D. (1987). *An early start to science*. London: MacDonald Educational.

ROSKOS, K. (1988). Literacy at work in play. *The Reading Teacher*, *48*, 562–568.

ROSKOS, K. (1990). A taxonomic view of pretend play. *Early Childhood Research Quarterly*, *5*, 495–512.

ROUTMAN, R. (1991). *Invitations: Changing as teachers and learners, K-12*. Portsmouth, NH: Heinemann.

SCHACHTER, F. F. (1979). *Everyday mother talk to toddlers: Early intervention*. NY: Academic.

SCHICKEDANZ, J. (1986). *More than the ABC's: The early states of reading and writing*. Washington, D.C.: National Association for the Education of Young Children.

SCHOGGEN, P. & SCHOGGEN, M. (1985). Play, exploration and density. In J. F. Wohlwill, & W. V. Vliet (Eds.), *Habitats for children: The impacts of density* (pp. 77–95). Hillsdale, NJ: Erlbaum.

SCIENCE & EDUCATION DEPARTMENT. (1975). *A language for life (The Bullock Report)*. London: HMSO.

SNOW, C. (1983). Literacy and language: Relationships during the preschool years. *Harvard Educational Review*, *53*, 165–189.

SNOW, C. & GOLDFIELD, B. (1982). Building stories: The emergence of information structures from conversations. In D. Tannen (Ed.), *Analyzing discourse: Text and talk*. Washington, DC: Georgetown University Press.

SORENSON, M. (1981A). Setting the stage. In L.L. Lamme (Ed.) *Learning to love literature* (pp. 13–27). Urbana, IL: National Council of Teachers of English.

SORENSON, M. (1981b). Storytelling techniques. In L.L. Lamme (Ed.), *Learning to love literature* (pp. 28–36). Urbana, IL: National Council of Teachers of English.

SPRADLEY, J. (1979). *The ethnographic interview*. NY: Holt, Rinehart & Winston.

STANOVICH, K. E. (1986). Matthew effects in reading: Some consequences of individual differences in the acquisition of literacy. *Reading Research Quarterly*, *21*, 360–406.

STAUFFER, R.C. (1970). *The language experience approach to teaching reading*. NY: Harper & Row.

STEIN, N. & GLENN, C. (1979). An analysis of story comprehension in elementary school children. In R. O. Freedle (Ed.), *Advances in discourse processing*. Norwood, NJ: Ablex.

SULZBY, E. (1985). Children's emergent reading of favorite storybooks: A developmental study. *Reading Research Quarterly*, *20*, 458–481.

TABA, H. (1962). *Curriculum development: Theory and practice*. NY: Harcourt, Brace and World, Inc.

TEALE, W. & SULZBY, E. (1986). *Emergent literacy: Writing and reading.* Norwood, NJ: Ablex.

TIZARD, B. & HUGHES, M. (1984). *Young children learning.* Cambridge, MA: Harvard University Press.

TORREY, J. (1969). Learning to read without a teacher: A case study. *Elementary English, 46,* 550–68.

TOUGH, J. (1982). Language, poverty, and disadvantage in school. In L. F. &. D. C. Farron (Eds.), *The language of children reared in poverty* (pp. 3–18). New York: Academic Press.

TREVARTHEN, C. & HUBLEY, P. (1978). Secondary intersubjectivity: Confidence, confiding and acts of meaning in the first year. In A. Lock (Ed.), *Action, gesture, and symbol.* London: Academic Press.

VYGOTSKY, L. S. (1962). *Thought and language.* Cambridge, MA: M.I.T. Press.

VYGOTSKY, L. S. (1978). *Mind in society: The development of higher psychological processes.* Cambridge, MA: Harvard University Press.

WANNER, E. & GLEITMAN, L. R. (1982). *Language acquisition: The state of the art.* NY: Cambridge University Press.

WELLS, G. (1985). *The meaning makers.* Portsmouth, NH: Heinemann.

WILLIAMS, R., ROCKWELL, R. & SHERWOOD, E. (1987). *Mudpies to magnets: A preschool science curriculum.* Mt. Rainier, MD: Gryphon House.

WOOD, D., McMAHON, L. & CRANSTOUN, Y. (1980). *Working with under fives.* Ypsilanti, MI: High Scope Press.

YADEN, D., SMOLKIN, L. & CONLON, A. (1989). Preschoolers' questions about pictures, print convention, and story text during reading aloud at home. *Reading Research Quarterly, 24,* 188–214.

ZAIS, R. (1976). *Curriculum: Principles and foundations.* NY: Harper & Row.

INDEX

Copyright Acknowledgments